# ESCAPE FROM DEMOCRACY

The orthodox view of economic policy holds that public deliberation sets the goals or ends, and then experts select the means to implement these goals. This assumes that experts are no more than trustworthy servants of the public interest. David M. Levy and Sandra J. Peart examine the historical record to consider cases in which experts were trusted, with disastrous results, such as in the field of eugenics, the regulatory use of security ratings, and central economic planning. This history suggests that experts have not only the public interest but also their own interests to consider. The authors then recover and extend an alternative view of economic policy that subjects experts' proposals to further discussion, resulting in transparency and ensuring that the public obtains the best insights of experts in economics while avoiding pitfalls such as expert bias.

David M. Levy is Professor of Economics at George Mason University. He has worked with Sandra J. Peart at the University of Richmond for fifteen years, and both have codirected the Summer Institute for the History of Economics. He is a distinguished fellow of the History of Economics Society.

Sandra J. Peart is Dean and Professor in the University of Richmond's Jepson School of Leadership Studies. She is a former president of the History of Economics Society and President of the International Adam Smith Society.

# Escape from Democracy

*The Role of Experts and the Public in Economic Policy*

**DAVID M. LEVY**

George Mason University

**SANDRA J. PEART**

University of Richmond

# CAMBRIDGE
## UNIVERSITY PRESS

One Liberty Plaza, 20th Floor, New York, NY 10006, USA

Cambridge University Press is part of the University of Cambridge.

It furthers the University's mission by disseminating knowledge in the pursuit of education, learning, and research at the highest international levels of excellence.

www.cambridge.org
Information on this title: www.cambridge.org/9781316507131

© David M. Levy and Sandra J. Peart 2017

First published 2017

Printed in the United States of America by Sheridan Books, Inc.

A catalogue record for this publication is available from the British Library.

Library of Congress Cataloging-in-Publication Data
Names: Levy, David M., author. | Peart, Sandra, author.
Title: Escape from democracy: the role of experts and the public in economic policy / David M. Levy, Sandra J. Peart.
Description: New York, NY: Cambridge University Press, 2017. | Includes bibliographical references and index.
Identifiers: LCCN 2016024201| ISBN 9781107142398 (hardback) | ISBN 9781316507131 (paperback)
Subjects: LCSH: Economics. | Economics – Sociological aspects. | Economic policy. | Expertise. | Citizen participation. | Democracy.
Classification: LCC HB71.L544 2016 | DDC 330–dc23
LC record available at https://lccn.loc.gov/2016024201

ISBN 978-1-107-14239-8 Hardback
ISBN 978-1-316-50713-1 Paperback

Democratic action is *hard*. It means government by discussion, and the organization of discussion itself, as I said before, involves the main problems. Not much intercommunication is even theoretically possible. As the world is built, the cards are heavily stacked in favor of centralization. Even in one direction, communication is bad enough; ... as to inter-communication – even with two persons there is an insoluble problem of dividing the time for both between speaking and listening; ... with larger numbers, the limitation increases rapidly.

Frank Knight (1951)

# Contents

x                               *Contents*

# Figures

# Tables

# Acknowledgments

This book has been a long time in coming to fruition and consequently we have many individuals and organizations to acknowledge here. We began thinking about experts as we presented our research on eugenics at the History of Economics Society, the American Economic Association, and the Summer Institute for the Preservation of the History of Economics. Colleagues in those venues, including Dan Hammond, Eric Schliesser, Andrew Farrant, Ed McPhail, Maria Paganelli, Niccola Tynan, Tim Leonard, Charles McCann, and the late Laurence Moss were most helpful and encouraging. The Summer Institute in those years received financial support from the Earhart Foundation.

Subsequent versions of some chapters were presented at the History of Political Economy Workshop at Duke University, the American Economic Association, the History of Economics Society, and the Joint Statistical Meetings. We received encouragement and helpful comments from M. Ali Khan, Barkley Rosser, George DeMartino, Craufurd Goodwin, Kevin Hoover, Bruce Caldwell, and Roy Weintraub. Colleagues, including Tyler Cowen, Peter Boettke, Alex Tabarrok, Deirdre McCloskey, Roger Koppl, Arye Hillman, Ross Emmett, Steven Durlauf, and Virgil Storr have been helpful along the way. To help assist with our thinking, we organized a Liberty Fund colloquium on experts in 2009; the colloquium was most useful to our thinking about the discussion tradition. Emily Chamlee-Wright encouraged us to write a chapter for her edited volume on discussion: that chapter forms the basis for Chapter 2. Portions of other chapters have appeared in print and are reprinted with permission here.

We are grateful for permission to print previously unpublished writings. We thank Jo Ann Burgess for permission to publish the correspondence of James Buchanan. We thank Laura Hicks of the Foundation for Economic Education (https://fee.org/) for permission to publish Orval Watts's letter

xvi                          *Acknowledgments*

to Rose Wilder Lane. We thank Noel L. Silverman, on behalf of the Little House Heritage Trust, for permission to publish Rose Wilder Lane's letter to Orval Watts. We thank Leah Donnelly of the Special Collections Division of George Mason University Library for permission to publish manuscripts in the Clark E. Warburton Papers. We thank James Poterba, on behalf of the National Bureau of Economic Research, for permission to publish the correspondence among the participants in the NBER corporate bond study. We thank Manfred Lube, on behalf of the University of Klagenfurt / Karl-Popper-Library, for permission to publish Karl Popper's letter to Gordon Tullock. We thank Ning Wang for permission to quote Ronald Coase's unpublished words.

Chapter 2 first appeared in 2015 as "On 'Strongly fortified minds': Self-restraint and cooperation in the discussion tradition," in *Liberal Learning and the Art of Self-Governance* edited by Emily Chamlee-Wright (pp. 35–49). We thank the editor and the publisher, Taylor & Francis, for permission to reprint. An earlier version of Chapter 6 first appeared in the *Journal of Economic Behavior & Organization* Vol. 78, April 2011 (pp. 110–125). We thank the editor, William Neilson, and the publisher, Elsevier, for permission to reprint. An earlier version of Chapter 9 appeared in 2016 in *The Oxford Handbook of Professional Economic Ethics*, edited by George F. DeMartino and Deirdre N. McCloskey (pp. 635–650). We thank the editors and the publisher, Oxford University Press, for permission to reprint. An earlier version of Chapter 10 first appeared in *Public Choice* as "Tullock on motivated inquiry: expert-induced uncertainty disguised as risk" Vol. 152, April 2012 (pp.163–180). We thank the editor, William Shughart, and the publisher, Springer, for permission to reprint. Chapter 12 first appeared in the *Eastern Economic Journal*, Vol. 34, Winter 2008, pp. 103–114. We thank Nature Publishing Group & Palgrave Macmillan for permission to reprint.

David Levy acknowledges financial support from the Earhart Foundation and the Pierre and Enid Goodrich Foundation that allowed us to hire research assistants for the study of textbooks reported in Chapter 6. Without the efforts of Adam C. Smith, Emily Skarbek, and Michael D. Thomas, the research could not have been accomplished. The economics department at George Mason University provided funds for August Hardy's assistance with the manuscript preparation. The Center for Study of Public Choice provided research support, and Jane Perry has read and reread the manuscript.

Neither of us has served in a consulting role while working on the book manuscript. We did undertake a consulting project on research and development for Statistics Canada, in 2006. David Levy's service on the

Professional Ethics Committee of the American Statistical Association was unpaid, as such things are usually measured.

Sandra Peart acknowledges the support and encouragement of her sons, Nathan and Matthew, and of Craig Heinicke. David Levy remembers his parents and is grateful for Nicholas and Michelle.

When we began the project, Richard Ware, Gordon Tullock, and James Buchanan were alive. Buchanan told us that we should visit Ware to learn about G. Warren Nutter. There we first saw the letter from W. W. Rostow. Tullock told the profession that economists were no different than anyone else. Buchanan by himself saved the Knightian tradition for a little while as a viable alternative to orthodoxy.

Finally we thank Karen Maloney and her staff at Cambridge University Press.

# PART I

# INTRODUCTORY THEMES

# 1

# Introduction

One who is to act for another with special competence, superior to that of his principal, and with fidelity, must be picked for competence and trustworthiness by some intuitive process, and must then be trusted. Sanctions of the sorts found in every society no doubt help in securing trustworthiness. About all these matters we have little knowledge, and the one thing that can be said with assurance is that (peace to the shade of Jeremy Bentham!) no machinery of sanctions can conceivably function without very large aid from moral forces.

Frank Knight (1947, pp. 29–30)

## 1.1 Introduction

The twenty-first century is surely the century of consultants, advisors, and experts. We listen with great interest to pundits who make predictions about an election, the World Series, or the Super Bowl. When we rebalance our portfolio, buy a house or a car, or adopt a healthier lifestyle, we visit websites where experts advise us about how best to proceed. Consultants are hired at every turn. In higher education they offer advice on bringing in a class at the appropriate discount rate; developing a strategic plan that will please multiple constituencies; or planning for a capital campaign. Academia is not unique in this regard; throughout the for-profit and the nonprofit world we seek and rely on the advice of experts – those outside the organization who will independently verify our thinking or point us in a new direction. Sometimes, this is a simple process of validation: we on the inside have a hunch that, for instance, higher rates of discount will yield greater retention rates at a college; the consultants we hire collect the data and perform the analysis that yields the advice we were looking for in the first place.

And this specialization and division of knowledge are good.[1] We want doctors and dentists to be experts and we rely on the engineering expertise of those who design our cars and the rides at Busch Gardens. No one who has visited a dentist in the last few years would wish to return to the dental practices of even ten years ago. If we decide to put a new policy in place – for instance to increase a discount rate for superior students at a college – we need reliable estimates of the costs and benefits associated with this change.

It is straightforward to observe and appreciate the benefits associated with access to expertise. There is, first, the simple fact that our lives have been greatly improved as a consequence of experts who made living easier by building bridges, discovering new medical techniques, and producing washing machines and countless other devices. In part for this reason, we typically defer to the experts. We put them on TV, YouTube, blogs, and the radio. Experts testify in court cases and before Congressional and Senate hearings. Political leaders and judges defer to them. Doctors – themselves experts – read evidence of the efficacy of a treatment and they rely on the expert scientists who conducted the trials. Experts rate securities, and firms and individuals base investment decisions on these expert-backed ratings. Experts tell us at what rate China and India are growing, what the balance sheet at the Federal Reserve looks like, and whether to expect high winds with the storm that promises to come through our region soon.

But another aspect of expertise has now burst into public attention, the failure to replicate a large number of results reported in scientific journals.[2] Marcus Munafo, the coauthor of a 2015 *Science* study that could replicate fewer than half of the results reported in a hundred articles in leading psychological journals,[3] explained the problem in terms of motivation and he pointed to the incentives facing the researcher:

---

[1]  As Nathan Rosenberg, L. E. Birdzell, Jr., Deirdre McCloskey, and many others have shown, living standards in the West have increased dramatically in a matter of a few hundred years. Although the increase in human thriving has not been uniform and there are distributional issues to consider, much of the overall increase in well-being is attributable to engineering and other scientific discoveries (Rosenberg and Birdzell 1986; McCloskey 2010). To this, McCloskey adds the language of commerce. We will return to this in Chapter 2.

[2]  An instance that has received a good deal of attention recently is the high school student's disreplication of a claim published in the *Oxford Journal of Social History* (Jensen 2002) that signs saying "No Irish Need Apply" did not exist, despite the widespread belief to the contrary. Rebecca Fried demonstrated (Fried 2015) that in fact "No Irish Need Apply" was a commonplace in the newspaper advertisements of the period.

[3]  http://science.sciencemag.org/content/349/6251/aac4716. The authors cite the work of John P. A. Ioannidis whose model of the search for statistical significance predicted the problem

If I want to get promoted or get a grant, I need to be writing lots of papers. But writing lots of papers and doing lots of small experiments isn't the way to get one really robust right answer. What it takes to be a successful academic is not necessarily that well aligned with what it takes to be a good scientist.[4]

Unfortunately, the consequences of such motivated inquiry have occasionally been severe. Perhaps the best-known example followed a 1998 article published in *The Lancet* that asserted that childhood vaccines against measles and other diseases led to higher rates of autism. We now know that the author concealed his financial interests and the biased estimation procedures that strongly influenced his results. Obviously the editors, who had no such interests, were not aware of the concealment. Had the private goals of the author and the statistical procedures been obvious to the editors, or even suspected, there is no reason to believe the article would have been published. Experts – and here we simply defer to authority – claim that this widely diffused result has led to a disastrous fall in the vaccination rates.[5]

In what follows, we focus on experts in economics because it is easier for us to read the technical literature in economics than in other fields. Thus, our attention is confined to those who have a claim to scientific authority in economics and who use their expertise to influence policy, broadly construed. Such experts have attained great stature over the last century, and some notoriety recently.[6] The influence of the Chicago School of Economics in creating a neoliberal world is controversial in large part because their

(Ioannidis 2005). http://journals.plos.org/plosmedicine/article?id=10.1371/journal.pmed.0020124

[4] https://www.theguardian.com/science/2015/aug/27/study-delivers-bleak-verdict-on-validity-of-psychology-experiment-results

[5] A Wikipedia article "Alexander Wakefield" attempts to keep up with the studies evaluating the impact. http://en.wikipedia.org/wiki/Andrew_Wakefield.The retraction is in http://www.thelancet.com/journals/lancet/article/PIIS0140-6736(97)11096-0/abstract. This belated retraction was important enough to make the major news outlets, for example the *Wall Street Journal*, February 3, 2010. "The Lancet's Vaccine Retraction: A Medical Journal's Role in the Autism Scare" and *NPR*, "Lancet Renounces Study Linking Autism and Vaccines," http://www.npr.org/sections/health-shots/2010/02/lancet_wakefield_autism_mmr_au.html.The study's impact is asserted widely: Jeanne Whalen and Betsy Mckay, "Fifteen Years after Autism Panic, a Plague of Measles Erupts Legions Spurned a Long-Proven Vaccine, Putting a Generation at Risk" *Wall Street Journal* June 19, 2013. http://www.wsj.com/articles/SB10001424127887323300004578555453881252798.

[6] The motion picture, *The Inside Job* documents a good deal of embarrassing economic advice in the period before the 2007 financial crisis. Jonathan Gruber's statements about the private benefits of nontransparency demonstrated the power of YouTube. Gruber's apology for casual usage of the principle of rational ignorance was that he was not an expert on politics. http://radio.foxnews.com/2014/12/11/jonathan-gruber-to-congress-im-not-an-expert-on-politics/

claims of expertise seem to have overruled democratic institutions.[7] In that context, Chicago School experts in economics are viewed by some as akin to physicians who prescribed the bitter medicine of "shock therapy" with the admonition, "take this, we know what's good for you."

Economists were concerned with questions such as the motivations of economic experts and the replicability of their results long before the "shock treatment" characterization of economic advice.[8] These misgivings, largely out of the public eye, have gradually reformed submission policies for academic journals in economics. Publication of applied statistical articles is now often contingent upon submission of the data as well as the computer commands to implement the statistical procedures. This is a remarkable change from the era in which data sharing was voluntary, motivated only by scientific duty, as an editorial in the *Journal of Political Economy* in 1975 informed its readers (Stigler 1975).

In line with such concerns, we hold that all inquiry is motivated. This follows from our presumption that all experts have at least some private (as opposed to purely public) motivations. As is well known, throughout his career James Buchanan made the simple but important claim that policy

---

[7]  Juan Valdes examines the role of economists in Pinochet's Chile (Valdes 2008). Andrew Farrant and Edward McPhail and Leonidas Montes discuss new evidence on Milton Friedman's role in Chile (Farrant and McPhail 2013; Montes 2015). Valdes focuses on the University of Chicago's economics department and offers the view that their advice was inspired by the teaching of Frank Knight: "The community of economists risen to a Platonic category as 'the scientific community' was also seen in Knight's writings as the appropriate model for the 'free society'. The Chicago School, then, developed a vision of itself as the community of true economists, 'having the gift of faith, steadfast witnesses to the social glory and redemptive power of the market system'. More than economists in the restricted sense, they became social or moral philosophers; they tended to form – to use a Weberian concept – 'a rational sect'" (Valdes [1995] 2008, p. 80). A variation on this is found in Klein (2007, pp. 60–61) who views Knight's 1933 contribution as teaching his students to treat economic theory as above discussion. Valdes misses Knight's discussion of the collective-action problem among economists in a democracy, an issue A. C. Pigou addressed the following year. We discuss that in Chapters 2 and 9.

[8]  Thomas Mayer used the replication criterion to ask whether economics is a science: "Neither originality, logical rigor, or any other criterion is as ranked as 'essential' by so many natural scientists as was replicability" (Mayer 1980, p. 170). Such concerns were the background for the replication project of the *Journal of Money, Credit and Banking* (Dewald, Thursby, and Anderson 1986; Feigenbaum and Levy 1993). In Chapter 4 we return to Mayer's attempt to replicate the body of empirical work linking current consumption to anticipated income (Mayer 1972). Chapter 11 addresses the question of motivated nontransparency. The history of concerns as well as the state of econometric replication as of 2015 is described by Duvendack, Palmer-Jones, and Reed (2015). There is now a replication network to help establish connections among researchers and to help the interested keep up-to-date. http://replicationnetwork.com/

makers are neither more nor less public spirited than the public.[9] We have used the phrase "analytical egalitarianism" to describe the presumption that people are all approximately the same messy combination of interests. In our view, it is now time to apply this homogeneity claim not only to policy makers but also to the experts who influence policy.[10] This book extends analytical egalitarianism to economic experts who influence policy, and this explains our cautionary approach to expertise: If one suspects the expert has a point of view not fully in line with that of society writ large, then one might be well advised to take precautions against the uncritical adoption of the expert's advice.

It is important to emphasize at the outset that we do *not* claim that experts in economics are untrustworthy or greedy, at least no more so than the rest of us. Instead, our position is that they are humans and like the rest of us they are subject to motivations to do good for all and to do good for themselves. Sometimes, by contrast (and sometimes to our peril, we suggest), people presume that experts pursue *only* the truth or that bias is costly for them because their only interest is the pursuit of truth. But when experts' models have alternative uses, when they are instruments for policy or to please those with whom they are connected, the motivations become more complicated. Our main concern in the book is how to ensure that the public obtains the best insights of experts in economics while avoiding the pitfalls associated with uncritical deference.

## 1.2 Discussion

The vision described in section 1 of the Chicago School economist as a physician, is actually antithetical to the teaching of Frank Knight, a founder of Chicago economics, for whom democracy is *government by discussion*. In Part II we offer a reconstruction of Knight's view in which expertise is constrained by democratic consensus. Most important, independent of the "school" of economics in which expert advice originates, this book advocates for an alternative account in which the economist as expert is constrained by discussion and transparency. Such a constraint, we argue, may prevent policy disasters such as those detailed in Part III. Discussion works

---

[9] See Buchanan's 2003 essay, "Public Choice Politics without Romance."

[10] This is consistent with Erik Angner: "Economists-as-experts are overconfident, I would argue, not because they are different from everyone else, but because they are just like everyone else" (Angner 2006, p. 7). The insistence that economists are subject to the same biases and limitations as everyone else is stressed by W. Kip Viscusi and Ted Gayer (Viscusi and Gayer 2015). We thank William Shughart for the reference.

both ways: by ensuring that results can be discussed and checked, it leads to the publication of trustworthy results; by allowing for results to be discussed and checked, it helps foster a healthy amount of skepticism.

We recognize in Part II and again in Part V that it is both messy and quite difficult to constrain experts by discussion. Our point in Part II is that the benefits associated with discussion may be great. There we shall read J. S. Mill's explanation of how moderation in expression is important for those who dissent from social conventions. Mill put this view into practice, and as a consequence his views on contraception expressed in his definitive *Principles of Political Economy* were considered at the trial that led to a de facto legalization of the dissemination of contraceptive information in a form that poor women could afford. The larger context of the trial is considered in Chapter 5. In the context of our examination of the benefits of discussion, Chapter 2 also reviews experimental evidence on how cooperation is enhanced by discussion.

In Part III we suggest that the costs of neglecting fuller discussion may be quite high, and they include the trampling of human desires and well-being through the adoption of sterilization policies to prevent births that experts deemed unwanted. Part V offers some recommendations for obtaining consensus and constraining experts that are less costly than discussion among an entire polity. Perhaps not surprisingly, given the obvious difficulties associated with discussion among large numbers, Knight drew attention to these. Chapters 11 and 12 offer ways to overcome the intractability of discussion among large numbers by relying on a random draw from the full public.

## 1.3  Linear versus Cyclical Policy Goals

A key question in this book is whether policy goals are determined once and for all and then implemented by experts (what we call the linear model) or whether they are determined in an ongoing process of review and discussion (what we call the cyclical process). The dominant point of view about the role of (economic) experts in a democracy uses the linear model. In this formulation, society articulates ends through a process of democratic discussion. Experts are then tasked with finding the means (optimal solutions) to achieve those predetermined ends in something akin to an engineering calculus. A second point of view, which we defend, takes ends and means as determined simultaneously. Ends are articulated and means are proposed but these proposed means and even the ends are subject to continued review and discussion. The ends and means are then refined and the process continues.[11]

Unfortunately, all too often the role for review and discussion is minimal in the process of implementing policy. Indeed, once a decision is made, the overwhelming temptation for those in charge is to *avoid* continuous review and discussion. We argue that the separation of democratically established goals and means is costly at best and dangerous at worst. The linear model depends on experts being both trustworthy and effective. It neglects the temptation associated with power, with having the means to achieve an end that, once chosen, becomes disassociated from the people who apparently chose it. There is no guarantee that those who implement a policy are trustworthy or effective or that they are impervious to the temptations associated with power. Nor is there any reason to believe that they will choose the means that best serve the articulated goals of the group instead of the means that best serve their private goals.

The linear model presupposes that experts are faithful servants of society's goals, that they have no goals other than those of the group. But that is precisely what analytical egalitarianism warns against: experts, like the rest of us, are not *only* faithful servants of society's goals. Like the rest of us, they have and pursue their own goals and sometimes at the expense of the public.[12]

This problem associated with the linear model is known in the economics literature as "regulatory capture." After goals are agreed on, those who implement them may use their authority to achieve their own, private goals. Charles Wolf coined the helpful term "internalities" to describe the private goals of those entrusted with implementing public policy (Wolf 1979). Regulatory capture by those with such private goals is now seen as a central explanation for government failure.[13] A theme of this book is that, like the policy makers themselves, experts who provide advice to policy makers and

---

[11]  In Chapter 2, we consider Amartya Sen's analysis of the different approach to the problem of social choice taken by Kenneth Arrow and James Buchanan in the early 1950s in which "government by discussion" is the central question. Arrow took for granted that policy cycling is undesirable, whereas Buchanan disagreed. What was the basis of their disagreement? In his essay on ancient logic, Adam Smith warned that the coherence of many doctrines "of abstract Philosophy ... have arisen, more from the nature of language, than the nature of things" (1982, p. 125). In this context it is worthy of notice that Ariel Rubinstein recently pointed out how our language is crowded with transitive relationships to indicate direction (Rubinstein 2000).

[12]  The source of William Easterly's "technocratic illusion" that he combats in his masterful study (Easterly 2013) is the linear modeling approach to policy.

[13]  See Schuck (2014, pp. 109–10); Levy and Peart (2015a).

who design the means of implementation may also be subject to regulatory capture.

## 1.4  Exogenous versus Endogenous Goals

The question of whether it is generally appropriate to take group goals as exogenous will be central in what follows, because if goals are exogenous there is nothing to discuss. Of course, this is not a new insight. We shall see in Chapters 2 and 3 that the question has a long history in the economics literature. And, in 1961 James Buchanan explained to Kermit Gordon[14] that the difference between the economics tradition in which he participated, that of Knight and his students, and the orthodox economics tradition to which he thought Gordon adhered, was that Knight, Buchanan, and their followers did not take group goals as exogenously determined.

The temptation to take goals as exogenous is simple: exogenously determined goals offer tractability. The temptation of tractability allows us to link our work with Philip Tetlock's research on alternative styles of reasoning. Following Isaiah Berlin's use of the fragment of the Greek poet Archilochos, Tetlock distinguishes between "hedgehogs" and "foxes" (Tetlock 2005). Hedgehogs know one big thing, the trick that always works, and foxes know many things that rarely work.[15] As Tetlock explains it, the problem with hedgehogs relative to foxes is that they are not equally open to disconfirming evidence:

… hedgehogs bear a strong family resemblance to high scorers on personality scales designed to measure needs for closure and structure – the types of people who have been shown in experimental research to be more likely to trivialize evidence that undercuts their preconceptions and to embrace evidence that reinforces their preconceptions. (2005, p. 81)

Such trivialized evidence was apparent in the treatment of Soviet growth by some economists. When predictions of Soviet growth failed to materialize, a wealth of confounding factors was provided to "explain" the failure of the prediction. We offer a detailed study in Chapter 6.

Without knowledge of personality type or the ability to look back at events of earlier decades, how might economists use Tetlock's insight? The

[14]  Gordon shortly after would become a member of President Kennedy's Council of Economic Advisors.
[15]  Guy Davenport provides an interpretative translation of the fragment: "Fox knows eleven-tythree tricks and still gets caught; Hedgehog knows one but it always works" Davenport (1980, p. 57).

issue of whether group goals can be taken as exogenous may provide the means by which to move from hidden psychological traits to observable models. If group goals are taken to be exogenous, the implementation of policy is fundamentally an engineering calculus. But once the goals are taken as endogenous in an ill-understood process, as those in the tradition of Knight suggest, then implementation is contingent on the shifting goals, and ambiguity pours into the analysis. Yet perhaps ambiguity is the preferred, if previously unheralded, alternative: this book examines the consequences of succumbing to the temptation to escape from the messiness of democracy and defends another – perhaps lost – tradition of review and discussion as checks to the temptation to impose a policy choice, despite strong and perhaps valid objections. Thus, the problem of deferring to experts in the absence of discussion and transparency looms large in what follows.

Vernon Smith has described an additional problem associated with experts, how experts in one area gain credibility outside their immediate sphere of specialization:

... experts often get their reputations in narrow specialties and are no better in solving problems outside their area of expertise than a random citizen off the street. But we expect them to have an absolute advantage over less accomplished people on all topics.[16]

The puzzle is how those without disciplinary competence can view themselves, and be viewed by disinterested spectators, as having the weight of scientific authority behind their recommendations.[17] We consider this issue in Chapters 5 and 6, when we examine how those outside the immediate problem of interest accepted the recommendations of the specialists, and in Chapter 10, when we examine Michael Polanyi's discussion of how scientific authority can be uniform given the limitations of time and specialization. Polanyi described a plausible condition of overlapping competence by which those in neighboring competence examine the claims of those in nearby areas. Gordon Tullock compared economics with the science that Polanyi described and concluded that economics was not a science in Polanyi's sense because concealment persisted in economics. Without

---

[16] Smith (2008, p. 186). We thank Jonathan Wight for the reference.
[17] Perhaps this explains why a single article in *The Lancet* poisoned sensible parents' decisions not to vaccinate their children. They must have known that the leading antivaccination advocate is a television performer rather than a physician, but the article, published in such an esteemed journal as *The Lancet*, carried great authority. Retracting the article did not restore vaccinations to the status quo prior to publication. This is the problem of stickiness when models are instruments for beliefs and leadership positions.

transparency there is no reason to believe that Polanyi's secondary experts – those without the competence to actually check the assertions of primary experts – will all have the same views. What is more plausible is clusters of secondary experts around each group of primary experts. What is needed to dissolve such factions, Tullock argued, is the complete lack of concealment, complete transparency.

## 1.5 Transparency

Secrecy is a central theme of the chapters in Part IV. We begin with contemporary reactions to John Law's monetary reform that led to the Mississippi Bubble. But contemporary images and texts from 1719 and 1720 assert that Law was involved in an alchemical fraud that depended critically on concealment. The episode, discussed in Chapter 7, illustrates how worries about transparency and expertise are very old, indeed.

Life is finite, so people cannot check everything they believe, even if they knew how far back to go. Thus, deference, like expertise, is inevitable and generally a good thing. How then to deal with the associated nontransparency? At least two possible approaches exist. First, one might accept the nontransparency as fact and attempt to find a second opinion from an independent source. Second, one might appeal to Francis Galton's information aggregation theorem of median estimates (or the generalization thereof) and infer truth from consensus.[18] Unfortunately, people often neglect the independence assumption these both require and, if so, this creates a nontransparent nontransparency. They depend on some unknown party whose work is endlessly repeated as if in a cosmic echo chamber, and they think all the voices are independent. And they let down their guard. They fail to see the stickiness and focus only on the consensus. Even as great a statistical economic thinker as George Stigler made this mistake, moving from consensus to truth without checking whether the consensus was obtained independently (Levy and Peart 2008b).

One of the systematic themes we shall develop in the book is that transparency is a complicated concept. It is often idealized as a binary state, where an institution is conceptualized as transparent (state 1) or not (state 0). This idealization makes transparency akin to truth: 1 if true and 0 if false. But we will argue that transparency is fuzzier than this; it allows some

---

[18]   See Francis Galton (1907a, 1907b), reprinted in Levy and Peart (2002) and generalized in Peart and Levy (2005). In Chapter 12 we return to Galton's example of a jury deliberation as an instance of democratic procedure.

or perhaps all values between 1 and 0. In this case, a proposal might offer a method to move from less to more transparency. Our approach, discussed in Chapter 11, recognizes that full transparency is incentive incompatible and seeks instead to induce more transparency.

We can also think of transparency in hierarchical terms. In such a setting, transparency becomes the institutional analogue of states of awareness (Halpern and Rêgo 2009). Suppose that people are unaware of a fact. Hierarchy, then, characterizes this situation because (1) people may be aware that they are unaware of this fact or (2) they may be unaware that they are unaware of this fact. In economic theory perhaps the best example of a nontransparent institution where there is transparency about the nontransparency is the used-car market. In the used-car market buyers are unlikely to have the same information about the quality of the used car as the seller. But consumers all know this. The difficulty of finding an acceptable used car is a matter of folk wisdom; indeed the title of George Akerloff's paper in which he studied the used-car market, "The market for lemons" (Akerloff 1981), pays tribute to this folk wisdom. The nontransparency here is known; it is itself transparent. When the nontransparency is transparent, it makes sense to propose an institutional reform that moves us closer to state 1. We take up this challenge in Part V.

When the nontransparency is itself nontransparent, the problem is more difficult. The *Lancet* article alleging a positive relationship between vaccine and autism relied on concealed information that would have led the referees to reject it. Returning to economic policy, the controversy surrounding Jonathan Gruber's remarks to the effect that transparency would have been an impediment to the legislation he advocated suggests that the nontransparency in that instance was unknown, at least by some.[19] His remarks sparked much outrage; on both sides of the spectrum, politicians reacted to the admission that legislation had been deliberately crafted to be murky and nontransparent so that "stupid" voters would be fooled. Judging from the expressed surprise and anger that followed the discovery of his remarks, this subterfuge had not been anticipated from an economist whose competence was certified by his colleagues at the Massachusetts Institute of Technology [MIT]. Consumers of economic expertise may have already learned that the used-car model is a useful one to apply to economic experts. In the context of policy analysis this suggests that it would be wise to consider ways to induce transparency of experts, to render transparency incentive compatible. This is the subject of Chapter 11.

---

[19] https://www.youtube.com/watch?v=G790p0LcgbI

## 1.6 Sympathetic Bias

Since experts operate within groups that share methods, affinities, and perhaps ideological attachments, they may well be motivated to obtain results consistent with those of their group and to render their methods nontransparent to those outside the group. Thus, we also take a page in what follows from Smith's work on sympathy – connections that, he argued, form and persist among those who are closest to us socially – and "factions." Smith famously argued that people are prone to sympathize with those most like them; and they may then seek approbation from those with whom they have sympathetic connections.[20] He recognized that this may have devastating consequences that span collusion to war and he observed that employers are "every where and always" in a tacit combination to keep wages low (Smith 1904 I.8.13). We explore Smith's idea of sympathetic bias in Chapters 9, 10, and 11.[21] There, we extend Smith's terminology and think about people with sympathy for their system as well as experts who form sympathetic connections with their clients.[22] We explore different institutional structures – rules – that determine how expert judgment is produced, and we seek ways to minimize the costs associated with obtaining unbiased advice. The goal is to generate plenty of unbiased expert judgments, for instance, by making transparency incentive compatible or, if that is unattainable, by making nontransparencies transparent. If people see that they are deferring to a process they fail to understand, they can take precautions. If they do not see this nontransparency, they might fail to do so.[23]

[20] As noted earlier, this suggests that experts might be "captured" by regulators or those in industry without engaging in behavior that would be considered a financial conflict of interest. We return to this concern in Chapter 9. The long-time economics columnist for the *New York Times*, Leonard Silk, expressed his shock at learning about the politics of economic advisers (Silk 1972); Leland Yeager discusses William Allen's then unpublished interviews with economists who served in government (Yeager 1976; Allen 1977).

[21] Appealing to sympathetic motivation avoids the problem of thinking about an institution based on an exchange of approbation as if it were the same as an exchange of material goods. R. C. O. Matthews quotes Matthew Arnold on the "damage done to the morale of school-teachers by the introduction of a 'payment by results' system in the 1860s." (Matthews 1991, p. 747). Samuel Bowles offers powerful evidence on differences between the exchange of approbation and the exchange of money (Bowles 2008). We return to this in Chapter 9.

[22] Daylan M. Cain, George Loewenstein, and Don A. Moore focus on experts who might exploit their clients (Cain, Loewenstein, and Moore 2005); in Chapters 9 and 11, we also consider expert-client pairings who form sympathetic groups at the expense of the public.

[23] Asymmetric information is one justification for ethical codes, for example, Matthews (1991). To this we add the argument that asymmetric information is a much more serious problem when there is asymmetric information about the asymmetric information itself.

## 1.7 Ideology

Although there may be ideological dimensions associated with expertise, in what follows we challenge the commonly held position that expert advice is readily collapsed into a one-dimensional debate over the scope of government, with the left or progressive position arguing for more intervention, and the right or conservative position arguing for less.[24] Ronald Coase, the last avowed representative of the Knightian tradition with a Chicago address studied in Chapter 3, was hardly a Fabian socialist. Yet despite their political differences the Fabians relied on Coase's expertise to guide their discussion about ending the British Broadcasting Corporation's monopoly (Levy and Peart 2014b). Perhaps the greatest debate in economics during the first two-thirds of the twentieth century concerned the possibility and/or desirability of a centrally planned economy. Economists of the right – Ludwig von Mises and F. A. Hayek are the key names involved in the debate – asserted that a centrally planned economy could not possibly be more productive than a market economy. They were opposed by economists of the left – Oskar Lange and Abba Lerner were the key names on this side – who asserted that a centrally planned economy could perform at least as well as a market economy.

On the central planning debate, we have nothing to say here. What interests us instead is something that was common to both positions, the supposition that the experts who direct a planned economy would be disinterested, that they would not exploit their positions for self-interested purposes (Levy and Peart 2008c). We provide details of this episode in Chapter 6; here, we emphasize that, as far as their conceptions of the nature and scope of experts were concerned, economists on the left were indistinguishable from those on the right.[25] Thus, one of the few Soviet experts who came close to correctly characterizing Soviet growth was G. Warren Nutter, an economic advisor for Senator Goldwater and Assistant Secretary of Defense for President Nixon. Nutter's credentials are clearly conservative. Yet Nutter's analysis was central to Walt Whitman Rostow's argument

---

[24] Our account is consistent with that of William Barber: "The phenomenon on display here is thus not Chicago-specific, but (to borrow a Marshallian phrase) is a 'specie of a larger genus.' And the central characteristic of that genus is an attitudinal one: namely, an unquestioning faith that its teachings will uplift the human Condition" (Barber 1995, pp. 147–48). We thank George DeMartino for the helpful reference.

[25] One of the sustained themes in Easterly's *Tyranny of Experts* is that the tradition of using political orientation to characterize debates about the relationship between experts and the public is remarkably unhelpful (Easterly 2013).

in his *Stages of Economic Growth* (Rostow 1960). Rostow was an important advisor to both Presidents Kennedy and Johnson. Those are unimpeachable liberal credentials.

In a letter to Nutter written a month before President Kennedy's murder, Rostow refers to their shared view on Soviet growth and their isolation from the economics establishment. The issue that separated Nutter and Rostow from the establishment was clearly not their varied political views. Instead it was simply how one should characterize the expert-guided economy and the motivations of economic experts. Despite their political differences, they agreed that one needed to be wary of the advice of the experts and the motives of those who provided the data on economic growth. If the experts were correct that Soviet power was growing more quickly than that of the United States, perhaps this would prompt an earlier war with the power.

## 1.8  Systems Gone Wrong

We began our work on Soviet growth after we came to a hiatus in our work on eugenics. Eugenics, as we have come to understand, is another policy linearization in which implementation of the public goal of so-called racial perfection was entrusted to experts. It is now clear that eugenic policy, not only in the Hitler era but also in the United States until the 1970s, was a policy disaster. Yet strange things happened in the course of our study of eugenics. When we started, naïvely, we relied on the standard scholarly work of English language economists. The searchable archive of academic journals, Digital library of journals and books (JSTOR), was new then, making it possible to document omissions in a way that is nearly impossible by reading printed materials. We discovered that important studies of the economic associations were simply silent on the topic of eugenics. When we proposed a session on eugenics at the American Economic Association's annual meeting, it was accepted but we were encouraged not to use that word in the session title.

Perhaps because the studies of eugenics and Soviet growth were formative in our research on expertise, we have been prompted to inquire what we can learn from worst-case examples. The goal more generally is to learn from this history. A common feature of the case studies in Part III is that each is characterized by a lack of transparency. As we shall demonstrate in Chapter 7, images of John Law's role in the Mississippi Bubble, stressed the "occult" or hidden nature of his expertise. One lesson we learn from these cases is the importance of worst-case thinking in a second-best world (Lipsey and Lancaster 1956–1957). In Chapter 8 we examine how investors learned to trust the experts in rating agencies who played a role in the recent financial crisis. The first academic study of ratings, in 1938, put forward an avowedly worst-case statistical method for dealing with the obvious expert bias. Moreover, we demonstrate there that the practice of banking regulators for decades either mimicked or employed worst-case methods. The question then is why we forgot this worst-case approach to expertise.[26]

To impose organization on public knowledge, experts in economics frequently use a model. There are many different ways of thinking about models, from toys that mimic larger things to austere logical constructs that unify a whole universe of discourse. For our purposes, a model is a consistent organizational framework for examining the world.[27] So, the public advice of experts may flow from a publicly available model. College textbooks in economics introduce students to the standard models used by professional economists. Successful textbooks are lucrative and they also offer nonmonetary rewards for the author – namely, fame. The author of the most important economics textbook of the twentieth century, Paul Samuelson, quoted by David Colander and Harry Landreth, explained it this way: "Let those who will, write the nation's laws if I can write its textbooks" (Colander and Landreth 1996, p. 28). Supposing Samuelson to be correct, the textbook and its models give the expert a claim to approbation, to respect, and to a position of authority or leadership. Public models thus serve as instruments to private rewards. But as Tetlock's work suggests, there is also a dark side to Samuelson's point. If the expert abandons the model, he or she must abandon some claim to fame and fortune or to intellectual leadership. In turn, the expert's private interest might lead him or her to stick to a model somewhat longer than appropriate.

The immediate objection to this concern is that if the model is public what difference does it make what the incentives are?[28] As the following chapters will reveal, however, it is not always clear that so-called public models are quite as public as they seem to be. The textbook model of production

---

[26] Even the exposition of worst-case analytics by Richard Woodward and Richard Bishop supposes that the expert policy advice is unbiased (Woodward and Bishop 1997).

[27] An extensive treatment of the nature and meaning of models for economists is provided by Mary Morgan and Margaret Morrison (Morgan and Morrison 1999).

[28] Discussion surrounding the creating of a code of ethics for economists focused on how economists work with public models. See *The New York Times*, December 30, 2010, http://www.nytimes.com/2010/12/31/business/economy/31economists.html?pagewanted=all&_r=0 George DeMartino's *Economist's Oath* examines the debate surrounding the desirability of a code of professional ethics for economics (DeMartino 2011). See also Stephen Ziliak and Deirdre McCloskey's *The Cult of Statistical Significance* (Ziliak and McCloskey 2008) and Thomas Mayer (Mayer 1993).

trade-offs that we study in Chapter 6 is consistent at any moment in time, but it was inconsistent over time in some nontransparent fashion. Needless to say, if the author provides notice to the reader that an error has been detected and corrected, there is no problem whatsoever. But without such a notice it might be prudent to worry about whether the researcher is holding on to an inconsistency over time.

As we noted earlier, perhaps the single greatest account of the use of models – he called them "systems"[29] – was offered by Smith. Smith taught that people use systems of the mind to reform themselves and society. He also warned that this is dangerous because system builders may sacrifice people to the system itself. We will return to this insight frequently in the following chapters. In line with Smith, we worry about what happens when an expert is so caught up in the linear policy that he or she is willing to sacrifice some transparency in the conveyance of implementation.

Smith's insight about the role of systems, lost for many years, becomes critical when we explore the role of experts in governance. A much-neglected positive tradition in economics and political philosophy takes governance to be a truth-seeking activity. If this is so, the role of legislation is to find the correct answer to social issues and, since those involved in the legislative process are truth seekers, this will all work out nicely. Knight developed this approach in the 1930s and John Rawls revived it in his 1971 *Theory of Justice*. But Knight's students at the University of Chicago and elsewhere instead developed an alternative, preference-based theory of legislation. In this alternative, largely due to the work of K. J. Arrow and Buchanan, there is still a commitment to truth seeking as a normative goal of economists, but as noted previously, Buchanan's "politics without romance" recognized that all of us, legislators included, are self- as well as public-spirited.

## 1.9  Some Possible Remedies

In Part V, we turn to possible remedies, ways to help ensure that the public gets the best out of experts. The critical question is how to respond to

---

[29]  Smith's word "system" is capacious enough to include models. Systems might be thought of as the overarching commitments of the expert. One of the advantages of thinking in terms of systems is that the word encompasses situations in which the expert, who wishes to obtain a particular result, might change an estimation technique or a model in some nontransparent manner. We use the term *system* to cover various model manipulations including ones that violate consistency, a property critical to the logical concept of "model." See Quine (1969, p. 305). Examples of systems that are not consistent models, discussed in Chapter 6, speak against Machlup's (1965) view that logical contradictions are not a substantial worry.

motivated inquiry. We use this term to describe motivations that are wider than the pursuit of the public good of truth. We shall make the case that any response must depend in part on whether the disinterested or those in other factions are aware of the motivations at work. Since new reports of scientific retractions are now easy to find – the blog *Retraction Watch* accompanies many a morning coffee[30] – we cannot take public unawareness of nontransparency of motivated inquiry as a fixed condition. If academic journals in economics have changed their data submission policies, it seems reasonable to expect other changes will be forthcoming. There is also the possibility of deeper reform; in Chapter 11 we point to an institution in the American constitution, trial by jury, in which such matters are routinely addressed.[31]

Section 1.1 sketched the position that experts are people characterized by a messy bundle of private and other-regarding interests, and that experts may seek bias since it is a private good for them. Plato long ago recognized this conundrum with the philosopher kings in his *Republic*. His problem was a political one, because he proposed that the guardians (his experts) be rulers. And his solution, famously, was to purify the experts, to remove self-interest from consideration to the extent possible, to propose that guardians must not own property or have families. This was in keeping with his pre-supposition that the purity of the guardians was the only answer. Otherwise they too would need watching and, as Plato pointed out, "it would be absurd that a guardian should need a guard" (*Republic* 403e). The platonic social purification is perhaps the most popular approach to align the interests of experts and the public good. Economists such as Knight (1951) and W. H. Hutt (1936), whose politics are far from those of Plato but who also grappled with the collective-action problems among expert economists, offered variations on Plato's proposal for experts.

Our overarching approach is different. Instead of Plato's frankly unattainable hierarchy of pure ruler and self-interested ruled, we offer a more circular order of the sort captured in Fleeming Jenkin's exchange diagram that graced the cover of our earlier book (Figure 1.1), *The "Vanity of the*

---

[30] http://retractionwatch.com/

[31] The proposal in Chapter 12 to reimagine regulation in terms of a jury trial with opposing experts would require the imposition of the legal rules of discovery. A weaker form of discovery imposed without (it seems) sufficient discussion is already creating a good deal of controversy (Thacker and Seife 2015). The severity of the controversy can be judged from the resulting removal of the paper from the PLOS site http://blogs.plos .org/biologue/2015/08/13/the-fight-over-transparency-round-two/. The details are discussed here: http://retractionwatch.com/2015/08/24/following-criticism-plos-removes-blog-defending-scrutiny-of-science/

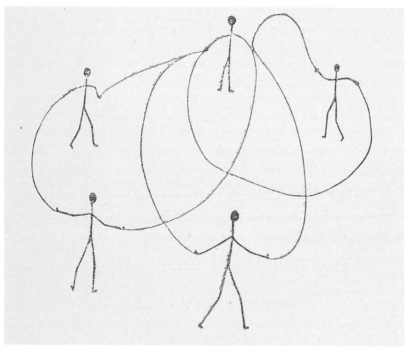

Figure 1.1. Fleeming Jenkins's exchange diagram.

*Philosopher": From Equality to Hierarchy in Post-Classical Economics.* We advocate mutual monitoring, a form of exchange of ideas and information characterized by mutual awareness of motivations, benefits, and temptations, in short, characterized by reciprocity and induced transparency.

Instead of "better" people watching "worse" people, we suggest that people must watch each other. Our concern is that those who rely on others' expertise do not let down their guard or defer to someone's expertise too readily.

More specifically, our recommendations are designed to better align incentives associated with expertise. None is sufficient in and of itself, but various combinations will attenuate the potential failures associated with uncritical acceptance of expertise. First, Chapter 9 considers how a code of ethics can serve as a warning sign about a collective-action problem. Next, as good economists and in parallel with our remark at the outset about obtaining a medical opinion from not one but two or more doctors, we argue in Chapter 10 that competition is a key limiting factor. If experts arrive at a consensus too quickly, without making room for competing views and expertise, there is a real danger that the public will defer to an unchallenged expert judgment. An open, competition-rich, scientific environment has a better chance of offering the community of experts, and the public, competing views.[32] For example, if we know that the advice has an upward bias, then there are methods for removing at least some of the bias by using one of the lower estimates. Although this is a simple proposal, it also has a subtle consequence. If the advice givers know their advice will be adjusted downward, each one of them may face less pressure to bias upward. Because the advice has less influence there is less gain from biasing it.

If one danger of expertise is that the expert becomes overly attached to his or her system, a second and related problem is that the expert may not fully disclose to his clients everything about the system that produced the results. Chapter 11 turns to the American legal system as an exemplar that overcomes motivated concealment. To the extent that data sets can be analyzed using different estimation techniques, it is terribly important that the data – and techniques – be shared widely so that they may be replicated and challenged. When the famous statistician, Karl Pearson, conducted his study of Jewish "inferiority," he made clear the techniques that underscored his argument; as we note in Chapter 5, this transparency enabled those who came after him to challenge his conclusion. What the less knowledgeable reader may have missed is that Pearson's practice in this context deviated from the elaborate statistical philosophy he defended elsewhere.

We shall also argue in favor of mechanisms to render the nontransparency – as it relates to *how* the information or advice is generated, – transparent. At times, expert wisdom seems to contradict ordinary experience of the public. Economic experts, as we have said, often have access to information that is not common knowledge. Sometimes the expert relies on technique to convince a client, suggesting the model is too "complicated" or "complex" fully to convey to the client.[33] Although we acknowledge that complex models and explanations are difficult to convey in simple terms, we urge resistance to this position.

Proverbial wisdom can be an alternative to complex models. When the housing bubble was picking up steam, and rating shopping was being discussed in the *Wall Street Journal*, we wondered how securities that contained nothing but mortgages could receive the same rating as those of the

---

[32] Allen interviewed Gordon Tullock and reported that Tullock "would never award 'a research contract; you should always have at the very least two' independent studies – and 'offer to each of them the possibility of criticizing the other'" (Allen 1977). Tullock's systematic views on scientific inquiry are discussed in Chapter 10.

[33] Paul Romer recently coined the term *mathiness* to describe how concealment operates in service to faction in research papers in mathematical economics (Romer 2015).

US government. Surely there would be an undue correlation of assets from only one sector of the economy. But this would imply that all the eggs are in the same basket, in violation of proverbial wisdom. The Chairman of the Federal Reserve System, Alan Greenspan, who has access to very complex models, had declared in testimony to Congress that a nationwide housing bubble was impossible since houses in Portland Maine could not be moved to Portland Oregon in search of higher prices.[34] So, the trick was to have a regionally diversified portfolio of mortgages. If the market believed Greenspan, as it certainly was profitable to do, mortgage money from the "bubble proof" securities would flow into housing markets all over the country to create the "impossible" bubble (Levy and Peart 2008a). That was an obvious mistake.

What was less obvious is why the ratings, which were known to be the product of rating shopping, were believed in the first place. Chapter 8 provides our explanation. When security ratings entered regulation, the experts of the Federal Deposit Insurance Company /National Bureau of Economic Research were precluded from revealing any information about the differences among the rating agencies. We know there were differences because of an earlier privately-financed dissertation that could freely report the remarkable differences the author documented. The belief that any rating is as good as any other is the basis of rating shopping. And of course with rating shopping, there may be an irresistible pressure for rating inflation.

The housing bubble meltdown is full of stories about banks that neglected proverbial wisdom about diversification and instead chose to hold a dangerously large proportion of their assets in the stock of government-sponsored enterprises, Fannie Mae and Freddie Mac. Experts assured investors that these latter assets were essentially the same as, no more risky than, government securities. The fact that the returns on government sponsored enterprises were higher than those on government securities might have suggested that people who buy and sell such assets were worried about them. There is another proverb that pertains here: if something seems too good to be true, it is probably too good to be true. As noted earlier, the idea of deference looms large in the following chapters. Supposing that experts' conceptions of "what is good for the public" are also influenced by what is good for the experts or for a group of people with whom they are closely connected, uncritical deference may lead us all to believe an expert when we should not. The expert can then take advantage of – perhaps even

---

[34]   https://www.federalreserve.gov/boarddocs/testimony/2005/200506092/default.htm

manipulate – the information gap between what he or she knows and what we are able to find out.

If experts come to agree independently, or when their interests are opposed, perhaps we should trust the result. But what if they are not independent? Suppose an MIT economist would not speak about a policy for fear of giving credence to a University of Chicago economist?[35] This is our concern in Chapter 10. There we examine the difficulty that arises when expert consensus is the result of social pressure to present a united front to the outside world. In those cases – which are difficult to distinguish from the former – the public should be skeptical. If experts gain influence from consensus, breaking with consensus is costly and it would be naïve to presume otherwise. This is why Tullock's worry that economic practice allows concealment is so important: with concealment we can expect faction to prevail.

The foregoing suggests that an improved public understanding of the motivations of experts itself will better align public and private interests in a world filled with experts. The *Wealth of Nations* exposes the pretensions of merchants as disinterested experts; as noted earlier and in accord with Smith, we suggest that, generally, experts are motivated by a combination of private and public interests. From this understanding, we can appreciate that any defense against the predation of expertise needs to be dynamic. We will offer components for the toolkit. Competition, reputation, transparency, and ethics are all included in the package. We shall also, throughout, provide some thoughts on how such second-best solutions might emerge, whether in the context of the application of policy or the development of new policy or a rule of conduct. Second-best devices, as we shall see in Chapter 11, are of great help when there is an impediment to some best policy, a constraint, and when pressing on regardless of this impediment would lead to disaster. The impediment that concerns us most is the non-transparency of expertise.

One institution that may allow the public to obtain the best from experts is trial by jury. We examine this framework in detail in Chapter 11, where we stress the institutional features, that each side relies on contending experts and the members of the jury surely realize that the experts are biased in their clients' favor. With that understanding and the rule of discovery that

---

[35] The case, witnessed by Leo Rosten and described in a letter to Milton Friedman is discussed in Milton and Rose Friedman's joint autobiography (Friedman and Friedman 1998, p. 218). A copy of the letter is in the William Baroody Papers at the Library of Congress. All Rosten tells Friedman is that the economist in question is not Samuelson.

subjects evidence to hostile eyes, responsible decisions can be made by a random section of the public. The jury is small enough for discussion; it fits in a small room. Although it is implausible in the extreme to think that a large democracy could have a discussion, it is entirely plausible that a random draw from the public could do so. Consequently, we suggest that something akin to jury trials might be a viable means by which to obtain the benefits of expertise in the regulatory setting.

## 1.10  Concluding Thoughts

We pause, finally, in a moment of reflexivity to say a few words about the apparent contradiction inherent in a work of this sort. Although we write about the ethics of expertise, we too are subject to the motives we attribute to experts. We are, after all, claiming some expertise about expertise. We claim no more (nor less) self-interest in the pursuit of this project than characterizes anyone who writes a book: like them, we seek to persuade. In ways that we shall highlight at the appropriate times later, we subject ourselves to the same ethical norms we recommend for other experts – transparency and reciprocity being most important. We also welcome skepticism among our readers and we hope for competition in the market for expertise about expertise! There are few books of this sort in the economics profession and that may in and of itself be a sign that economists have yet fully to acknowledge the implication of our argument that *we should apply the tools of economics to the economists who use them.*

We take this aspect of analytical egalitarianism as a moral obligation. As our systems are supposed to apply to the world, a model that yields to the modeler a higher capacity than it gives to the modeled is an assertion that the modeler is entitled to more than the modeled.[36] This violates reciprocity. So, we see a deep problem with the truth-seeking assumption at least when it is made without condition. Truth is a pure public good, so truth seeking is selfless in a way that seeking the private good of happiness is not likely to be. The notion that a truth-seeking modeler supposes agents who are self-seeking suggests to us that the modeler wishes to mend the world. This in itself is fine – we all wish to make the world a better place. But the harm occurs and our skepticism arises because the truth seeker has

---

[36] In this spirit we find Mark Weisbrot and Dean Baker asking precisely the right question: "… it is not clear that the economists and the professional staff at the IFIs [International Financial Institutions] are held accountable for their performance in the same way as they advocate other workers should be held accountable" (Weisbrot and Baker 2004, p. 3).

placed him- or herself outside the model and wishes to improve the world by improving others but not him (or her)-self.

In a world of transparency, the only sensible decision is to trust experts: if we expended the resources on obtaining their knowledge, we would make the same decision that they recommend. However, when transparency fails, that trust can be a catastrophe. If we think in terms of the general theory of the second best in which we accept the existence of constraints that cannot be removed, a world in which transparency is a pipedream, what *is* possible is to make the nontransparency itself transparent. The used-car market is the economist's paradigm of a nontransparent market. Because everyone knows about that nontransparency, people participate in this market with as much awareness as is feasible. Given that knowledge, people can work to reform the market or take precautions. This is what we are attempting to achieve with the book: we wish to ensure that those who purchase expert advice do so with their eyes wide open, alive to the hidden nontransparencies and able fully to benefit from a marketplace for well-discussed ideas rich in competition, reciprocity, and ethical conduct.

# PART II

# THE DISCUSSION TRADITION

One of the clearest demarcations between classical political economy and post-World War II economics is the role of the language. This history is our concern in Part II. In Chapter 2, we begin with Adam Smith and J. S. Mill. For Smith, trade itself depends on language; it is fundamentally an act of persuasion. For Mill, discussion is central to self-government. In his view, people arrive at the goals of the group through discussion. Through discussion they also learn to moderate their language so as not to offend and, indeed, to persuade. For Mill, discussion is also the means by which one learns one's own biases and one comes to challenge belief with evidence.

When economists lost interest in language, they lost the ability to move from individual to group goals. For many years after, the collective action problem – described by the colorful label of the prisoner's dilemma – was seen as insurmountable. But economists like everyone else looked at the empirical world and they noticed a good deal of cooperation. Experimental economics emerged as an important subdiscipline of economics and the question was posed using experimental methods: what if individuals are allowed to communicate in a collective-action setting?

One of the regularities of experimental economics that has now been firmly established is that language induces cooperation. Chapter 2 reviews these findings as reported in a survey article by Elinor Ostrom and her colleagues as well as two later metastudies. We also briefly discuss two papers that we, along with coauthors, published to test whether the role of language is more than a signal conveying information. The experimental results speak to the issue of the endogeneity of group goals. Communication among group members is different from a message from outside. It is, instead, the means by which goals are established.

Chapter 3 provides our account of the "Knightian moment" in which discussion briefly flourished in economic analysis. As Knight uses the term *discussion*, it precludes persuasive speech. It is, instead, constrained by deference and fairness, by ethics. We show that, many decades later, John Rawls was struck by Knight's approach to discussion. Two of Knight's students, George Stigler and Milton Friedman, who early in their careers considered themselves Knightians, wrote only one article together, a 1946 study of the consequences of rent control. Their article obtained a modest celebrity in recent years for its ingenious use of the San Francisco earthquake as a natural experiment. At the time, however, economists realized the significance of its approach: the article placed allocation by the market on the same moral plane as allocation through politics. Because of this, the article was quite controversial.

Chapter 4 examines how discussion largely disappeared from the economics literature with the advent of new welfare economics. In 1932 Knight's friend, Lionel Robbins famously made the compelling case that even if we know scientifically that demand curves slope down, we do not know scientifically how to compare the well-being of one person with that of another. Robbins's colleagues, Nicholas Kaldor and John Hicks, responded to this challenge by arguing that any policy that increased physical output allowed the possibility of transfers that made everyone richer. From this idea of possible transfers emerged New Welfare Economics, which was said to be value-free and which offered a seemingly scientific warrant for economic policy analysis. We suggest in what follows that with the rise of Kaldor-Hicks efficiency, the implementation of expert advice became akin to engineering to obtain efficiency. The space for discussion in the formulation or implementation of goals shrank markedly as a result, whereas the role for the expert became less about exploring options and goals and more about designing mechanisms to obtain efficiency. So, as economists began to posit exogenous goals, the role of the economist shifted from participant in democratic deliberations to that of economic engineer.

Late in his life, Samuelson reminisced about Robbins's contribution. We quote his words as epigram to Chapter 4 because his witness is invaluable. Robbins's position was unpopular with economists, Samuelson remembered, because Robbins offered policy advice as a voter equivalent to other voters. There was, in Robbins's view, no scientific warrant for policy without consent. In our view, Robbins's caution was well-founded: We demonstrate in Section 3 just how costly it has been to impose exogenously determined goals on people without adequate review and discussion.

2

# On "Strongly Fortified Minds"

## Self-Restraint and Cooperation in the Discussion Tradition

Public reasoning is not only crucial for democratic legitimacy, it is essential for a better public epistemology that would allow the consideration of divergent perspectives. It is also required for more effective practical reasoning. It can bring out what particular demands and protests can be restrained in interactive public reasoning, in line with scrutinized priorities between a cluster of quite distinct demands. This involves a process of "give and take" which many political analysts, from Adam Smith and the Marquis de Condorcet in the eighteenth century to Frank Knight and James Buchanan in our time, have made us appreciate better.

A. K. Sen (2012)

## 2.1 Introduction

We are all subject to wishing that a thing be true or at least provisionally correct, so that our prior beliefs are confirmed. Indeed, John Stuart Mill recognized this in his 1843 *Logic*, a tour de force in making the case for inductive logic. Mill wrote:

We cannot believe a proposition only by wishing, or only by dreading, to believe it.... [Wishing] operates, by making [a person] look out eagerly for reasons, or apparent reasons, to support opinions which are conformable to his interests or feelings; ... whoever was on his guard against all kinds of inconclusive evidence which can be mistaken for conclusive, would be in no danger of being led into error even by the strongest bias. There are minds so strongly fortified on the intellectual side, that they could not blind themselves to the light of truth, however really desirous of doing so. (Mill 1973, p. 738)

Mill placed his faith in education – including, significantly, robust discussion – as at least a partial correction for this failing. In his view, discussion was the means by which individuals come to more fully understand what they believe. More than this, in the classical view of economics, the exchange of words and discussion constitutes the means by which we come to moderate our selfish impulses and, increasingly, to cooperate.[1]

Accordingly, this chapter explores some unappreciated benefits of discussion, in particular the importance of discussion as a correction to bias and a means by which society's goals are endogenously determined and constantly checked and revised.[2] People come to appreciate the goals of others through discussion with them. Through discussion, they come to appreciate difference and point of view. Discussion is part and parcel of a healthy skepticism of expert recommendations and policy formulations that presume exogenous goals.

Accordingly, we demonstrate in what follows that beginning with Smith and continuing through the experimental economists and Amartya Sen (2012), economists have expounded on the rich moral and material benefits associated with discussion – benefits that contribute to a well-governed social order.[3] The role of economists from Adam Smith through Frank Knight and his student, James Buchanan, in explaining the benefits associated with discussion has been neglected both within economics and throughout academe. The requirements for discussion, as these economists used the term, are stringent. Reciprocity and civility are needed and so, too, is real listening and moral restraint. In this tradition one accepts the inevitability of an individual "point of view" and the good society is one that governs itself by means of an emergent consensus among points of view. To emphasize the common themes in this neglected tradition, we shall refer to it as the "discussion tradition."

## 2.2  Discussion, the Self, and Trade: Adam Smith

Perhaps the first and hardest bias is the bias that places the self at the center of the universe. Without language there is no other, and hence no requirement for reciprocity or civility: the sense that one resides at the center of the universe simply persists. With language, we convey our sense of self to others, and we learn how others perceive our self and our sense of self. We also learn about others; we exchange ideas and emotions with them.

---

[1]  The Mill passage we quote comes from the section of *Logic* that concerns fallacies. In this and in many other areas, it is helpful to read Mill and Richard Whatley together. See Levy and Peart (2010).

[2]  Martha Nussbaum focuses on argumentation, as opposed to discussion, and she suggests that we must continue to support Socratic pedagogy on college campuses. See Nussbaum (2010, pp. 46–61). We seek to broaden the focus to include all forms of communication.

[3]  Most recently, Deirdre McCloskey has argued that the material benefits associated with persuasion are significant. See McCloskey (2010, p. 385ff).

The first lesson about discussion, then, is that language forms the basis for imaginative exchange, for the placing of one's self in another's shoes, and for giving and receiving approval or approbation.[4]

For Smith, this first type of exchange, the exchange of approbation, helps us become moral persons. As is well known, Smith distinguished between praise and praiseworthiness in *The Theory of Moral Sentiments*, and he held that we are all subject to the desire to be praiseworthy. Although we may not always know how to obtain the approbation of others, we observe people's reactions to our acts and we come to understand what constitutes appropriate or virtuous conduct by observing what is generally approved. We come to moderate our actions in order to obtain general approval. We come to understand that we are not the center of the universe and we behave accordingly:

A very young child has no self-command; but, whatever are its emotions, whether fear, or grief, or anger, it endeavours always, by the violence of its outcries, to alarm, as much as it can, the attention of its nurse, or of its parents. While it remains under the custody of such partial protectors, its anger is the first and, perhaps, the only passion which it is taught to moderate. By noise and threatening they are, for their own ease, often obliged to frighten it into good temper; and the passion which incites it to attack, is restrained by that which teaches it to attend to its own safety. When it is old enough to go to school, or to mix with its equals, it soon finds that they have no such indulgent partiality. It naturally wishes to gain their favour, and to avoid their hatred or contempt. Regard even to its own safety teaches it to do so; and it soon finds that it can do so in no other way than by moderating, not only its anger, but all its other passions, to the degree which its play-fellows and companions are likely to be pleased with. It thus enters into the great school of self-command, it studies to be more and more master of itself, and begins to exercise over its own feelings a discipline which the practice of the longest life is very seldom sufficient to bring to complete perfection. (Smith 1790; III.1.64)

The first significant benefit of (face-to-face) language, of discussion, in Smith's view is, therefore, that it induces moderation and perhaps even something we would today refer to as tolerance. It is through language, and the exchange of approbation over time, that we come to understand what is generally approved and we try to act accordingly. To the extent that we succeed, we become virtuous individuals. Importantly, for Smith all that is required for this is the exchange of approbation that occurs in language: civility and virtue emerge from our general desire for approval.[5]

---

[4] Language is the mechanism by which approval is conveyed, just as it is required for material exchange. We return to such trades in section 2.5.

[5] What can thwart this moderating influence of discussion, of course, is faction: the desire to obtain approval from one subset of the polity. When one belongs to a faction, one cares

In terms of governance, in the discussion tradition we are led to accept that ours is only one of many points of view in the search for consensus. Discussion is also a means by which our imaginative capacity is stretched to include at least partial understanding of the goals and arguments of others.[6]

This partial understanding of the goals of others is central to Smith's account of the material benefits of exchange. The argument in his lectures, delivered between the publication of the *Theory of Moral Sentiments* and the *Wealth of Nations* makes the case most clearly. Here Smith linked the desire to persuade, a central piece in the discussion tradition, with exchange. To make a persuasive argument in favor of an exchange, Smith argues, we need to imagine how the exchange will benefit our would-be trading partner.[7]

As noted, Smith famously held that without discussion there is no trade; with discussion there is. Without the ability to converse, creatures like greyhounds and mastiffs are, therefore, unable to obtain the material benefits attendant on language:

The strength of the mastiff is not in the least supported either by the swiftness of the greyhound, or by the sagacity of the spaniel, or by the docility of the shepherd's dog. The effects of those different geniuses and talents, for want of the power or disposition to barter and exchange, cannot be brought into a common stock, and do not in the least contribute to the better accommodation and conveniency of the species. Each animal is still obliged to support and defend itself, separately and independently, and derives no sort of advantage from that variety of talents with which nature has distinguished its fellows. (Smith1904, I.2.5)

In contrast, humans have access to language and that enables them to obtain the benefits of specialization, trade, and cooperation:

Among men, on the contrary, the most dissimilar geniuses are of use to one another; the different produces of their respective talents, by the general disposition to

---

about approval from that group rather more than approval from everyone; consequently one might grandstand, showboat, or behave poorly toward those who are not in the group to obtain the group members' approval. Smith was well aware of this problem. We will return to factions in Chapter 10.

[6]  Our account is in line with that in Nussbaum (1997, p. 93) in which she links liberal education via imagination to an improved capacity for compassion. In the nineteenth century, major figures in the discussion tradition, Mill and Whately, were important in the larger antislavery movement. See Peart and Levy (2005) and Levy and Peart (2005).

[7]  "If we should enquire into the principle in the human mind on which this disposition of trucking is founded, it is clearly the natural inclination every one has to persuade. The offering of a shilling, which to us appears to have so plain and simple a meaning, is in reality offering an argument to persuade one to do so and so as it is for his interest ... That is bartering, by which they address themselves to the self interest of the person and seldom fail immediately to gain their end" (Smith 1982, vi.57, p. 352). The passage is taken from the student notes at the 1763 lectures.

truck, barter, and exchange, being brought, as it were, into a common stock, where every man may purchase whatever part of the produce of other men's talents he has occasion for. (Smith 1904, I.2.5)

Discussion is also the key means by which wealth is produced and increased over time. In today's vernacular, it is via discussion that we are able best to decide who should do what and when.

There is, then, an external economy in the realm of knowledge associated with discussion among free people. One dramatic example occurred at a celebrated dinner party hosted by Aaron Director with guests from the economics department at the University of Chicago. At this dinner, Ronald Coase famously changed the minds of his colleagues on the question of externalities and property rights. George Stigler described the conversation:

When, in 1960, Ronald Coase criticized Pigou's theory rather casually, in the course of a masterly analysis of the regulatory philosophy underlying the Federal Communications Commission's work, Chicago economists could not understand how so fine an economist as Coase could make so obvious a mistake. Since he persisted, we invited Coase (he was then at the University of Virginia) to come and give a talk on it. Some twenty economists from the University of Chicago and Ronald Coase assembled one evening at the home of Aaron Director. Ronald asked us to assume, for a time, a world without transaction costs. That seemed reasonable because economic theorists, like all theorists, are accustomed (nay, compelled) to deal with simplified and therefore unrealistic "models" and problems. (Stigler 1988, p. 75)

It was this thought experiment that led to a deeper understanding of the role that property rights (and other social institutions that reduce the costs of exchange) play in fostering overall efficiency as individuals bargain with one another in a market context. We call attention to the deep respect that the Chicago economists and Coase had for each other. They discussed what divided them and through this discussion they changed the course of twentieth-century economics.[8]

## 2.3 Discussion and Learning: J. S. Mill

As noted at the outset, Mill believed that education was a means by which we come to fortify ourselves against bias. Although he was for the most part silent on the source of such priors, Mill was convinced that we come to rid

---

[8] Today, in an increasingly complex society in which knowledge is partial and local, many key innovations are similarly the result of discussion and collaboration among those who bring their separate expertise to the table.

ourselves of false beliefs and to understand true ones through discussion.[9] In Mill's view, all people[10] are capable of being "guided to their own improvement by conviction or persuasion":

Rectifying … mistakes, by discussion and experience. Not by experience alone. There must be discussion, to show how experience is to be interpreted. Wrong opinions and practices gradually yield to fact and argument: but facts and arguments, to produce any effect on the mind, must be brought before it. (Mill 1984, p. 306)

Silencing discussion "is an assumption of infallibility," the presumption of perfection.[11]

For Mill, we first come to know a thing by knowing what is said about it:

[T]he only way in which a human being can make some approach to knowing the whole of a subject, is by hearing what can be said about it by persons of every variety of opinion, and studying all modes in which it can be looked at by every character of mind.

If, instead, we simply believe what we are told, we fail fully to understand the proposition and our belief might well be called "superstition."[12] (Mill 1977, p. 232)

So, knowledge is better understood once experienced or discussed.

[9]   What Mill called "false beliefs" might today be referred to as "implicit bias"; see Greenwald and Cooper (2006). Consistent with the argument in section 2.5, Greenwald and Cooper maintain that such biases are malleable and they suggest that biases against "out group" individuals are reduced by intragroup interactions.

[10]  Mill provided the qualification that those who are childlike had yet to acquire this capacity. In his 1867 Inaugural Address at St. Andrews, Mill reiterated, "improvement consists in bringing our opinions into nearer agreement with facts; and we shall not be likely to do this while we look at facts only through glasses coloured by those very opinions. But since we cannot divest ourselves of preconceived notions, there is no known means of eliminating their influence but by frequently using the differently coloured glasses of other people: and those of other nations, as the most different, are the best" (Mill 1984, p. 226).

[11]  "To call any proposition certain, while there is any one who would deny its certainty if permitted, but who is not permitted, is to assume that we ourselves, and those who agree with us, are the judges of certainty, and judges without hearing the other side" (Mill 1977, p. 223). In Chapter 6, we show how the silencing of an academic textbook had a deleterious effect on the analysis of the growth of the Soviet Union. F. A. Hayek refused to endorse William F. Buckley's continuation of the attack on the Keynesian economics textbooks (Buckley 1951). See Peart and Levy (2013a).

[12]  "The fact, however, is, that not only the grounds of the opinion are forgotten in the absence of discussion, but too often the meaning of the opinion itself. The words that convey it, cease to suggest ideas, or suggest only a small portion of those they were originally employed to communicate. Instead of a vivid conception and a living belief, there remain only a few phrases retained by rote; or, if any part, the shell and husk only of the meaning is retained, the finer essence being lost. The great chapter in human history which this fact occupies and fills, cannot be too earnestly studied and meditated on" (Mill 1977, p. 247). See also Mill (1984).

[T]here are many truths of which the full meaning *cannot* be realized, until personal experience has brought it home. But much more of the meaning even of these would have been understood, and what was understood would have been far more deeply impressed on the mind, if the man had been accustomed to hear it argued *pro* and *con* by people who did understand it. The fatal tendency of mankind to leave off thinking about a thing when it is no longer doubtful, is the cause of half their errors. A contemporary author has well spoken of "the deep slumber of a decided opinion." (Mill 1977, p. 250)

It is also important to know and perhaps to learn from one's critics, to develop a "steady habit of correcting and completing" our opinion "by collating it with those of others."[13] Arguments that try to silence discussion often, in Mill's view, hide behind a pronouncement that we must avoid discussing an extreme case.[14] Like Smith, Mill recognized the problem of faction; discussion may not break down the barriers of factionalized or party interests. Although discussion may not successfully penetrate and alter the minds of those whose views have been hardened by faction, it will, nonetheless be useful to the "calmer and more disinterested bystander," one who has yet to become factionalized.

I acknowledge that the tendency of all opinions to become sectarian is not cured by the freest discussion, but is often heightened and exacerbated thereby; the truth which ought to have been, but was not, seen, being rejected all the more violently because proclaimed by persons regarded as opponents. But it is not on the impassioned partisan, it is on the calmer and more disinterested bystander, that this collision of opinions works its salutary effect. Not the violent conflict between parts of the truth, but the quiet suppression of half of it, is the formidable evil. (Mill 1977, p. 259)

Free discussion leads to moderation, although here Mill suggested that the incentives are asymmetrically aligned. In a twist on Smith's theme, Mill argued that those who speak against received wisdom must practice moderation more systematically than those who hold received opinions:[15]

---

[13] We might also hold conversations with people in the past: "To question all things; never to turn away from any difficulty, to accept no doctrine either from ourselves or from other people without a rigid scrutiny by negative criticism, letting no fallacy, or incoherence, or confusion of thought, slip by unperceived; above all, to insist upon having the meaning of a word clearly understood before using it, and the meaning of a proposition before assenting to it; these are the lessons we learn from the ancient dialecticians" Mill (1977, pp. 229–30).

[14] This sort of reasoning is the basis for the common exercise on college campuses of randomly assigning students to a "point of view" and then asking them to argue a conclusion that may well be contrary to what they bring to the classroom. As they do so, students may come to better appreciate the weight of their opponents' arguments.

[15] In Chapter 5 we observe the consequence of Mill's own practice of moderation in discussion. His very delicate consideration of contraception in his *Principles of Political Economy*

In general, opinions contrary to those commonly received can only obtain a hearing by studied moderation of language, and the most cautious avoidance of unnecessary offence, from which they hardly ever deviate even in a slight degree without
losing ground: while unmeasured vituperation employed on the side of the prevailing opinion, really does deter people from professing contrary opinions, and from
listening to those who profess them. (Mill 1977, p. 249)

Teachers consequently for Mill had a special obligation to teach from
different perspectives:

If teaching, even on matters of scientific certainty, should aim quite as much at showing how the results are arrived at, as at teaching the results themselves, far more, then,
should this be the case on subjects where there is the widest diversity of opinion
among men of equal ability, and who have taken equal pains to arrive at the truth.
This diversity should of itself be a warning to a conscientious teacher that he has
no right to impose his opinion authoritatively upon a youthful mind. His teaching
should not be in the spirit of dogmatism, but in that of enquiry. (Mill 1984, p. 249)

The discussion tradition that recognizes the inevitability of a point of
view can be contrasted with a tradition that idealizes anonymity, in which,
because scientific knowledge is presumed anonymous, the scientist ought
not to have a point of view. In one sense, the issue is trivial. If everyone
agrees, then there is nothing interesting to discuss. More dangerously, however, those with power can easily stigmatize those without power on the
basis that the powerful are impartial and have no point of view but the stigmatized do. The "impartial" are, therefore, better than the stigmatized and
thus are to be trusted with power. The fundamental moral issue is respect
for personal autonomy carried by a reciprocity norm. One is aware of one's
point of view and by reciprocity one accepts that all other moral agents are
entitled to their own point of view. Open discussion is thus the signature of
this mutual respect. Moreover, the respect for others carries with it a commitment to a seriousness that leaves open the possibility of being persuaded
to alter one's point of view.[16]

---

made it implausible that the topic was itself an obscenity, an argument that Annie Besant
advanced with great force in her trial.

[16] As emphasized earlier, in Smith and Mill's telling discussion is characterized by listening
and civility – that is, the imaginative exchange of positions. It is worth noting that we have
moved a long way from this idealized state: discussion today in the political, artistic, and
intellectual realms very often entails only posturing (to which we return in Chapter 4)
and, worse, a sort of shrill yelling. Although our main concern in the book is the role of
discussion in the policy-making context, it is worth noting here that, as such shrillness
has perhaps ratcheted up on college campuses, and discussion of different points of view
and experience is perceived to be unsafe, it is unsurprising that we see increased calls on
college campuses for "trigger warnings" to allow the less powerful to disengage.

## 2.4 Fair Play and Language

In the twentieth century, a helpful treatment of the role of moral restraint in discussion is found in the papers collected by his students and younger colleagues in Frank Knight's 1947 *Freedom and Reform*. Knight's dictum that he attributed to Lord Bryce – democracy is government by discussion – (Knight 1947 p. 391) has attained a status in recent years as a substantial improvement over the approach to "social choice" laid out by Kenneth Arrow (1963). Arrow's initial formulation supposed that the preferences of the agents in the political process remained unchanged in the process of voting. If preferences reflecting desires were fixed, a theorist of liberal democracy could take the society's goals as exogenous. If, however, discussion has any role to play in governance, preferences might alter in the course of discussion (Buchanan 1954; Sen 1995). Here is Sen's recent judgment:

> By clarifying the role of that momentous engagement in a truly outstanding pair of articles in the *Journal of Political Economy* in 1954, Buchanan immensely enriched the subject matter with which social choice as well as public choice has to be centrally engaged. In contrast with Arrow's initial inclination – as he put it – "to assume … that individual values are taken as data and are not capable of being altered by the nature of the decision process itself," Buchanan had to insist that seeing "democracy as 'government by discussion' implies that individual values can and do change in the process of decision-making" (Arrow, 1963 and Buchanan, 1954). It can be claimed that it is only through Buchanan's expansion of Arrow's departures that we can do justice to the Enlightenment enterprise of advancing rational decision making in societies, which lies at the foundation of democratic modernity. (Sen 2013)[17]

Sen's final sentence alludes to the issue of whether governance is an occasion for learning. Consistent with liberal tenets, Arrow had assumed that everyone's views count and he then demonstrated that, given participants with fixed, coherent desires, the only way to obtain coherence at a group level was to give up liberality and let the decision be made by a single individual.[18] For decades after Arrow first published his formulation Buchanan protested against Arrow's assumption that nothing is learned in the democratic process. Buchanan challenged Arrow's assumption of fixed desires and Sen points us to Buchanan's objections in the passage above. The key problem, to which Sen draws our attention, is that Arrow's formulation

---

[17] John Rawls's dependence on Knight's 1935 *Ethics of Competition* in *Theory of Justice* is discussed in Chapter 9.

[18] Arrow 1963, pp. 83–84) addressed Knight's and Stigler's argument about the importance of consensus. We discuss Knight's influence on Stigler's early work in Levy and Peart 2008b and Chapter 3.

assumes there is no learning in the course of discussion. The group's goals are exogenously determined.

Knight, who was Buchanan's teacher at Chicago, described how preferences might change in the course of discussion. People enter into discussion in part because they are discontented with themselves:

> In contrast with natural objects – even with the higher animals – man is unique in that he is dissatisfied with himself; he is the discontented animal, the romantic, argumentative, aspiring animal. Consequently, his behavior can only in part be described by scientific principles or laws. (Knight 1947 p. 237)

Real discussion, as Knight sees it, is rare because it depends on public-spirited participants:

> Genuine, purely intellectual discussion is rare in modern society, even in intellectual and academic circles, and is approximated only in very small and essentially casual groups. On the larger scale, what passes for discussion is mostly argumentation or debate. The intellectual interest is largely subordinate to entertainment, i.e., entertaining and being entertained, or the immediate interest of the active parties centers chiefly in dominance, victory, instructing others, or persuading rather than convincing, and not in the impartial quest of truth. (1947, p. 349)

Knight saw the conflict in the discussion tradition between attempting to implement one's point of view by any means available and truth seeking. Yet by requiring that economists in the discussion are truth seekers and allowing that ordinary people seek their own interests, Buchanan and Knight introduced a motivational heterogeneity – some people in discussion seek the truth, and others seek their own happiness. The solution to this paradox is close at hand as long as we can accept ethical rules of conduct as constraints for all who enter into the discussion. In an extension of Buchanan and Knight, we propose that participants in the discussion bind themselves ex ante with rules of conduct that constrain how they argue their points of view.

Agreement on such constraints depends strongly on an awareness that those who participate in discussion generally have a point of view. Viewing the contending parties' views as equally deserving of respect is a critical step in the argument. It seems unlikely that constraints on discussion will come about without an awareness that, without them, unwanted results will emerge. Smith's principle of moral reform held that before we change ourselves or society, we need to come to view our own actions from the vantage point of outside observers. If we see others offering biased advice and we think poorly of the practice, then there is hope for a reformation. It is helpful to notice that for Smith there is little distinction between individual and social reform (Levy and Peart 2013a). This is taken for granted when Knight describes humans as the unique dissatisfied animal. But he did not lay out any plausible process of reform. He could not have availed himself of *Theory of Moral Sentiments* since, when Knight wrote, *TMS* was known only to specialists. The greatest of these, Knight's colleague Jacob Viner, had offered the judgment at the University of Chicago sesquicentennial celebration of the *Wealth of Nations* that there was a deep inconsistency between it and Smith's early book (Viner 1927).

Thus, one of the most promising developments in the last four decades has been the recovery by economists of Smith's *Theory of Moral Sentiments*. The recovery of the *Theory of Moral Sentiments* and the overcoming of Viner's objections has had a considerable impact on the interpretation and the development of experimental economics. Many puzzles in the experimental results became coherent when viewed in light of Smith's *TMS*. To this line of research we turn next.

## 2.5  Discussion and Cooperation: Experimental Evidence

The recovery of the *Theory of Moral Sentiments* by experimental economists (V. Smith 1998, 2008; Ashraf, Camerer, and Loewenstein 2005) brought about a sea change in how economists deal with the experimental regularities of cooperation and sharing. There is perhaps no stronger experimental evidence than the conclusion, confirmed in many experimental studies, that discussion strongly enhances cooperation. As guides to a large literature we point to a wide-ranging survey of the literature from 1992 and two meta-analyses, one from 1995 and one from 2010. Twenty years ago Elinor Ostrom and her colleagues (Ostrom, Walker, and Gardner 1992) summarized a large body of empirical work, which addressed the neoclassical economic (Hobbesian) commonplace that language did not matter. They described the empirical findings:

i) In one-shot social dilemma experiments, communication alone leads to substantial improvements in outcomes.
ii) In repeated social dilemma experiments, repeated communication alone leads to substantial improvements in joint outcomes.
iii) In field settings of repeated social dilemmas, participants invest substantial time and effort monitoring and imposing sanctions on one another (1992, p. 405).

Three years later, David Sally published a meta-analysis of the experimental evidence from 1958 to 1992 (Sally 1995). Sally noted that the standard

model of rational choice had problems accounting for the observed regularities, and "This incongruity is widest with respect to the role of language
in encouraging cooperation" (Sally 1995). A meta-analysis in the 2010
*Journal of Conflict Resolution* summarized the results of experiments studying the impact of communication on cooperation as follows:

> Among the most researched solutions to social dilemmas is communication. Since
> the late 1950s, it has been well known that communication enhances cooperation
> in social dilemmas. This article reports a meta-analysis of this literature … and finds
> a large positive effect of communication on cooperation in social dilemmas … This
> effect is moderated by the type of communication, with a stronger effect of face-to-
> face discussion … compared to written messages … The communication-cooperation
> relationship is also stronger in larger, compared to smaller, group social dilemmas.
> Whether communication occurred before or during iterated dilemmas did not statis-
> tically affect the communication-cooperation effect size. (Balliet 2010)

Thus a robust set of experimental evidence confirms the insight that
discussion is a key to determining and achieving group goals. Members
of a group are more likely to realize that, as a group, they would be well
advised to cooperate, when discussion about the goals is allowed. This
leaves open the question, however, of the role of experts in the endogenous determination of such goals through discussion. In most public
goods experiments, the institutional structure is flat: there may be a first
mover but there are few if any information advantages created in the
structure of the game. Everyone hears the same instructions and then
the group members begin to discuss contribution levels and make their
contributions.

We have argued in Chapter 1 that experts are self-interested as well as
public-spirited and that, consequently, transparency is a key to ensuring
that groups obtain the benefits associated with expertise. To obtain some
experimental evidence on the role of transparency in the determination of
group goals, we designed a public-goods experiment in which we allowed
a communicator, the leader,[19] to convey a message to others in the group
about how much to contribute to the public good. The most natural way
to introduce language into economics is to suppose that it functions solely
as means to exchange information in support of coordination of plans. The
first question then is whether this is all there is. In the technical literature,

---

[19] In these experiments we characterized the communicator as a leader. Whether he or she
might be conceptualized as an expert is another matter. Clearly, however, she is offering
advice on the contribution level that would be best for the group. Group members may
defer to advice carried in language even when they are aware that the advice might not be
trustworthy.

the phrase "cheap talk" is used to suggest that the costs of neglecting the role of language are small.

To address the role of language in supporting cooperation we, along with our colleagues Daniel Houser, Kail Padgitt, and Erte Xiao, conducted a series of experiments (Levy, Padgitt, Peart, Houser and Xiao 2011; Houser, Levy, Padgitt, Peart, and Xiao 2014). The rules of the game were explained to all participants, and their understanding was checked before play began, to ensure that the *rules* were transparent. Thus, although there was some nontransparency throughout the *play* of the game, this play occurred in the context of transparent rules. As in the experiments described, players in the game chose how much to contribute to a public account and a private account. Collectively, players have an incentive to put all their contributions in the public account, but individually each has an incentive to put all contributions into the private account.

One novelty in our setup was the selection of a leader who suggested an amount to be contributed to the public account. This was one way in which language entered the experiment. But there was another place for language. Before the game was played, each player wrote a platform or recommendation for the group's play. Proposed platforms were distributed to all players. Two methods were used to select the group's leader. In the first, the player who proposed the winning platform was the selected leader. Second, the leader was selected at random from the players. The leader then made a nonbinding suggestion for contributions to the group account. Not surprisingly given the studies reported earlier, our experiments induced more cooperation than in experiments without language. Moreover, the results clearly indicated that the leader elected on the basis of a proposed platform was more effective in eliciting contributions than a leader selected at random.

To further study how language matters, we compared contributions in the context of a message that emerged endogenously from the group versus a corresponding message from a computer. The message was the same; only the source differed. In the former case the message emerged endogenously to the group's discussion; in the latter, it was exogenously determined. We coined the term *really cheap talk* to suggest that even if the cost of human language is small, as *cheap talk* suggests, an exogenous message is smaller still. The results were predictable – contributions collapsed in really cheap talk.

The second sequence of experiments focused on the question of transparency in the course of discussion and advice. In the initial experimental setup, the leader could suggest an amount and contribute without the others being aware of how his or her conduct matched his or her suggestion.

Two variations were then imposed. In the first, all the players were told what the leader suggested and also what the leader contributed to the public account in the previous round. In the second, the information given to the players included a random component to make the transparency imperfect. The results were striking and very much in line with our presupposition that transparency is important in achieving the benefits of cooperation: the higher the transparency, the higher the level of contributions to the public account.

Essentially the experiment explored the motivational force of the age-old aphorism, "Do as I say, not as I do." One simple interpretation of this saying is that it warns against hypocrisy, as when children dismiss parental advice that runs counter to their parents' observed behavior. Aware that the motivational force of advice can be weakened by the presence of a gap between saying and doing, people who give advice (including parents) might be motivated to follow their own suggestions of selflessness (for example, to save more and smoke less). But this supposes transparency, that what they do is observable.

The issue with advising selfless behavior, of course, is that it may be individually costly to follow. Consequently, if we were able to get away with doing so unseen, we each have the incentive to give such advice but not to follow it. This insight, that transparency links private motivations and social consequences, dates at least to Smith's 1759 poetic statement:

If we saw ourselves in the light in which others see us, or in which they would see us if they knew all, a reformation would generally be unavoidable. We could not otherwise endure the sight. (Smith 1790, III.i.93)

A hundred years later, in an argument against the secret ballot (which he viewed as a nontransparency in the selection of leaders) Mill suggested that secrecy attenuated social motivations:

the point to be decided is, whether the social feelings connected with an act, and the sense of social duty in performing it, can be expected to be as powerful when the act is done in secret, and he can neither be admired for disinterested, nor blamed for mean and selfish conduct. But this question is answered as soon as stated. (Mill 1986, p 1214)

If Mill is correct, transparency would yield more public-spirited actions.

Although economists work and live in language, their models of how agents act largely neglect the role of communication, whether face-to-face, spoken, or written. Certainly this is true of textbook economics in which our agents rarely speak to each other.[20] If we are to take language seriously, we need to begin at a foundational level and ask the most rudimentary questions. In a well-studied experimental context, does it matter whether the message, a fragment of language, comes from a person in the group or from an unknown process? Our experimental evidence demonstrates that it does. Although this may seem to be an obvious result – of course people matter! – the faceless and nameless agents in countless models where information is surely being transmitted suggest that we have underappreciated (and understudied) the connection between the person and the advice.

Second, we have experimental evidence to address the question: Does it matter if the advisor is not actually willing to follow his or her own advice? Perhaps the best question to a doctor in the face of a recommendation to suffer through a treatment in the perhaps slim hope that it will yield better health: "would you undergo this treatment yourself in the same situation?" The Madoffs or the Pearsons of the past who advised horrible investments or horrible immigration restrictions surely would never have wished to suffer the consequences of their recommendations themselves.

So, in this same (public good) experimental context, we asked whether it matters if the advisor, the message sender, acts to follow his or her own advice. The answer is, resoundingly, that it does. This reinforces our argument, made throughout the book, that a transparency that allows those who receive advice to see how the expert/leader behaves is important. We would suggest that there is an ethical imperative for the expert to reveal that his or her actions are (or are not) in accord with the advice offered and that anyone who follows the advice of the expert should scrutinize the expert's actions as much as possible in order to see whether he or she is indeed acting in accord with the advice.

Smith provides a valuable guide to this body of research because, as we have noted and unlike the economists of the next two centuries, he anchors trade in language. Although Smith has a reputation of individualism, there is no mistaking his concern for how membership in a group influences one's conduct. The group could be a family, neighborhood, college campus,

---

[20] George Stigler might have been one of the last great neoclassical economist even to joke about this when he pointed out that the agents economists study can talk. He asked what chemistry would be like if an element of oxygen insisted that it was actually argon (Stigler 1966, p. 8). Unfortunately, Stigler never published his lecture considering how Smith's explanation of trade depends on language. We know of the lecture only because one of us was witness. Roger Koppl reminded us that we should not forget Fritz Machlup's "If matter could talk" (Machlup 1978).

commercial association, or a nation; Smith analyzes the impact of many such groups on individual choice (Levy and Peart 2009a). But perhaps the group to which he gives the most substantial attention is that of a religious body. His celebrated defense of religion independent of government is offered as a means of moderating the tenor of discussion among religious leaders (Levy and Peart 2009a, 2013a). Here, in a passage that deserves to be quoted at length, Smith offers evidence of an American field experiment on the nature of discussion. This is where we see Sen's give and take most clearly expressed:

> The interested and active zeal of religious teachers can be dangerous and trouble-some only where there is either but one sect tolerated in the society, or where the whole of a large society is divided into two or three great sects; the teachers of each acting by concert, and under a regular discipline and subordination. But that zeal must be altogether innocent where the society is divided into two or three hundred, or perhaps into as many thousand small sects, of which no one could be considerable enough to disturb the public tranquility. The teachers of each sect, see-ing themselves surrounded on all sides with more adversaries than friends, would be obliged to learn that candour and moderation which is so seldom to be found among the teachers of those great sects ... (Smith 1904, V.1.197)

In the statement we quoted earlier, Sen argued that Knight and Buchanan progressed a step beyond Smith's enlightenment project with their appeal to government by discussion. Smith holds clearly and distinctly that justice is central to a well-governed society. He also makes the case that factionalized religion presents a clear danger to social order because religious doctrine is the path by which the duty of justice is diffused. The danger is that the dictates of impartial justice will be suspended for the benefit of one's fellow sectarians (Levy and Peart 2013a). The path away from that danger is, for Smith, to alter the terms of discussion.

## 2.6  Conclusion

If the foregoing insights, beginning with Smith and carried through Mill to Knight, Buchanan, and Sen are correct, do they provide any guidance for how we think about policy formulation and the role of experts? We take several lessons from the political economists who work in the "discussion tradition."

That tradition suggests there may be real and unappreciated benefits associated with discussion about group goals. Although many policy mak-ers and educators pay lip service to discussion, they less frequently pro-vide evidence of the benefits of discussion. Three major benefits have been sketched. Smith emphasized, first, the development of a moral sense that emerges as one begins to see oneself as a part – and only a small part – of the universe. Mill accepted this argument and added a second benefit: conversation is corrective. Discussion yields insight into bias and profound learning. The Knight–Buchanan–Sen tradition takes a step beyond Mill to suggest that through discussion one becomes aware and self-aware. One may change one's position in the course of discussion; one may come to appreciate that exogenously determined group goals sometimes come at an enormous, and unacceptable, price: the sacrificing of individual desires and goals.

Experimental evidence confirms these insights and strongly suggests that discussion and transparency facilitate cooperation with others when private and group interests are not fully aligned.[21] Although parties may begin as concerned only with the self or their group, they come to perceive their interconnectedness in the course of discussion. A well-governed society requires that people enter into the spirit of laws and cooperate when their material interests urge them in another direction. Experimental evidence confirms the importance of discussion in encouraging such cooperation. Thus, we can extend these findings to suggest that the benefits from discussion of expert findings, group goals, and policy recommendations are both moral and material, and in either event they are significant.

Most importantly, discussion requires respect for others and their points of view. The same respect for others and their actions is required in Smith's account for considerations of justice to have motivational force. For Smith, people come into the world with two foundational principles: an instinct to trade and an instinct to persuade, and, in fact, he conjectured that these are actually the same principle (1904, I.2.2). The experimental evidence suggests that Smith's conjecture holds. Modern writers tend to think of governance and justice in terms of trade, that is, whether material dealings are fair and equitable. But if Smith is correct, the question of whether discussions take place in a fair and equitable manner is prior.

---

[21] This is consistent with the claim that universities may serve to develop social capital; see Trani and Holsworth (2010, p. 6).

3

# The Knightian Moment

There seem to me to be two essential ways of approaching the study of problems of political, social, and economic organization. The first way is that of setting up independently certain criteria or goals for achievement and to examine existing and potential institutions in the light of their performance or expected performance in meeting these criteria ...

The second approach is that which deliberately avoids the independent establishment of criteria for social organization (such as "efficiency," "rapid growth", etc.), and instead examines the behavior of private individuals as they engage in the continuing search for institutional arrangements upon which they can reach substantial consensus or agreement.

James Buchanan
Letter to Kermit Gordon, September 17, 1960

## 3.1 Introduction

In Chapter 2 we traced a tradition in economics from Adam Smith through John Stuart Mill and into the twentieth century from Frank Knight through James Buchanan to Amartya Sen. In that tradition, goals are determined endogenously, through a "process of 'give and take'" as Sen described it, rather than imposed exogenously on a people. The question that arises is what role remains for experts and expertise? In this chapter we examine the program of expertise put forward most forcefully by Knight in the twentieth century and extended by his students through the late twentieth century.

Our concern in this chapter shall be, first, how economists in this tradition viewed their roles as proponents of policy making, as experts. Second, we shall be concerned with their recommendations for the determination of group (societal) goals and the implementation of those goals. Perhaps most important, using what economists did and said in various policy contexts, we attempt to describe their roles in the determination and the implementation stages of policy making. We do not present an exhaustive list of economists' participation in various policy debates; instead we consider a number of examples that, taken together, suggest an approach to policy analysis, recommendation, and implementation that fits in the discussion tradition described in Chapter 2. In the cases we explore here, economists attempted to place themselves within the economy rather than outside it, participating in the discussion as members of the polity with information advantages that they were willing to eradicate by sharing information.

Between the onset of the marginalist period of economics (ca. 1870–1890), and the modern period (ca. 1945) the discussion tradition flourished. What distinguishes these years from what followed was the emphasis on public discussion in the determination of an ideal policy. To use the phrase Knight adopted from James Bryce, a disciple of the central figure in mid-nineteenth-century British political economy, J. S. Mill, democracy is government by discussion. As such, the group determines its goals endogenously through discussion. This endogeneity of group goals stands in stark contrast to the now orthodox economic approach. We refer to those who hold this older view as "Knightians" and we suggest that the episodes described next represent a "Knightian moment" in economics, one that soon passed and has since been eclipsed.[1]

We acknowledge at the outset that in the view of influential studies of the Chicago School of Economics, Knight's influence there was minimal.[2] For our purposes, the "Chicago School" is too coarse a characterization: not all economists at Chicago were Knightians; some, such as George Stigler, were briefly Knightian and then became less so; and some Knightians were never associated with Chicago.[3]

[1] We defer until Chapter 4 giving a detailed treatment of the passing of the Knightian moment and what replaced it; for now, it suffices to note that in the post-Knightian tradition, discussion does not enter into the determination of goals; instead group goals are inferred from the inarticulate revealed preferences of individuals comprising the group.

[2] See, for instance, Reder (1982, p. 6): "Like the profession at large, Knight's students absorbed his ideas, but did not use them as points of departure for their own work." Reder adds a footnote: "Stigler's dissertation in the history of economic thought (1941), written under Knight's supervision might constitute an exception to this statement. However, Stigler's research in areas other than *Dogmengeschicte* is not particularly Knightian." Perhaps the most Knightian of Stigler's technical contributions is known as "Stigler's diet problem." His "absurd" solution, the least palatable diet one can imagine, is the result of taking biophysical goals asserted by authorities as the precise ends of human life and working out the consequences. The absurdity suggests that there is something wrong with the short list of goals (Stigler 1945; Levy and Peart 2008b).

[3] When Arnold Harberger came to the University of Chicago, the economics department acquired an unqualified advocate for the non-Knightian new welfare economics (Harberger 1954), discussed in Chapter 4.

The notion that group goals are endogenous, determined in a deliberative discussion, has further implications for the role of an expert in democracy. For Knight, the role of the economic expert was twofold: 1) economic experts take the values (norms) of the society as given; 2) proposals for change should be submitted for discussion in a democratic process. Such a brief statement requires at least one amplification. By "values" and "norms," the group is not limited to what economists think of as "ends." Society may well have norms that preclude certain means from consideration. The term that Knight's friend Lionel Robbins used for this was *conventions*.

What are the requirements to satisfy Knight's idea of discussion? Knight's statement in the 1933 preface to the London School reprint of *Risk, Uncertainty and Profit* – unfortunately, not included in the papers collected in the widely available 1935 *Ethics of Competition* – is most illuminating. As he uses the term, discussion is, minimally, noncoercive. But more than this is required. Discussion differs from persuasion. It requires laying out the evidence and then allowing the evidence to do the work of persuasion, an objectivity that is perhaps impossible to attain in human conversation:

> The crux of the whole matter lies, I think, in the concept of discussion. As a plain matter of fact, we do not discuss problems with natural objects, and we do, or may, with human beings. But discussion must be contrasted with persuasion, with any attempt to influence directly the acts, or beliefs, or sentiments, of others. Discussion is a cooperative quest of an impersonally, "objectively" right (or best) solution of an impersonal problem. It cannot be an attempt to "sell" a solution already reached, or it is not discussion. (Knight 1933, p. xxxiii)

We begin by examining Stigler's writings when he was still highly influenced by Knight. The great technical challenge to the Knightian approach, as we shall detail in Chapter 4, was the creation of a value-free welfare economics that supposed economists knew people's goals – higher material income – and could create policies that accomplished these goals. Economists in this view did not need to ask anyone to discuss matters about the policy consequence of hurts and helps because they supposed it was possible for policy winners to compensate losers. In 1943 Stigler attacked the emerging field of new welfare economics by producing a hypothetical policy that would increase material income but violate shared norms.

The second example is the argument advanced by two Knightians, Friedman and Stigler, in their 1946 pamphlet *Roofs or Ceilings?* Here, Friedman and Stigler put forward a series of possible policy responses to housing shortages. Their Knightian position stressed the endogeneity of group goals, determined by some process in which everyone had equal weight in the discussion. What most incensed free-market advocates outside the Knightian tradition was that their pamphlet left room for a non-market solution to the dearth of housing. This episode illustrates that the requirements for a Knightian discussion are substantial.

We turn next to some aspects of the wide-ranging debate over how to conceptualize savings. Early in the twentieth century (and beforehand), savings was supposed to be the observable consequence of one's capacity to imagine the future. An inferior ability to so imagine the future, combined with the supposition that such an inferiority was inherited, was thought to disqualify a person's children from full participation in democratic discussion. It was a small step to eugenic policies, the subject of Chapter 5. Here, we consider the foundational empirical claims in which Friedman's 1958 *Theory of the Consumption Function* played such an important role.[4] We examine how Friedman's work challenged the central tenant of the secular stagnation thesis in which savings was regarded as a residual, something that happens to people. Savings is not, from this point of view, endogenous at even an individual level. Friedman held by contrast that on balance people save about the same proportionate amount of their permanent income. In another instance in which the discussion tradition ranges across traditional labels of left and right, we demonstrate that Paul Samuelson was one of the many advocates of Friedman's consumption work.

We turn finally to perhaps the clearest articulation of the Knightian vis-à-vis the orthodox tradition. The context is a 1960 application to the Ford Foundation from the Knightians of the University of Virginia's Thomas Jefferson Center, Buchanan, Warren Nutter and Ronald Coase. Kermit Gordon and his colleagues at the Ford Foundation concluded that the Knightians were committed to small government and unregulated markets, a narrow sort of liberalism. Buchanan explained that their commitment was to a worldview of analytical egalitarianism in which group goals are endogenous and agents in the model choose their ideal policy. He failed to convince the Ford Foundation officials that theirs was a different sort of liberalism than a dogmatic small government position. The application for funding was denied, putting in motion forces that led to the demise of the Center as a stronghold of the Knightian tradition at the University of Virginia.

What links these episodes? As noted earlier, political differences are neither necessary nor sufficient to explain who fits into the discussion

---

[4] Given the critical role of statisticians in the articulation of eugenic theory and policy responses, it is not a surprise that Friedman encountered such views. See (Friedman and Friedman 1998, p. 618).

tradition: Friedman was attacked from the right; while Samuelson joined with Friedman on the consumption function.[5] Instead, our argument in this chapter is that these examples demonstrate a Knightian moment – a time when a significant portion of economists were willing to take seriously the idea of discussion and the endogeneity of goals. Accordingly, they offered their recommendations for discussion; they saw themselves as part of the group about which they wrote. As such, their role as experts was one of sharing information and expertise and then allowing the discussion to occur. Theirs was a more modest and a more constrained role as expert than we shall see in another period, when the Knightian moment had passed.

## 3.2  Frank Knight's Disciple, George Stigler

In 1943 Stigler put forward a Knightian challenge to "new welfare economics," defending classical economic policy against what was then becoming the new orthodoxy. Two important technical assumptions entered into the debate that followed between Stigler and Samuelson. First, there was the question of whether people have preferences over policies or whether they care only about material goods affected by policies. In his Knightian period, Stigler held the former; whereas Samuelson's position's was unclear. He denied that Stigler's policy was a real instance of new welfare economic policy and he asked Stigler where he might find these shared goals (Samuelson 1943). The latter query was seconded by Kenneth Arrow (1963, pp. 83–84). In his later review of Samuelson's *Foundations* Stigler made the point that Samuelson's economics depended critically upon exogenous preferences and, even with that assumption, new welfare theory did not seem to have real policy applications.

Stigler began the 1943 article with an objection to the presumption that the group would endorse any and all efficient policies. His example, that of paying thieves to prevent theft, strongly suggested that people may well have preferences over policies:

Consider theft; our present policy toward this means of livelihood probably has adverse effects on the national income. Prevention of theft and punishment of thieves involves substantial expenditures for policemen, courts, jails, locks,

---

[5]  This is not to deny some ideological affinity, as argued in Reder (1982) and others. Many who align with what we have called the discussion tradition also align themselves with small government. We will examine this point in much more detail in Chapter 6 when the issue is how to model the Soviet Union, not whether the United States ought to emulate it. For now, our argument is that right/left politics is too blunt an instrument to explain where economists land in the examples that follow.

insurance salesman, and the like. By compensating successful thieves for the amounts they would otherwise steal, we save these resources and hence secure a net gain. (If this policy leads to an undue increase in declarations of intent to steal, the retired successful thieves – who, after all, have special talents in this direction – may be persuaded to assume the police functions.) (1943, p. 356)

Since it would "outrage our moral sensibilities to pay voluntary tribute to thieves," something must be wrong with the presumption that efficiency suffices to determine policy. Stigler sketched the alternative, in which he leaned heavily on discussion by the group:

The familiar admonition not to argue over differences in tastes [*de gustibus non est disputandum*] leads not only to dull conversations but to bad sociology. It is one thing to recognize that we cannot *prove*, by the usual tests of adequacy of proof, the superiority of honesty over deceit or the desirability of a more equal income distribution. But it is quite another thing to conclude that therefore ends of good policy are beyond the realm of scientific discussion.

For surely the primary requisite of a working social system is a consensus on ends. The individual members of the society must agree upon the major ends which that society is to seek. (1943, p. 357)

Stigler cited the 1943 paper in the first full edition of the *Theory of Price* (1946, pp. 15–16) as articulating a Knightian view of the law (Knight 1947, p. 62): "it is the fundamental tenet of those who believe in free discussion that matters of fact and logic can (eventually) be agreed upon by competent men of good will, that matters of taste cannot be.... " Consensus in deep goals was as critical to policy as consensus about theory and fact was to science.

Stigler returned to this argument in 1948 when he reviewed Samuelson's *Foundations of Economic Analysis* in the *Journal of the American Statistical Society* (Stigler 1948). Here he also emphasized the importance of fixed preferences for Samuelson's enterprise. Without this assumption, Samuelson's theorems are necessary truths, imposed on the world rather than discovered in the world:

There is a free variable in his system: the tastes of consumers. These tastes are not observationally (or operationally) defined, so any contradiction of a theory derived from utility theory can always be attributed to a change in tastes, rather than an error in the postulates or logic of the theory. (Stigler 1948, p. 604)

Stigler noted that Samuelson's theory of value was only that; the book contained no worked example of a policy defended by value-minimized methods. He returned to the theme of a consensus of goals.[6]

---

[6]  Stigler (1948, p. 605): "... welfare economics of the Hotelling variety (i.e., somewhat free of value judgments) also receives considerable attention (Chap. 8). I persist in my belief

## 3.3 Free-Market Experts and Ordinary People

*Roofs or Ceilings?* was published in 1946 by the Foundation for Economic Education. It has since attained modest celebrity for its pioneering use of a natural experiment as an identifying restriction in thinking about movements in demand and supply: the 1906 San Francisco earthquake was a true exogenous event that reduced the supply of housing. In their pamphlet, Friedman and Stigler first presented the case for the supply shock and then laid out alternative responses to the shock: rationing by prices; or rationing by government policy.[7] The piece was immediately and severely criticized by Ayn Rand. As the objections were contained in private letters to friends, which remained unpublished until 1995 (Rand 1995, pp. 320–32), Friedman did not learn of them until late in his life.[8] He did, however, provide answers to objections such as Rand's in his 1991 "Say No to Intolerance" in which he discussed the ideas of both Rand and Ludwig von Mises (Friedman 1991). We can appreciate Friedman's answers once we know more about Rand's 1946 objection.

For a useful starting point to understand the dispute between Rand and the Knightians, consider the recent study of the free-market movement by Jennifer Burns:

This dispassionate tone infuriated Rand, who saw *Roofs or Ceilings?* through the lenses of her experience in Communist Russia. Friedman and Stigler's use of the word "rationing" particularly disturbed her. She did not know such usage was standard in economics, instead flashing back to her days of near starvation in Petrograd. "Do you really think that calling the free pricing system a 'rationing' system is merely confusing and innocuous?" she asked in an angry letter to Mullendore, a FEE trustee. She believed the authors were trying to make the word "respectable" and thus convince Americans to accept permanent and total rationing. Focusing entirely on the hidden implications of the pamphlet, Rand saw the authors' overt

---

that this is one of the less fertile areas that modern economists till; it is symptomatic that we have elaborate instructions on how to form welfare judgments that do not depend on value judgments, but we have no illustration of the application of this technique to a real problem of contemporary policy. Samuelson indeed offers much support for this skeptical view, by this enumeration of the assumptions of the new welfare economics (p. 222ff.), most of which are held to be partly invalid … When economists are writing freely on desirable policy, that is, when they are not writing on methodology, the disputes are almost always over how the economic system works, and not over the goals that should be sought. Thus, although I disagree with some of the policy recommendations in Samuelson's recent textbook, I do not differ (except in emphasis) from the goals that they are intended to subserve."

[7]  *Roofs or Ceilings* was included in the first edition of *Readings in Economics*, the collection to accompany Samuelson's textbook, Friedman and Stigler (1952).

[8]  Her letter is a "footnote" to an old controversy (Friedman and Friedman 1998, p. 621).

argument against rent control as "mere window dressing, weak, ineffectual, inconclusive and unconvincing."

Rand believed that Friedman and Stigler were insincere in their argument against rent control because they failed to invoke any moral principles to support their case. And when they did mention morality, it was to speak favorably of equality and humanitarianism. (Burns 2009, p. 117).

Burns perhaps downplays Rand's anger – she opened her letter characterizing the pamphlet as a defense of theft and concluded by labeling the unnamed authors as "two reds" (Rand 1995, pp. 320–27) – but more importantly the account also neglects the central argument in Friedman and Stigler.

In fact, the standard terminology when Friedman and Stigler wrote was much as Rand suggests. Their piece defends rationing by the market as opposed to rationing in a political system and in doing so they used the term in a radically new way. Before their pamphlet appeared, rationing had been used by economists with very different perspectives to describe *alternatives to* prices but not the work that prices do. Knight himself used rationing to signify an alternative to prices; as did Abba Lerner whose contribution to new welfare economics rivals Samuelson's.[9] In 1942 Friedman had offered rationing as a term for the general class of allocation mechanisms. One member of the class – "bare-shelf rationing" – was simply for store owners to do nothing when the demand for a product rose.[10]

The approach in *Roofs and Ceilings* was radically different. The argument put prices in the same category as government allocative mechanisms. Rand was not the first reader to object to this use of the term *rationing*. Before the publication of *Roofs or Ceilings?*, Orval Watts, who at the time served as editor for the Foundation for Economic Education, wrote to Rose Wilder Lane to ask what she thought about their use of the word *rationing*.[11] In his letter,

---

[9] Knight (1933, p. 56): "The problems of the apportionment of tasks and rewards might be solved for a complicated, technical civilization by an autocratic, theocratic, or militaristic giving of orders and rationing of produce in which the individual would have no voice in the least detail either of his work or his enjoyment." Lerner (1944, p. 50): "Rationing also sacrifices the optimum allocation of goods in a round-about attempt to prevent the rich from outbidding the poor."

[10] Friedman (1942, p. 317): "… to take a highly unreal extreme, sellers of consumers' goods might simply refuse to raise prices despite the high level of demand, permitting, instead their shelves to empty and bare-shelves rationing to replace price rationing."

[11] Watts's editorial labors are clear in Daniel and Claire Hammond's publication of the Friedman–Stigler correspondence (Hammond and Hammond 2006). Watts had earned a PhD in economics at Harvard doing his thesis work under the direction of T. N. Carver; Rose Wilder Lane reviewed the first American Keynesian textbook and subsequently campaigned to have it removed from college campuses (Levy, Peart, and Albert 2012). The consequence of this is considered in Chapter 6.

Watts quoted the paper at considerable length without informing Lane about the author so she might well have thought that it was Watts's own terminology. Lane wrote back immediately. We include transcriptions of the correspondence.[12] The reader can judge whether Lane caught a glimpse of the young Milton Friedman and George Stigler.

THE FOUNDATION FOR ECONOMIC EDUCATION, INC
IRVINGTON-ON-HUDSON, NEW YORK

July 26, 1946

<u>Returned for reference.</u>
Mrs. Rose Wilder Lane
Route 4, Box 42
Danbury, Connecticut
Dear Mrs. Lane:

What do you think of the following:

"War experience has led many people to think of rationing in terms of OPA forms, coupons and orders.

"But this is a superficial view; everything that is not as abundant as air or sunlight must, in a sense, be rationed. That is, whenever people would like to have more of something than can be had for the asking, whether bread or theater tickets, blankets or haircuts, there must be some way of determining how it shall be distributed among those who want it.

"The method of rationing scarce goods in a free economy has been the method of the auction sale. As demand for any goods increases relatively to supply, competition among buyers tends to raise its price. This rise in prices causes buyers to ask themselves again just how much of this article they really want at the higher price and how they can use it more sparingly, carefully and economically. In this way the rise in price reduces consumption down to the supply. At the same time, the increase in price encourages producers to expand outputs."

Sincerely,
*Orval*
V. Orval Watts

*In particular, I wish to know how you react to the use of the term "rationed" in the 2nd and 3rd paragraphs.*

---

[12] The letters are in Box 9 of the V. Orval Watts Papers at the Hoover Institution. The folder holds what seems to be a complete version of the editorial suggestions for revision and important responses to Rand's letter that have not been published. One of the responses was by Ivan Bierly, whom Friedman would later thank for helping to bring about *Capitalism and Freedom* (Friedman 1962a, p. xv).

R 4 Box 42
Danbury, Connecticut,
July 27, 1946

Dear Orval Watts,

My immediate reaction is that I don't like it. When the idea itself is examined, logically it is correct, but the way in which it is expressed seems to me tricky, self-conscious, "show-off," smart-alecky, designed for effect on a reader, and therefore oblique and unsuccessful.

I would not add to the confusion-of-meanings already existing, by juggling with the meaning of the word, rationing. At present it means, to 140 million Americans, "The Government's" control of distribution of goods, by means of ration stamps. And that's near enough. People don't like it, there is a dammed-up emotional reaction against it that's ready to back up any rational attack on it. As a matter of <u>tactic</u>, instead of confusing them by telling them that there's always rationing, I'd let the meaning of the word stand as it is and make a straight all-out attack on rationing.

Rationing is an arbitrary, artificial, clumsy, crude, attempt to do by force and threats what people naturally do smoothly and efficiently when they're let alone. Without rationing, people really do what rationing fails to do; they do it so easily and well that they don't realize that they are doing it. Americans have always, steadily, distributed more goods more evenly to more persons, year after year and decade after decade. Lenin and Hitler, by rationing, try to give everyone a motor car, for instance. Americans, without rationing, did it. Rationing seems to be a method of distributing goods fairly, because everyone knows about rationing. The real method of distributing goods fairly doesn't seem to be a method at all, because it works so well that no one thinks about it. The real method is this: etc.

That, roughly, seems to me to be a much better approach. Also I think that the fact that the individual customer is the boss who runs the real method of fair distribution should always be stressed and emphasized. In your second quoted paragraph, a change from "buyers" to "each buyer," (and use of singular instead of plural pronouns, of course) would be in line with what I mean. Actually, it is the customer's decision not to buy (rather than "the rise in price") that reduces consumption to the supply. (Not "reduces... down." The root, duc, carries the meaning of, down, with the re prefix. Literally, "to lead once more" means to lead <u>down</u>; I conjecture, because of the pack-train's rest on the mountain top.)

I'm sorry if I've attacked your baby, but this is the answer to your question.

RWL

Lane's immediate response was to criticize the use of rationing, to claim that although it was logically correct that prices ration goods, to say that prices are a rationing mechanism was unhelpful and "smart-alecky," a usage that put government action on the same moral ground as the market place. For Lane, the marketplace was the high moral ground; and no discussion would make it otherwise. Friedman and Stigler, by contrast, placed price rationing and political rationing on equal status in the class of allocation methods up for discussion. What their approach did, and why it provoked such a quick and critical reaction from Lane, is that it allowed for a discussion of the problem of price ceilings as one form of allocation among others. It thereby allowed that policy is the outcome of a determination of goals. Social goals are endogenously determined in the course of discussion rather than being exogenously set by a group of free-market experts. The *Roofs or Ceilings?* essay was in line with Knight's teaching whereby ends are given by discussion and proposed means are given by demonstration that can be checked by ordinary people. For Lane, that was precisely the problem with the pamphlet; in her view, the goal is determined exogenously by experts who then show how to attain it.

Many years later Friedman clarified how he objected to the Randian enterprise of expert-prescribed goals. In the transcribed 1991 talk, "Say no to intolerance" he attacked both Rand and Ludwig von Mises for being intolerant. He praised both of them for bringing young people into the free-market movement, but he spoke about how he was troubled by their appeal to a priori considerations and their denigration of statistical and empirical considerations. He argued that von Mises considered economic science to be restricted to matters of necessary truths. In Friedman's view, the necessary truths in question, Rand's "A is A" or Mises's appeal to purposive behavior, were not a sufficient basis for social science.

How did Friedman extract value-laden inferences from the purely actual? He appealed to shared goals, arrived at through a process of democratic discussion: he suggested that there are in fact *actual* values that people share. (Burns quotes Rand in her objection to Friedman and Stigler's acceptance of equality and humanitarianism as the guiding norms.) The question was, then, which policy – price rationing or political rationing – moves society closer to the actual shared goal. For Friedman, these are matters for discussion.

### 3.4 Milton Friedman's Consumption Function

We have suggested that the Knightian moment is characterized by a presumption of government by discussion in which goals are determined endogenously. In this section we show that Milton Friedman's theory of consumption also fits in this tradition.[13] The discussion tradition supposes that the discussion is open to all, and to their future children, subject to

---

[13] We make no claim that Friedman's body of work taken as a whole fits in the discussion tradition.

some agreed upon minimal requirement.[14] In opposition, it was held that there were people who ought not be allowed to have children because their time preference was sufficiently high to induce social destruction. In *A Theory of the Consumption Function* Friedman laid out a theory in which all agents, rich or poor, are self-aware and they make consumption and savings choices consciously and concurrently. Friedman thereby departed from two separate strands of work by economists. Late in the nineteenth and well into the twentieth century, economists had held that savings at the individual level was "planned," a conscious decision, but some people were said to save "too little" because they were inherently myopic. We touch on this tradition only briefly here and will return to it in Chapter 5 when we take up the role of economists in eugenic policy formation. Second, economists toward the middle of the twentieth century speculated about economic stagnation, and in the course of that analysis, they held that savings is a residual after consumption. In both of these conceptualizations, the goal – some level of savings in the aggregate and per capita – is specified exogenously; and the role of the economic expert expands to include advocating policies to induce or force savings.

Well into the twentieth century, time discounting was supposed to be a way to characterize peoples (groups) in a hierarchical order because time discounting attenuated the awareness of future consequences of choice.[15] In this literature, discounting the future increased as "foresight, self-control and regard for posterity" decreased (Fisher 1930, p. 374; Peart and Levy 2005). The inference from time discounting to inferiority depended on the presupposition that savings and thrift were unambiguously social goods.[16]

Friedman's consumption theory departed from the presumption that some groups of consumers are less rational than other groups. When he discussed time discounting in *A Theory of the Consumption Function*, it was

---

[14] Mill's important role in furthering the discussion of who gets to be part of the discussion is considered in Peart (2015).

[15] Fisher (1930, pp. 374–75): "The nations and people which have been most noted in the past for foresight, self-control, and regard for posterity are probably the Dutch, Scotch, English, French, German and the Jews, and the interest rate has been lower in general in the communities dominated by these people than in communities dominated by less thrifty people.... On the other hand, among communities and people noted for lack of foresight and for negligence with respect to the future of India, Java, the negro communities both North and South, the peasant communities of Russian, and the North and South American Indians." We return to this issue in Chapter 5. Friedman's results about the saving rate of African Americans continued to be cited for many years after the publication of his work. This is the one group for which his results directly addressed the eugenic commonplace we find articulated by Fisher.

[16] For a detailed examination of this position in early neoclassical thought, see Peart (2000).

in the context of persons with full awareness of the future. Agents might prefer present consumption to future consumption because they are aware that they will not be alive in the future. They might prefer present consumption to future consumption because they are aware that the characteristics of a good today are superior to its characteristics tomorrow. Because such considerations do not vary systematically across groups, Friedman notes them only to assume they are not sufficiently important to alter his argument (Friedman 1957, p. 12n8). Here Friedman's work can be viewed as a continuation of Knight's (1933, pp. 130–32) dissent from the long-time tradition that supposed a strong, predictable time discounting for all people.[17]

By the mid-twentieth century, economists began to speculate that agents consume and then whatever is left over might be thought of as savings. Here, savings happen without the saver being aware. The unaware saver became a central fixture in the secular stagnation debate that flourished for the better part of two decades, from 1930 to 1950. Perhaps the sharpest statement of this doctrine of the unaware saver is found in Lorie Tarshis's ill-fated textbook of 1947.[18] In it, Tarshis described saving as an "absence of activity":

Saving and investment are completely different. Investment is something active which helps determine income, while saving is merely a resultant, determined in part by the level of income. Investment measures the total amount spent by business firms, governments, and foreigners upon the products of the economy (after allowing for duplication); saving measures the amount of income (before taxes, and so on) not spent on consumers' goods. Hence, while investment represents a positive activity, saving is a mere absence of activity. Furthermore, saving is done – if a failure to act can be described as doing – by people in their capacity as income recipients, while investment is carried on by business and government units and by foreign buyers. Thus, saving and investment must be sharply distinguished. (1947, pp. 366–67)

Given the result in Keynesian theory that full employment equilibrium requires the equality of desired saving and investment, the supposition that

---

[17] Reder (1982) discusses neither Friedman's work on consumption nor Knight's on capital theory so he has no occasion to consider how Knight's skepticism about the necessity of discounting influenced his students. A denial of the rationality of time preference is found as late as Stigler and Becker (1977).

[18] Tarshis's role in the secular stagnation debate was clear to the critic of the doctrine, George Terborgh (1945, p. 13), who cited the 1938 *An Economic Program for American Democracy* by Tarshis and six others. Tarshis (1947, pp. 578–79) discusses the debate although he does not acknowledge there who wrote *An Economic Program*. We cite Tarshis's text because until 1961 (Ackley 1961) there are no stand-alone macroeconomics texts (Ackley 1978).

savings are made without intention makes room for expert economists to guide savings. This is clear from the introduction to Tarshis's text:

Most of the economic institutions we have inherited were not designed by economists; certainly the basic ones were not. In fact, they were not designed at all. Students of economic history can trace their gradual evolution under the pull and tug of various interest groups ... Anyone who has studied the development of these institutions will not be surprised to find that they do not always perform efficiently. After all, it is rarely enough that what we plan turns out as we planned it; it would be remarkable indeed if something which grew without planning should perform in just the way we want it to. If doctors had designed the human body, there would probably be no diseases. Likewise, if economists had designed the economy, the chances are that there would be no economic problems to worry about. As it is, the economist believes his job is to understand the existing economy in order that he can properly guide efforts to make it work efficiently. (1947, p. 5)

Friedman's consumption theory challenged two key assertions, that consumption increased with income but not in proportion; and that the marginal propensity to consume was less than the average. As is well known, his permanent income hypothesis suggested, in opposition to these perspectives, that low and high income persons consciously decided to save and that they saved the same amount proportionately to their income. Friedman's results offered a coherent reason to believe Simon Kuznets's earlier time series evidence that consumption rose in proportion to income (Kuznets 1942).

Friedman's consumption work, along with that of James Duesenberry and Franco Modigliani, was endorsed by Samuelson in the 1961 fifth edition of *Economics* (Samuelson 1948–1980, p. 217). There are no references in earlier editions to either Duesenberry (1949) or Modigliani (1949). Evidently Friedman, in Samuelson's eyes, not only proposed an important theory in its own right, but also opened the door for consideration of an entire class of theories. This is also Thomas Mayer's judgment after an extensive attempt to replicate the body of reported results linking consumption to income both current and projected (Mayer 1972).

The presentation in *Economics* modifies the elaborate graphics (Figure 3.1) that came to characterize the later editions of Samuelson's text. In the textbook version of the graph in Figure 3.1, savings is presented in blue to distinguish it from consumption items presented in green. The footnote to the graph tells the reader that the graph needs to be modified by Friedman's analysis! Footnote 3 tells the reader:

These data do not depict long-run behavior of each family when its income moves from a *permanently* low level to a *permanently* high level.

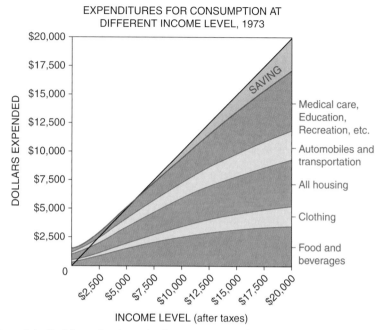

Figure 3.1. Paul Samuelson's graph of consumer expenditures. Reproduced by permission of McGraw-Hill Education Material from Paul A. Samuelson, *Economics*, Ninth edition, 1973, p. 209.

A few notes later, Samuelson comes back to the issue: "This warning, which appeared earlier in footnote 3, is worth repeating."

When thrift was an unambiguous virtue, the time discounting that was said to cloud the awareness of distinct groups of people to different extents was a central piece in the assertion of the warrant of economic experts to direct the choices of ordinary people. Indeed, it was central to the assertion, discussed in Chapter 5, of the ability of experts to remake by biophysical methods ordinary people themselves. With the flamboyant rise and destruction of Hitler, physically remaking people lost its appeal for at least a while. Nonetheless, experts lost no time in asserting their warrant to direct the choices of ordinary people into the consumption of things, the importance of which they were not aware. Friedman's empirically successful model of the fully aware saver, in the judgment of perhaps his oldest but certainly his most technically adroit critic, Samuelson, was a great blow against that particular line of argument. The claim of inferiority, now expressed as a so-called cultural difference, was revived in the 1960s. In his pioneering work on statistical discrimination, Kenneth J. Arrow refuted this claim. He did so by citing Friedman's result that there was no systematic difference in cross-racial savings rates (Arrow 1971, p. 4).[19]

## 3.5 The Thomas Jefferson Center Proposal to the Ford Foundation

In May 1960, the principals at the Thomas Jefferson Center [TJC] submitted a request for a ten-year grant in the amount of \$1.14 million to the Ford Foundation.[20] The proposal is remarkable for its emphasis, some forty years before this became fashionable in academia, on interdisciplinary connections. The aim of the Center is stated in the first paragraph of the proposal: "to promote enquiry into the problems of preserving and improving a free society." Faculty and students were to be "drawn from the several social science disciplines" and the Center was to focus on "political economy in its classical conception."

Buchanan and his colleagues at the Center staked out a number of claims in the proposal. The phrases "preserving and improving" society and "political economy in its classical conception," identified their approach with the methods and aims of economists in an older tradition of the eighteenth and nineteenth century. At the same time, the juxtaposition of preserving with improving left open the question about whether they were essentially conservative in point of view, or reform-minded. As the drama associated with the proposal to the Ford Foundation unfolded, this question was the crux of the matter. Those who opposed the Center judged it to be on the conservative side of the spectrum, whereas Buchanan and his colleagues regarded themselves as emphatically reform-minded.

In the proposal, Buchanan and his colleagues stated that they hoped to create and sustain a research program at the Center that brought together scholars with different disciplinary and political viewpoints. Thus they saw "a need in the scholarly community for a program of study directed toward major issues of policy in a free society, bringing to bear on those issues the analytical tools that have been and are being developed in the various social science disciplines." They called for a methodological change in economics, an "inversion" of practice in the academy to reverse the fifty-year tendency

---

[19] This is another example of how economists agreed across their political differences on the role of endogenous goals and discussion.

[20] The *TJC Annual Report for 1959* that accompanied the proposals lists the "Staff, Fellows, and Associates of the Center" publications in this order: James M. Buchanan, Ronald H. Coase, Otto Davis, G. Warren Nutter, James R. Schlesinger, D. Rutledge Vining, Alexandre Kafka, and Leland B. Yeager.

to increased narrowness and specialization. The proposal also contained a paragraph suggesting that the Center's aim "is not narrowly parochial" and that "cooperative arrangements [be established] with many excellent scholars in smaller institutions." Students, too, the proposal continues, would benefit from visiting other institutions and studying with non-Center faculty members.

When the TJC proposal came to the Ford Foundation, the Foundation staff embodied the consensus view of the economics profession.[21] The program articulated in the Foundation's Gaither Report (Ford Foundation 1949) contrasted the new economics that the Foundation intended to promote with an older style and "unrealistic" economics. The existence of a "school" was regarded as a potential sign of such outmoded and unrealistic thinking.[22] Kermit Gordon, the program officer with whom the TJC dealt, held sufficient stature in the economics profession that he soon after joined James Tobin and Walter Heller on the Council of Economic Advisors.[23] Thus, the reaction of the Ford Foundation to the TJC was not simply the reaction of one foundation among many but instead reflected the discipline's consensus.

It was the Center's perceived political and ideological leanings that provoked much of the discussion that followed. The commitment to "preserving and improving a free society" was interpreted by officials at the Ford Foundation as a commitment to conservative principles. Try as they might in the conversations that followed, the TJC faculty members were unable to shake that interpretation.[24] As we will see, in their view, the enterprise was not conservative but rather one also committed to reform via discussion.[25]

[21] We thank Craufurd Goodwin whose comments at the Duke University History of Political Economy seminar in 2014 provided the basis for this section.

[22] Ford Foundation (1949, pp. 71–72): "In many instances theories which are highly plausible or which conveniently serve the interests of particular groups have had long acceptance without adequate efforts to verify them in real-life situations. Dominant 'schools' of economic thought have from time to time constructed over-all 'systems' through the use of convenient but unrealistic abstractions, such as 'other things being equal' or the fiction of the 'economic man' ... Classical economic theory, for example, was developed long before the enormous expansion of government in economic life, before the technological developments which had led to increased concentration of economic control, and before organized labor acquired its important position in our economic structure."

[23] See Bernstein (2004, pp. 43–44). At the Duke University seminar, Goodwin compared Gordon's reputation in the circles in which he traveled with that of Aaron Director in Chicago circles; cf. Reder (1982).

[24] The claim that the enterprise was primarily conservative outlived the TJC; some thirty years later Charles Goetz expressed his dissatisfaction with the label (Goetz 1991, p. 15).

[25] An undated planning document that was never submitted to the Ford Foundation did, however, put things more narrowly: "The Center should be made up of scholars who

Following the submission of their proposal, Buchanan, Nutter and then-President of the University of Virginia (UVA) Edgar Shannon met with the representatives of the Ford Foundation, Tom Carroll and Kermit Gordon. Buchanan summarized his impressions of the August 31 meeting in a "Memorandum of Conversation with Ford Foundation" dated September 1, 1960: "The reaction of the Ford representatives must be considered to have been almost wholly negative." He continued to recount how the UVA representatives attempted to convince the Foundation representatives that the TJC was "unique," unlike any "comparable program in the country." Gordon then mentioned what may have been the crux of the matter: whether the TJC reflected "a single 'point of view.'" Buchanan attempted to dispel this conclusion, arguing that the program was "sufficiently broad" to "encompass wide and divergent points of view." Commonality existed in terms of "problems" examined as well as "an interest in the preservation of the free society" and a "common political and philosophical base" but "wide and divergent points of view" characterized the faculty at the Center.

In the aftermath of the meeting, Buchanan's September 1 letter to Coase was both realistic and yet hopeful. In Buchanan's view, Gordon was entirely uninterested in the substance of the proposal: "He consistently refused to be even so much as curious, and any meat of the conversation had to be introduced by Shannon or Nutter, or me." Like Nutter, Buchanan pointed to Gordon's apparent concern with the issue of a "unified point of view" at UVA, as opposed to Gordon's claim that there was no such unity at other, more respectable institutions. Gordon "raised the question about point of view," Buchanan wrote, "and with a completely straight face said he considered neither Harvard nor Yale to have a point of view. Warren really lit into him on this one." Buchanan suggested to Coase that Gordon was entirely opposed to funding the UVA proposal but he wondered whether Carroll might be induced to provide support if the Foundation could be persuaded that it was in the Foundation's interest to do so. Buchanan suggested that Coase might be "more effective" at convincing Carroll, and perhaps even Gordon, that the Foundation should support the Center.

Coase next wrote to Gordon to arrange for a meeting in New York. That meeting, too, was by all accounts unsuccessful. The October 20, 1961 memo that contains Coase's reflections on his meeting begins by stressing the

start from the philosophical premise that the free society is worth maintaining and who sense the dangers to the free society, especially brought about by the ever increasing role of highly centralized authority." ("The Thomas Jefferson Center for Studies in Political Economy and Social Philosophy." Small Special Collections, University of Virginia, President's Papers 1960. Series II, Box 16).

diversity he brought to the Center as an "Englishman" whose "personal relations with the English Socialists have always been excellent.": "In England,
although I am known as pro-American in foreign policy and anti-Socialist
in home affairs, my point of view has always been treated with respect by
those who held opposing views. Indeed, my personal relations with English
Socialists have always been excellent and with one member of the Cabinet
in the first Labour Government, I was on close personal terms. I was asked
to give evidence on behalf of the Fabian Society to the Beveridge Committee
on Broadcasting ..."[26] Coase mentioned "these facts to indicate that I am in
the habit of presenting my views with moderation and respect for opposing views." He hoped the meeting would clear up the Foundation's "evident
misunderstanding" about the unity of viewpoints at the Center.

Coase reportedly continued the conversation with his main point,
that the work at the Center was not propagandist in nature but a "serious
research programme"; Gordon responded that the Center was characterized by "a complete uniformity of the views" in the economics department
at UVA. Then Coase came to the crux of the matter: Gordon conflated the
Center's stated support for "individual liberty or the American Constitution
as a cover for opposition to Government intervention in the economic
system." Gordon also conflated the research program at UVA with that
at Chicago: "Mr Gordon clearly did not have a high opinion of the work
done at the University of Chicago. He instanced one member of the faculty
of the University of Chicago who had told him that 'if anything is profitable, it must be in the public interest'. I said that no-one at the University of
Virginia would make such a statement." All was to no avail: upon the conclusion of the meeting, Coase sank "deep in gloom": "I found Mr Gordon's
attitude terrifying. That night I could not sleep. I arose at 5 a.m. and began
to draft my first letter. By 9 a.m., I had completed it."[27]

On the other side of the correspondence, in an InterOffice Memorandum
dated September 21, 1960 Oskar Harkavy acknowledged Coase's connections at the London School of Economics (LSE) and remarked that the LSE
had connections with the British Socialists. Harkavy stated that the "point of
view" issue figured large in the conversation. In his recollection and in contrast with Coase's description of the conversation summarized in his memo,
he characterized Coase as opposing "all forms of government intervention in
economic affairs."

---

[26] Coase's memo and the testimony offered by the Fabian Society representatives to the
Beveridge Committee are available at Levy and Peart 2014b.
[27] The letter to Kermit Gordon is dated September 17, 1960.

Next followed Gordon's letter to Coase, dated October 7, 1960, in which Gordon conveyed his sense that any university "is under an obligation to foster the competition of ideas by welcoming to its faculty able scholars of divergent views." It was therefore appropriate, Gordon suggested, for the Foundation to inquire into "the university's allegiance to the principle of freedom of inquiry" and the "coincidence of outlook" among UVA's economics faculty.

In the correspondence that followed, Buchanan acknowledged *methodological* (though not ideological) unity at the TJC Center. His letter of October 17 to Kermit Gordon offers perhaps the clearest statement of the Knightian view that group goals are endogenous to discussion. We quote the central paragraph. First, Buchanan refers to a social welfare function approach in economics, a "social engineering" view in which goals are exogenous:

There seem to me to be two essential ways of approaching the study of problems of political, social, and economic organization. The first way is that of setting up independently certain criteria or goals for achievement and to examine existing and potential institutions in the light of their performance or expected performance in meeting these criteria. This approach, for purposes of exposition here, may be called the "social welfare function" or "social engineering" approach. It seems to characterize much of the current scholarship in the social sciences, and in economics especially. (Baroody Papers Box 79 Folder 10)

The approach of the TJC is said to differ from the social engineering approach in that it takes group goals to be endogenous to discussion:

The second approach is that which deliberately avoids the independent establishment of criteria for social organization (such as "efficiency," "rapid growth", etc.), and instead examines the behavior of private individuals as they engage in the continuing search for institutional arrangements upon which they can reach substantial consensus or agreement. (Baroody Papers Box 79 Folder 10)

The commitment to liberty is a requirement in that participation in the selection of goals is widespread. Otherwise there is no reason to believe the two approaches differ as long as we take the will of the despot or his economic adviser as exogenously determined.[28] On this principle one can easily appreciate why Buchanan would not tolerate dogmatists in the TJC. For dogmatists, goals are predetermined before discussion.

The context of Gordon's reaction is the consensus that scientific knowledge is anonymous knowledge. Since science does not hold a point of view,

---

[28] This principle might be the foundation of Buchanan's resistance to thinking of the economist as giving advice to the benevolent despot. (Buchanan 1959)

neither ought the scientist.[29] Concern for the point of view is at the heart of all the critical documents related to the Center's application for support. When the Ford Foundation turned down the TJC proposal, it prefigured a series of events that would soon destroy the Center at UVA and, even as the Center struggled to remain viable, the issue of "point of view" loomed large. Ironically, perhaps the closing of the Center contributed to the opposite of the Ford Foundation's goal of intellectual diversity: it removed one highly unusual methodological approach from the economics landscape and thereby moved the profession somewhat closer to a monolithic approach to economic problems.

## 3.6 Conclusion

In his foundational writings of the 1920s and 1930s, Knight asked a recurring question: how economists, experts on matters of fact, can change society. He provided a twofold method for moving forward. First, economic experts would explicitly accept the values (norms) of society as given, at least provisionally. Second, proposals for change should be submitted for discussion in a democratic process. The group may well have norms that preclude certain means from consideration and such preclusions would emerge from the discussion. In opposition to the Knightian approach, "new welfare economics" proposed to focus exclusively on increasing physical output. To refute this view, Stigler proposed a policy that would reduce the physical resources wasted by criminals but that would contravene a widely held accepted norm. The absurdity of paying criminals to not commit crimes was supposed to show the absurdity of new welfare economics.

Knight and his followers meant something very strict by "discussion." Discussion, in a Knightian sense, allowed no precommitment to one policy over another so that the case against political rationing and in favor of market rationing needed to start from a supposition that each was a rationing mechanism and to proceed from there. Thus, Friedman and Stigler gave up what promarket advocates considered to be the moral high ground when they redefined rationing to take away the stigma associated with it and placed the market and government rationing on the same footing.

---

[29] See Düppe (2011, p. 26): "Modern knowledge is anonymous knowledge; it is not an expression or in any meaningful sense a witness to those who bring this knowledge about." Roy Weintraub helped us here. Stigler (1966, p. 8) asked what chemistry would be like if the molecules analyzed could talk, trade, and lobby to get the chemist to report an outcome more favorable to their interests. Knight's influence lived a long time in the jokes in Stigler's texts.

Friedman's consumption work challenged the empirical basis of the claim that, because some classes and races showed less foresight, they were not fully capable of participating in democratic discussion. On the basis of his empirical work, he found neither such classes nor races. In his formulation, all were instead presumed equally capable of discussion and participation. This explains why some economists of the left, such as Samuelson and Arrow, applauded Friedman's findings.

At the center of Knight's technical approach to economics is the question for discussion: What is the alternative? What do we give up to get something? In the next chapter we consider what Knightian insights were given up when the economics profession adopted new welfare economics.

4

# The Rise of New Welfare Economics

## An End of Discussion?

Most economists resisted Robbins, because they thought there was nothing left by way of policy prescription, although Robbins never quite said that. He said: "As a scientist, I cannot tell you this. But, as a voter, I can tell you which way I would go."
Paul Samuelson
Suzumura and Samuelson (2005)

## 4.1 Introduction

The last two chapters have explored the emergence in economics of the discussion tradition, in which group goals are determined through a process of give and take that includes a wide set of participants. We have argued that this tradition culminated in a brief "Knightian moment" in which Frank Knight and his erstwhile followers participated. In this chapter, we examine what replaced the discussion tradition, paying particular attention to the expanded role for the economic expert in the new welfare economics that emerged in the mid-twentieth century. Although historians of economics have studied the adoption of increasingly technical methods in the latter half of the twentieth century, they have neglected the significance of the transition from endogenous to exogenous goals. As economics became akin to an engineering calculus to obtain efficiency, the space for discussion in the formulation or implementation of policy goals shrank markedly. At the same time, the role for the expert economist became less about exploring options and group goals and more about designing mechanisms to obtain efficient outcomes. As economists posited exogenous goals, the role of the expert economist shifted from participant in democratic deliberations to that of economic engineer.

We shall argue in what follows that the beginning of the transition is evident in the varied reactions to endogeneity and discussion in Lionel

Robbins's *The Nature and Significance of Economic Science [N&S]*, most notably by Nicholas Kaldor, John Hicks, and Paul Samuelson. We begin by discussing how Robbins, a contemporary and friend of Knight and the younger Knightians, suggested that cross-cultural variations in conventions might influence the conclusions of welfare economics. We propose to think of Robbins's "convention" as an equilibrium in a group discussion. Like Knight, Robbins insisted that within a culture, social goals were endogenously determined rather than exogenously specified by the economic expert. Indeed, his polemic against the usefulness of relying on the methodology of physics is precisely that market demand is unstable because people's tastes change over the course of discussion.

Robbins recognized how alluring it would be to posit stable preferences:

Suppose we are confronted with an order fixing the price of herrings at a point below the price hitherto ruling in the market. Suppose we were in a position to say, "According to the researches of Blank (1907–1908) the elasticity of demand for the common herring (*Clupea harengus*) is 1.3; the present price-fixing order therefore may be expected to leave an excess of demand over supply of two million barrels." How pleasant it would be to be able to say things like this! How flattering to our usually somewhat damaged self-esteem vis-à-vis the natural scientists! How impressive to big business! How persuasive to the general public! (Robbins 1949, pp. 107–08)[1]

These temptations were, however, to be resisted, notwithstanding the simplicity and tidiness of such analysis. For Robbins, economic science comprised the necessary truths that describe purposive behavior and it would be highly inappropriate to suppose stability of tastes.[2]

Another aspect of goal endogeneity in Robbins's account situates conventions within a culture. Robbins demonstrated that the policy proposals of both the Cambridge and the London economists depended on their judgment that all people were to be given equal weight in social-welfare calculations. He himself thought this was absolutely correct. Yet he acknowledged that such a weighting could not be proven to be correct in the same manner that one could prove that demand is negatively influenced by price. Instead,

---

[1]  Robbins continues, "The demand for herrings, however, is not a simple derivative of needs … It is a function of fashion; and by fashion is meant something more than the ephemeral results of an Eat British Herrings campaign; the demand for herrings might be substantially changed by a change in the theological views of the economic subjects entering the market … the availability of other foods … the quantity and quality of the population … the distribution of income within the community … Transport changes will alter the area of demand for herrings. Discoveries in the art of cooking may change their relative desirability."

[2]  This skepticism about demand stability is related to what Samuelson called the "bad element of Robbins's book," the claim that economic science is purely deductive from necessary truths (Suzumura and Samuelson 2005, p. 332).

Robbins recognized that equal weighting was a social convention, albeit one in which he participated. Outside his culture, Robbins admitted that the convention might well be different.

In response to Robbins's claim that the rule of equal weights enjoyed a nonscientific status, Kaldor and Hicks proposed a welfare economics, contra Robbins, that did not depend on weights given to individual hurts and helps. Kaldor asserted that the economist could justify a policy by demonstrating that all people might thereby be helped as long as winners could possibly compensate losers and still be better off. To this, Hicks added a production possibility set. And so new welfare economics emerged, an analysis that posited economic efficiency as the exogenously determined goal for society and then proceeded to demonstrate the means by which society would attain this goal. In Chapter 6 we shall consider how the production possibility function became the instrument to impose exogenous goals on cross-country economic analysis.

We turn finally to the full-fledged new welfare economics in which, we argue, Samuelson moved beyond Kaldor–Hicks by insisting on the transitivity of goals for society. Samuelson then formulated a social welfare function in which "possible" compensation was to be replaced with compensation "if necessary" (Samuelson 1965, p. 250). Transitivity of group goals essentially implied that people were not to change their minds in the course of discussion. In fact, new welfare economics ruled out discussion, just as it ruled out interactions of people within the group. The disagreement between Samuelson and Kenneth Arrow, discussed in section 4.3, clarified that new welfare economics did indeed spell an end to the tradition in which social goals emerged out of wide, possibly prolonged discussion.

## 4.2  Lionel Robbins and Goal Endogeneity

Robbins famously laid out the difference between economic science and conventional wisdom in his 1932 *Essay on the Nature and Significance of Economic Science*. For Robbins, economists accept the claims of economic science because they are necessary truths[3] and they accept nonscientific claims because they are conventional.[4] For Robbins, a working definition of

---

[3]  Economic science "is concerned with the disposal of scarce goods" (Robbins 1949, p. 75). "That goods are scarce and have alternative uses is a fact" (p. 76). "On the analytical side Economics proves to be a series of deductions from the fundamental concept of scarcity of time and materials" (p. 77). Scarcity of time is a central issue in Adam Smith's work (Levy and Peart 2013a).

[4]  Robbins 1949, p. 140; the full passage is reproduced later in the section.

Figure 4.1. "Pat" Adams's caricature of Lionel Robbins. Reproduced by permission of Jo and Carolyn Adams and the Archivist of the London School of Economics.

a convention is thus that people believe a proposition because it is believed by others. Economists and others accept conventions largely because other people accept them.

A talented caricaturist, A. R. "Pat" Adams, was a student at LSE in these days of high theory. We reproduce his caricature of Lionel Robbins in Figure 4.1

Robbins's book has been widely discussed and investigated. For our purposes, the question of importance is whether the book, and Robbins, remained agnostic toward "conventions" or goals or whether he saw a role for the endogenous formation of goals in a discussion-rich context. One reading of Robbins's argument is that he regarded everything outside of economic science – including goals and conventions – as exogenous to economic analysis. Indeed, some commentators situate Robbins in line with the Vienna Circle's claim that nonscientific statements such as "value judgments" are "meaningless" (Putnam 2004, p. 53). The preponderance of recent commentary,[5] however, suggests that there is little justification for

---

[5] See Howson (2011, pp. 1070–71). Huei-Chun Su and David Colander disagree with Putnam's reading of Robbins (Su and Colander 2013, p. 4). Their reading is set out in Colander (2009).

this interpretation.[6] In this reading, Robbins was not opposed to endorsing normative claims for policy-making purposes; his argument in *Nature and Significance* was that such claims rest on nondemonstrable scientific status.[7] More significantly, Robbins's economist is not as isolated as Robinson Crusoe himself. For Robbins, the economist who turns to policy analysis unavoidably draws on ethical claims that are part of a social convention. In particular, any claim about social well-being must invoke interpersonal utility comparisons and ethical presuppositions.

Robbins begins his essay by strongly insisting that the claims of economic science are accepted by all informed and fair-minded people:

> The efforts of economists during the last hundred and fifty years have resulted in the establishment of a body of generalisations whose substantial accuracy and importance are open to question only by the ignorant or the perverse. But they have achieved no unanimity concerning the ultimate nature of the common subject-matter of these generalisations. Robbins (1949, p. 1)

Economic science rests on unanimously accepted, necessary truths. Interpersonal comparisons of welfare, by contrast, rest on convention-ally accepted norms, such as everyone counts in the calculation equally. Robbins's argument that interpersonal comparisons are not a matter of economic science does not rest on a claim that they are meaningless, but instead reflects the simple point that cultural norms dictate how interpersonal comparisons occur. In some parts of the world, Robbins acknowledged, racists might insist that some preferences count more than others.[8]

---

[6]  Robbins uses the word *meaningless* only once in the text: "No doubt, *if* the change in demand or in cost conditions which led to its supersession had been foreseen, the disposition of resources would have been different. In that sense it is not meaningless to speak of a waste due to ignorance." (Robbins 1949, pp. 51–52). On the other hand the new welfare economists routinely use unspecified modal concepts such as "possible." We examine in section 4.3 how Samuelson's reformulation differs from Kaldor's.

[7]  Robbins returned to this point in his 1981 Ely Lecture where he strenuously argued in favor of "political economy" – as opposed to economics – in which value judgments were unavoidable (Robbins 1981, p. 6).

[8]  Samuelson points to this aspect of Robbins: "But, you see, most economists resisted Robbins, because they thought there was nothing left by way of policy prescription, although Robbins never quite said that. He said: 'As a scientist, I cannot tell you this. But, as a voter, I can tell you which way I would go.' This view can be traced back to David Hume, who was a great reductionist. I was ripe for that, because when I was an undergraduate student at the University of Chicago and studying sociology, I had to read William Sumner's *Folkways*. Sumner was a very conservative economist at Yale, but he was a great sociologist. He studied all cultures and showed how what was right in one culture was wrong in another and you could not prove by the methods of science which of them was correct." (Suzumura and Samuelson 2005, p. 332).

Unlike propositions such as "demand curves slope downwards," Robbins does not see how utilitarians who accept the convention of equality of capacity for happiness could scientifically prove this equality to someone who presupposed a hierarchy of capacity.[9] Deductive logic is insufficient to do so. Because the resulting weight of equality of people is not a necessary truth, interpersonal comparisons fail the unanimity test.

The critical pages for Robbins's argument about the nonscientific standing of equal capacity for happiness are 140 to 142; there, Robbins insists that although there is no scientific way to compare satisfactions across people, there are conventional ways to do so: "In Western democracies we assume for certain purposes that [people] in similar circumstances are capable of equal satisfactions." (Robbins 1949, p. 140). We reproduce these pages later with John Rawls's annotations.

Robbins's essay, with its controversial claim that interpersonal comparisons of utility were nonscientific, sparked a number of key responses. Roy Harrod responded to what he referred to as a "brilliant essay" in his 1938 Presidential Address to Section F of the British Association, published the same year in the *Economic Journal* with the title "Scope and Method of Economics." In the Address, Harrod admits to a "strong inner urge" to write on methodology, largely in response to Robbins's essay. He began with a fine restatement of Robbins's position. Appealing to Robbins's free trade inclinations flowing from the classical economists, Harrod then argued on Robbins's own grounds that the heirs to the classical economists could offer no scientifically-based policy advice on tariffs (1938, p. 396).[10] To proceed, economists must appeal to the postulate of equal capacity:

No; some sort of postulate of equality has to be assumed. But it should be carefully framed and used with great caution, always subject to the proviso "unless the contrary can be shown." In the case of the free-market arguments there is usually no characteristic attaching peculiarly to the beneficiaries of restriction other than that

---

[9]  Robbins's attack on the implicit racism in the economics of the period is evident in his discussion of a "series of thoroughly unscientific and question-begging remarks on national characteristics" (Robbins 1949), p. 70). The context is provided in Peart and Levy (2005).

[10]  We might answer Harrod on Robbins's behalf. Stipulate that free trade is optimal from a social point of view. Does this mean we wish to abolish all tariffs? Perhaps not. Consider the tariff that was part of the compensation to slave owners for the Act of Emancipation. Removing that tariff would mean breaking a political bargain agreed upon by people who were well aware of the benefits of free trade. History and context matter. Indeed, a case can be made that the abolition of protection on sugar imports from Jamaica created the impetus for Thomas Carlyle's racialized polemic in his "Negro question" (Carlyle 1849). J. S. Mill (Mill 1850) worried about the evils that would flow from Carlyle's defense of slavery.

they are beneficiaries. In the case of the uneven distribution of income, there are many special characteristics of the rich as a class to which due consideration must be given. (Harrod 1938, pp. 396–97)

Of course this concedes the case to Robbins save only that Harrod called economics what Robbins would later call political economy, with its mix of science and ethical claims (Robbins 1981).

Harrod offered an additional difficulty for policy advisors, one that he found more substantial than Robbins's original objection. To understand the distribution of income, Harrod argued, economists must possess knowledge of "social and political forces" that they generally lacked. In Harrod's view, economists might nonetheless continue to offer advice as long as they maintain a sense of "degree" and "proportion":

(ii) Objections may be raised on more general grounds which appear to me to have greater weight. The distribution of income is intimately connected with the balance of social and political forces, the study of which is outside the economist's province. In prescribing here he knows without being told that there are other considerations. This is not to say that he should avoid all questions with political entanglements, for then again he would be almost completely stultified. Most vested interests can whip up some political support. It is a matter of degree and sense of proportion. (Harrod 1938, p. 397)

In his response to Harrod (1938) Robbins wrote, "in practice, our difference is not very important." While those who objected to his characterization of economics held that "propositions based upon the assumption of equality are essentially part of economic science," Robbins differed: "I think that the assumption of equality comes from outside, and that its justification is more ethical than scientific." Practically speaking, their differences were less substantial: what would matter more for policy advice would be disagreement over whether all are to be treated as equals. On that matter, he and his critics strongly agreed in the affirmative:

But we all agree that it is fitting that such assumptions should be made and their implications explored with the aid of the economist's technique. Our dispute relates to definitions and to logical status, not to our obligations as human beings. In the realm of action, at any rate, the real difference of opinion is not between those who dispute concerning the exact area to be designated by the adjective scientific, but between those who hold that human beings should be treated as if they were equal and those who hold that they should not. (Robbins 1938, p. 641)

Robbins followed this with a statement that the best course of action is to presume equality.

John Rawls was, perhaps, the most significant philosophical commentator to evaluate the importance of Robbins's essay. Rawls came to *Nature and Significance* rather late, by way of Robbins's 1952 *Theory of Economic Policy in English Classical Political Economy.* In this latter text Robbins had explained the origin of the racial reference in *Nature and Significance* to his readers.[11]

Rawls's statement from "Two Concepts of Rules" in 1955 makes clear that he appreciated the normative claims in Robbins's writing:

> It is important to remember that those whom I have called the classical utilitarians were largely interested in social institutions. They were among the leading economists and political theorists of their day, and they were not infrequently reformers interested in practical affairs. Utilitarianism historically goes together with a coherent view of society, and is not simply an ethical theory, *much* less an attempt at philosophical analysis in the modern sense. The utilitarian principle was quite naturally thought of, and used, as a criterion for judging social institutions (practices) and as a basis for urging reform ... see L. Robbins, *The Theory of Economic Policy in English Classical Political Economy* (London, 1952).[12]

In "Justice as Reciprocity" prepared in 1959 but only published in 1971 Rawls interpreted utilitarianism, with the normative assumption of equal capacity *à la* Robbins, as "moral and political principles expressed in a somewhat technical language." He continued to add that, "when pressed," utilitarians invoked an assumption of "more or less" equal capacity: "When pressed they might well have invoked the idea of a more or less equal capacity of men in relevant respects if given an equal chance in a just society." (Rawls 1999, p. 222). The footnote to the passage recognizes that "Lionel

---

[11] "The Classical Economists placed themselves in a position of sharp contrast with all those thinkers who base their prescriptions for policy on ethical systems assigning absolute value to certain institutions or types of conduct – systems involving the sacrosanctity of particular institutions. On the Utilitarian view no institutions, no systems of rights, were sacrosanct. All were subject to the test of utility." (Robbins 1952, p. 178). It is in this reformist context that the convention of equal capacity for happiness becomes critical: "Among the English utilitarians the assumption was that each man's capacity for happiness was to be counted as equal. But it is easily possible to think of other assumptions which might be held to be equally binding; I have elsewhere quoted the example of Sir Henry Maine's Indian Brahmin who held that 'according to the clear teaching of his religion, a Brahmin was entitled to twenty times as much happiness as anybody else" (1952, p. 180).

[12] Rawls (1955, p. 19). The second paragraph of the preface to *Theory of Justice* confirms this: "Perhaps I can best explain my aim in this book as follows. During much of modern moral philosophy the predominant systematic theory has been some form of utilitarianism. One reason for this is that it has been espoused by a long line of brilliant writers who have built up a body of thought truly impressive in its scope and refinement. We sometimes forget that the great utilitarians, Hume and Adam Smith, Bentham and Mill, were social theorists and economists of the first rank; and the moral doctrine they worked out was framed to meet the needs of their wider interests and to fit into a comprehensive scheme" Rawls (1971 p. vii).

Robbins has insisted on this point on several occasions." (Rawls 1999, p. 222). Rawls agreed with Robbins that "the best way to defend the classical utilitarianism is to interpret these assumptions as moral and political principles" (Rawls 2000, p. xvi).

In his 1975 lectures on Henry Sidgwick, Rawls again discussed the basis for the equal weighting of individuals in what seems to have been his last systematic consideration of utilitarianism. Rawls begins with something new – the discussion between J. S. Mill and Herbert Spencer over equal rights and happiness. Rawls questions whether utilitarianism presupposes that individuals have an equal right to happiness, as Spencer argued, or, as Mill argued, whether the equal right to happiness is part of utilitarianism proper. Rawls thinks it obvious that Mill is correct (Rawls 2007, p. 400). He notes that Bentham and Mill assert that everyone has unit weight, but "Maine's Brahmin" insists on a twenty-fold weight for Brahmins relative to other people (Rawls 2007, p. 400). Then Rawls asks where the weights come from, and he concludes that equal weights must be a first principle:

We introduced a principle of equal claims for all sentient (or human) beings; and where did we get that? Not from its being the best way to maximize utility; for we have used it in defining utility. So it is a basic first principle perhaps; if so, then this needs to be made explicit.

For Rawls, Robbins's explicit assumption that the weights of individuals's capacity for happiness are unity, *regardless* of the facts of psychology, demonstrates that Robbins's doctrine departs from classical utilitarianism:

(4) Again, the standard assumptions that utilitarian writers often use may be a covert way of introducing or adding first principles. [Rawls's note: See Maine, *Lectures on the Early History of Institutions*: 399f.] This depends on how these assumptions are used and justified. If they are followed irrespective of the actual facts of individual psychology, then to this extent they are first principles; and mean, in effect: always treat people as if these assumptions hold. If so, these first principles must be explicitly noted; and once again, we no longer have the strict classical doctrine. [Rawls's note: Cf. Lionel Robbins, *The Nature and Significance of Economic Science* (London: Macmillan, 1932), p. 141.] (Rawls 2007, pp. 404–05).

Rawls's citation points to *Nature and Significance*, page 141 in which Robbins clarifies that in his view, ethical claims are *conventional* and are localized to a society. In Figures 4.2–4.4 we reproduce Rawls's annotations on his copy of Robbins's *N & S*. Beside the critical lines of argument (p. 142), Rawls indicates his approval with the judgment "Spendid!" Reproduced next are the pages in which Robbins contrasts scientific economics with "conventional assumptions." Maine's Brahmin is not directly

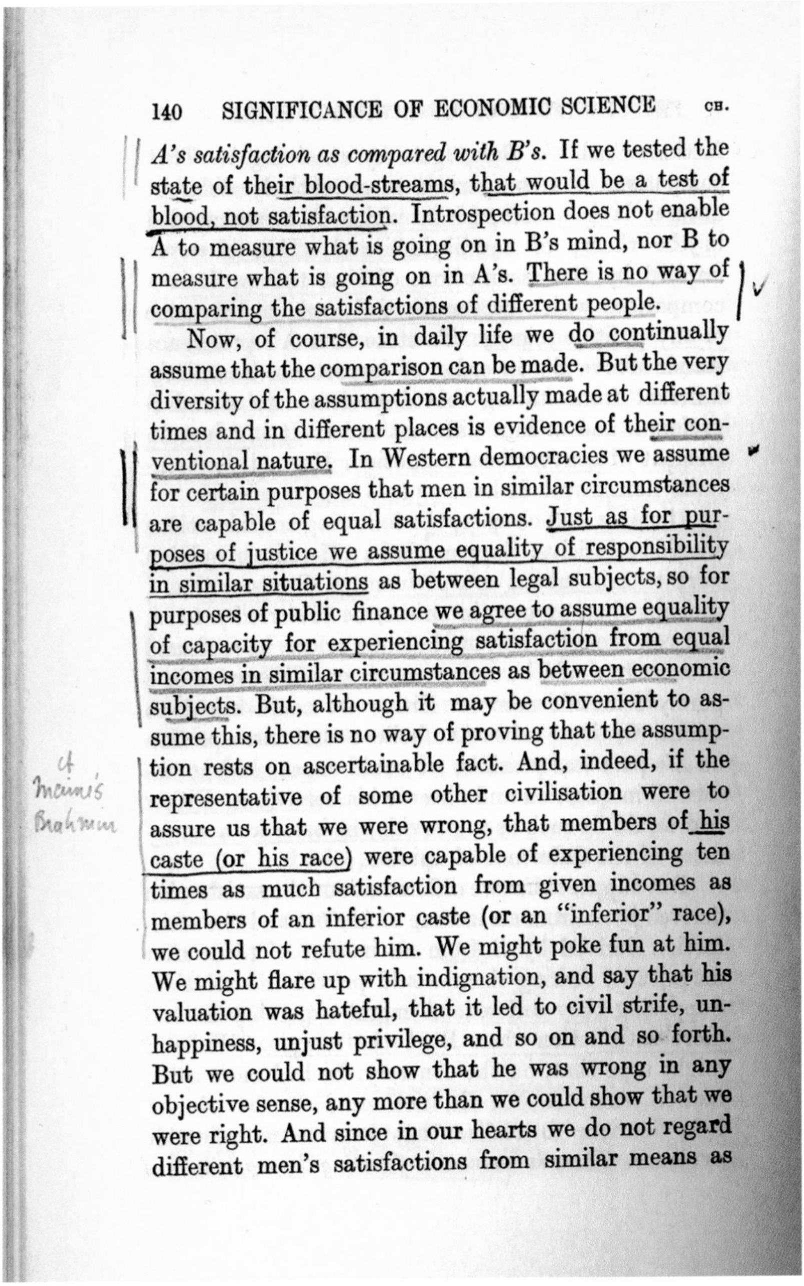

140    SIGNIFICANCE OF ECONOMIC SCIENCE    CH.

*A's satisfaction as compared with B's.* If we tested the state of their blood-streams, that would be a test of blood, not satisfaction. Introspection does not enable A to measure what is going on in B's mind, nor B to measure what is going on in A's. There is no way of comparing the satisfactions of different people.

Now, of course, in daily life we do continually assume that the comparison can be made. But the very diversity of the assumptions actually made at different times and in different places is evidence of their conventional nature. In Western democracies we assume for certain purposes that men in similar circumstances are capable of equal satisfactions. Just as for purposes of justice we assume equality of responsibility in similar situations as between legal subjects, so for purposes of public finance we agree to assume equality of capacity for experiencing satisfaction from equal incomes in similar circumstances as between economic subjects. But, although it may be convenient to assume this, there is no way of proving that the assumption rests on ascertainable fact. And, indeed, if the representative of some other civilisation were to assure us that we were wrong, that members of his caste (or his race) were capable of experiencing ten times as much satisfaction from given incomes as members of an inferior caste (or an "inferior" race), we could not refute him. We might poke fun at him. We might flare up with indignation, and say that his valuation was hateful, that it led to civil strife, unhappiness, unjust privilege, and so on and so forth. But we could not show that he was wrong in any objective sense, any more than we could show that we were right. And since in our hearts we do not regard different men's satisfactions from similar means as

*cf*
*manus*
*Brahmin*

Figure 4.2. John Rawls's annotation of Lionel Robbins's *Nature & Significance of Economic Science.* Reproduced by permission of Thomas Scanlon and Mrs. John Rawls for the Estate of John Rawls.

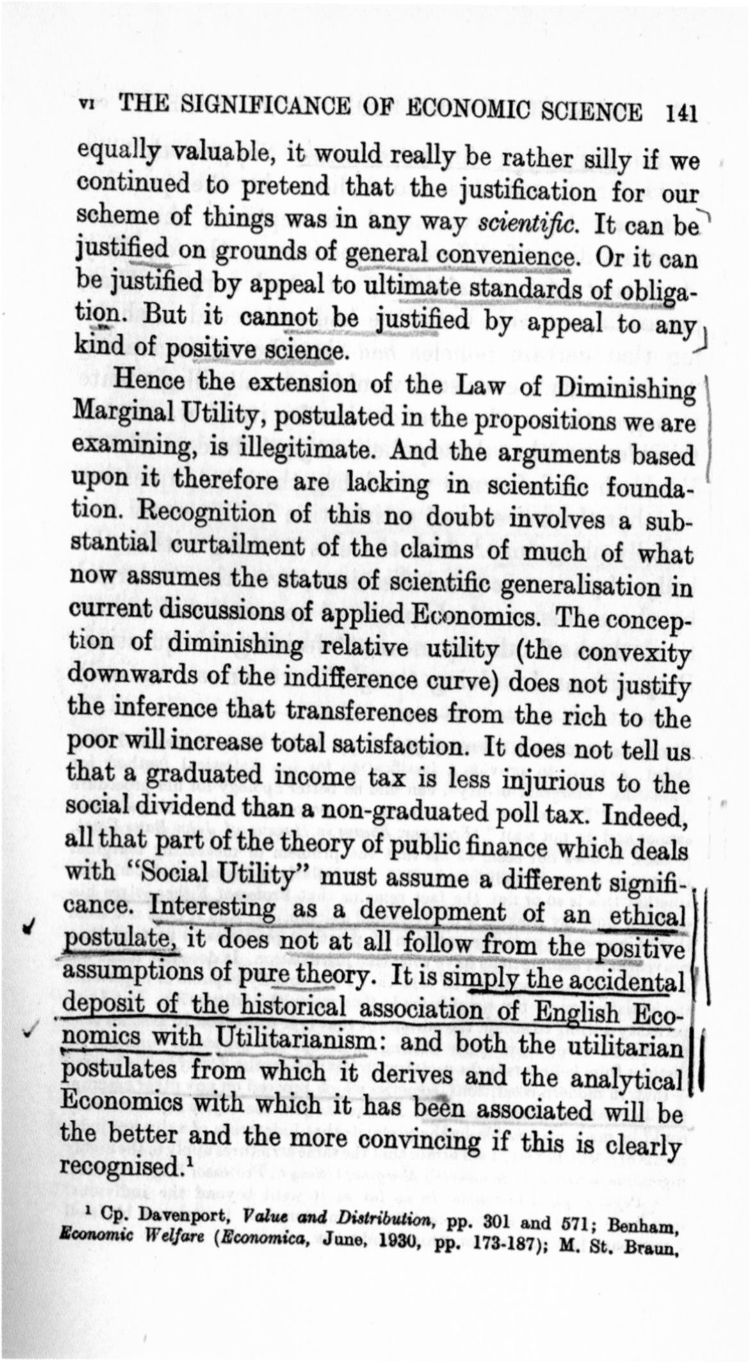

equally valuable, it would really be rather silly if we continued to pretend that the justification for our scheme of things was in any way *scientific*. It can be justified on grounds of general convenience. Or it can be justified by appeal to ultimate standards of obligation. But it cannot be justified by appeal to any kind of positive science.

Hence the extension of the Law of Diminishing Marginal Utility, postulated in the propositions we are examining, is illegitimate. And the arguments based upon it therefore are lacking in scientific foundation. Recognition of this no doubt involves a substantial curtailment of the claims of much of what now assumes the status of scientific generalisation in current discussions of applied Economics. The conception of diminishing relative utility (the convexity downwards of the indifference curve) does not justify the inference that transferences from the rich to the poor will increase total satisfaction. It does not tell us that a graduated income tax is less injurious to the social dividend than a non-graduated poll tax. Indeed, all that part of the theory of public finance which deals with "Social Utility" must assume a different significance. Interesting as a development of an ethical postulate, it does not at all follow from the positive assumptions of pure theory. It is simply the accidental deposit of the historical association of English Economics with Utilitarianism: and both the utilitarian postulates from which it derives and the analytical Economics with which it has been associated will be the better and the more convincing if this is clearly recognised.[1]

[1] Cp. Davenport, *Value and Distribution*, pp. 301 and 571; Benham, *Economic Welfare* (*Economica*, June, 1930, pp. 173-187); M. St. Braun.

Figure 4.3. John Rawls's annotation of Lionel Robbins's *Nature & Significance of Economic Science*. Reproduced by permission of Thomas Scanlon and Mrs. John Rawls for the Estate of John Rawls.

142    SIGNIFICANCE OF ECONOMIC SCIENCE    CH.

But supposing this were not so. Suppose that we
could bring ourselves to believe in the positive
status of these conventional assumptions, the com-
mensurability of different experiences, the equality
of capacity for satisfaction, etc. And suppose that,
proceeding on this basis, we had succeeded in showing that certain policies *had the effect* of increasing
"social utility", even so it would be totally illegitimate
to argue that such a conclusion by itself warranted
the inference that these policies *ought* to be carried out.
For such an inference would beg the whole question
whether the increase of satisfaction in this sense was
socially obligatory.[1] And there is nothing within the
body of economic generalisations, even thus enlarged
by the inclusion of elements of conventional valuation, which affords any means of deciding this question.
Propositions involving "ought" are on an entirely

*Theorie der staatlichen Wirtschaftspolitik*, pp. 41-44. Even Professor Irving
Fisher, anxious to provide a justification for his statistical method for
measuring "marginal utility", can find no better apology for his procedure
than that "Philosophic doubt is right and proper, but the problems of life
cannot and do not wait" (*Economic Essays in Honour of John Bates Clark*,
p. 180). It does not seem to me that the problem of measuring marginal
utility as between individuals is a particularly pressing problem. But
whether this is so or not, the fact remains that Professor Fisher solves his
problem only by making a conventional assumption. And it does not seem
that it anywhere aids the solution of practical problems to pretend that
conventional assumptions have scientific justification. It does not make me
a more docile democrat to be told that *I* am equally capable of experiencing satisfaction as my neighbour; it fills me with indignation. But I am
perfectly willing to accept the statement that it is *convenient* to assume that
this is the case. I am quite willing to accept the argument—indeed, as
distinct from believers in the racial or proletarian myths, I very firmly believe
—that, in modern conditions, societies which proceed on any other assumption have an inherent instability. But we are past the days when democracy
could be made acceptable by the pretence that judgments of value are judgments of scientific fact. I am afraid that the same strictures apply to the highly
ingenious *Methods for Measuring Marginal Utility* of Professor Ragnar Frisch.
    [1] Psychological hedonism in so far as it went beyond the individual
may have involved a non-scientific assumption, but it was not by itself
a necessary justification for ethical hedonism.

Figure 4.4. John Rawls's annotation of Lionel Robbins's *Nature & Significance of Economic Science*. Reproduced by permission of Thomas Scanlon and Mrs. John Rawls for the Estate of John Rawls.

quoted in *N & S* but Rawls's marginal note provides the reference. Rawls's annotations demonstrate his agreement with Robbins's argument that public finance in a democracy *presupposes* a shared conventional belief of equal capacity.

## 4.3 New Welfare Economics

We can now see why Robbins's *Nature and Significance* so rocked the economics profession. Essentially it undercut the status of the economist as policy advisor or expert by making the case that economists had no scientific warrant on which to base their advice. Economic scientists post-Robbins have the same warrant to express conventions as, to use Samuelson's phrase, any other voter. For Robbins, this was not such a problem – one might invoke ethics and discussion as the means to obtain goals and then proceed. Harrod, too, allowed that one might proceed to policy in a measured – but nonscientific – way.

But what if it were possible to reelevate policy advice to the status of science? This was the challenge that new welfare economics seemed to answer. In their attempt to reconstruct the scientific basis for policy analysis, the new welfare economists allowed, first, that interpersonal comparisons might be rendered unnecessary – as when output increased as a result of a policy intervention and all people might possibly be made better or no worse off through a series of compensations from winners to losers. Kaldor developed the formative statement of new welfare economics in which the economist continues to offer scientifically based economic policy advice notwithstanding Robbins's objections. As is well known, Kaldor appealed to the possibility of compensating those who lose from a policy shift:

In all cases, therefore, where a certain policy leads to an increase in physical productivity, and thus of aggregate real income, the economist's case for the policy is quite unaffected by the question of the comparability of individual satisfactions; since in all such cases it is *possible* to make everybody better off than before, or at any rate to make some people better off without making anybody worse off. There is no need for the economist to prove – as indeed he never could prove – that as a result of the adoption of a certain measure nobody in the community is going to suffer. In order to establish his case, it is quite sufficient for him to show that even if all those who suffer as a result are fully compensated for their loss, the rest of the community will still be better off than before. Whether the landlords, in the free-trade case, should in fact be given compensation or not, is a political question on which the economist, qua economist, could hardly pronounce an opinion. The important fact is that, in the argument in favour of free trade, the fate of the landlords is wholly irrelevant: since the benefits of free trade are by no means destroyed

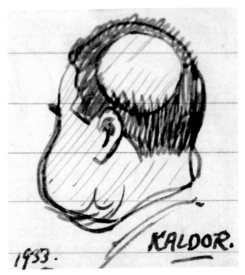

Figure 4.5. "Pat" Adams's caricature of Nicholas Kaldor. Reproduced by permission of Jo and Carolyn Adams and the Archivist of the London School of Economics.

even if the landlords are fully reimbursed for their losses. (Kaldor 1939, p. 551) [Emphasis in the original.]

Nicholas Kaldor as drawn by "Pat" Adams is seen in Figure 4.5.

This reopened the door to a "scientific" analysis of policy in which the goal is now improvement and improvement is defined as a situation in which any harms associated with a policy are possibly compensated by gains associated with it and all such compensations occur costlessly.[13] Hicks's article developed Kaldor's possible compensation criterion (Hicks 1939) and the new formulation has since been referred to as "Kaldor–Hicks compensation." Most importantly, Hicks made the production-possibility frontier into a central device in new welfare economics; in 1941 he referred to "a perfectly

---

[13] Arrow made the powerful case that "unaccomplished redistributions are irrelevant." (Arrow 1963, p. 45). Nonetheless, the Kaldor–Hicks criterion finds continued use in cost-benefit analysis, for example, Schuck (2014, p. 44). The fact that so many government programs fail even this test is grounds for reflection (Levy and Peart 2015a). The Kaldor–Hicks supposition that compensation is costless, an assumption that W. M. Gorman emphasized –"it seems clear that we accept the Kaldor criterion as intuitively reasonable because we think of compensation as a costless process" (Gorman 1955, p. 25) – may explain the origin of George Stigler's "Coase theorem" (Stigler 1966) as well as Ronald Coase's unhappiness with that "infamous theorem" (Coase 1991). Coase was interested in explaining how the world works so the zero transaction cost assumption was simply a starting point. Stigler's groundbreaking price dispersion work (Stigler 1961) supposed positive transaction costs in markets. In any event, Stigler would be unlikely to confuse actual positive transaction costs with possible zero transaction costs.

Figure 4.6. "Pat" Adams's caricature of John Hicks. Reproduced by permission of Jo and Carolyn Adams and the Archivist of the London School of Economics.

objective test which enables us to discriminate between those reorganizations which improve productive efficiency and those which do not" (Hicks 1941, p. 111). John Hicks as drawn by "Pat" Adams is seen in Figure 4.6.

Samuelson's 1947 *Foundations* was perhaps the high water mark for new welfare economics. Samuelson developed social indifference curves that depended only on transitivity. He began by allowing that any belief structure is "admissible":

Any possible opinion is admissible ... We only require that the belief be such as to admit of an unequivocal answer to whether one configuration of the economic system is "better" or "worse" than any other or "indifferent," and that these relationships are transitive (Samuelson 1965, p. 221).

He then called attention to Knight's worries about the endogenous goals of individual people within a culture.[14] Samuelson formulated his

---

[14] Samuelson (1965, p. 226): "As Professor Knight has ceaselessly insisted, Western Man is a hodgepodge of beliefs stemming from diverse and inconsistent sources. Fortunately his

compensation rule in modal language, adding the idea of compensation, "if necessary" to the Kaldor–Hicks idea: "Twere better that the Corn Laws be repealed, and compensation be paid, *if necessary.*" (Samuelson 1965, p. 250. Emphasis in the original.)[15]

Four years later, Arrow developed a theory of social choice in *Social Choice and Individual Values*. In this work he set out to answer the question, "Can such consistency be attributed to collective modes of choice, where the wills of many people are involved?" (Arrow 1963, p. 2). In what was widely interpreted as a theory of the political process, Arrow's analysis supposed transitivity of individual preferences and created what seemed to be plausible conditions in which social "preferences" were intransitive. Arrow further presumed that tastes were given: "We will also assume in the present study that individual values are taken as data and are not capable of being alternated by the nature of the decision process itself."[16] As is well known, his result called into question the soundness of the new welfare enterprise.

Almost immediately, economists who held with new welfare economics began to deny that Arrow's theory of social choice had any relationship to what they were doing. We see this most clearly in Ian Little's Samuelsonian response. Like Arrow, Little stipulated that tastes were given but Arrow's majoritarian principle required more structure than new welfare economics. Here we see with great clarity how a discussion that changed "tastes" – the terminology of that era did not allow for an easy distinction between ends and means that Stigler took for granted in his response to Samuelson – would create havoc in the new welfare economics:

life is sufficiently compartmentalized so that we can assume his various roles with a tolerable amount of ambiguity in each; and only the most introspective worry about this enough to become disorganized."

[15] Samuelson wrote his *Foundations* some years before its 1947 publication date (Stigler 1948). This was the period when the modal language that Samuelson used was becoming regularized. It is not entirely clear that his addition "if necessary" implies a difference from Kaldor–Hicks. The question is what does *necessary* mean? If it is read as obligatory, then there is no reason to believe that *necessary* would automatically imply actual. *Necessary* as obligation implies only possible plus an admonition (Lemmon 1977, pp. 50–52). Without the admonition to compensate, this would simply be Kaldor–Hicks. Samuelson apparently wished to add something to Kaldor–Hicks but he left undeveloped the mechanism by which policy might move from possible to actual compensation. Presumably, admonitions are carried in language and that would bring us back to discussion, which has no place in the motivations laid out in *Foundations*.

[16] Significantly for our interpretation of the transition from Knight to new welfare economics, Arrow acknowledged that this assumption represented a departure from Knight: "This, of course, is the standard view in economics theory (though the unreality of this assumption has been asserted by such writers as Veblen, Professor J. M. Clark, and Knight)" (Arrow, 1963, pp. 7–8).

Arrow wants to go much farther than this in two directions. He wants a "process or rule" which will produce a social ordering as a function of the tastes themselves. As I have tried to indicate, neither of these requirements really has anything to do with what is commonly thought of as welfare economics. Traditionally, tastes are given; indeed, one might almost say that the given individuals are traditionally defined as the possessors of the given tastes and that no sense is attached to the notion of given individuals with changing tastes (certainly the individual's "economic welfare" is not supposed to be comparable before and after a change of taste). (Little 1952, p. 425)

With such an attitude toward the nonsensicalness of changing tastes, it is of no surprise that Knight was not mentioned in Little's classic critique of welfare economics (1957). The dispute between Arrow and Samuelson seems to have continued unabated through the remainder of Samuelson's life (Suzumura and Samuelson 2005, pp. 343–45). Indeed, as late as 2005, Samuelson expressed unhappiness about Little's concession to Arrow.

## 4.4  Conclusion

Robbins had attempted to caution economists that when they entered into welfare analysis they left their scientific status behind. In response, new welfare economists attempted to reelevate policy analysis to scientific status. Perhaps unsurprisingly, as the second half of the twentieth century unfolded, economists qua scientific experts did not hesitate to step into policy debates.[17] In so doing they operationalized new welfare economics using cost-benefit analysis and advised governments about a myriad of reforms. Our present purpose is not so much to suggest that economists refrain from policy analysis as it is to suggest that we agree with Robbins that their warrant for doing so is rather more fragile than Hicks's "purely objective test" (section 4.3).

In the passage quoted in note 8 and as epigram for Part II, Samuelson acknowledged that Robbins's argument would undermine economists' scientific warrant to analyze policy. To answer Robbins's objections and save welfare economics as a viable field, economists attempted to reconstruct the scientific basis for policy analysis. To do so, they posited possible compensation of hurts and harms and exogenously determined social goals. They

---

[17] Recent examples include advice concerning the response to the financial crisis; bailouts; health care reform; environmental policy; and policies for economic development. On the latter, see Sachs (1991, 2005), Munk (2013) and Easterly (2013). DeMartino (2015) notes the tight consensus among economists in different analytical (and ideological) traditions (neo-Keynesians, and Austrians) on the widespread deregulation experiments of the 1980s and 1990s.

then moved forward with policy analysis using the criterion of economic efficiency as desideratum. But, as Arrow demonstrated, exogeneity of individual goals was insufficient for his approach to policy analysis. We close with some thoughts about what was lost when economists stopped allowing for discussion of those guides to policy that so preoccupied Robbins, conventions that rest on wide consensus rather than on demonstrated scientific truth.

Economists who rely on the Kaldor–Hicks framework and cost-benefit calculations in their analysis of policy reforms rarely acknowledge deep ethical challenges associated with doing so. As noted in section 4.2, there is, first, the question that so troubled Robbins of who measures the hurts and harms and how these measurements are established. What warrant do experts who know statistical methods have for the claim that they know the harm attendant on the imposition of the experts' policy shift? Such analysis also often ignores the challenges to new welfare economics posed by the multidimensionality of economic and social life: if some harms (benefits) occur in dimensions that are incommensurate with monetary rewards, even the assumption of *as if* compensation – let alone its *actual* implementation – is ill-specified.[18] In the following chapter, we shall see an example of a policy-imposed irreparable harm, when young women were subjected to forced sterilization. The role of sympathy was formative in the rise of eugenics because it was sympathy for the "unfit" that was supposed to impede the "law" of natural selection among humans. Sympathy in a more general context can generate interrelationships between the goals of people. For our purposes, sympathy motivates goal endogenity. It is goal endogeneity that the new welfare economists are at pains to deny.

A deep challenge to the new welfare economics is that of the "undue sanctification of the status quo" associated with the compensation principle (Arrow 1963, p. 45). If the status quo is unjust, then surely compensation would also be unjust. But perhaps not. Instead of the Corn Law case – an example selected by Harrod to question Robbins about his free-trade commitment – consider a status quo in which slavery exists. As is well known, Mill tirelessly opposed all forms of slavery. In recognition of his stature in the antislavery movement, he was elected to speak for freed slaves in a controversy over justice for people of all races.[19] Yet for Mill, the *actual* compensation to the slave owners was the paradigm

---

[18] This point is not original to our treatment; Sen (1979) and DeMartino (2015) provide more detail.

[19] For a full discussion of Mill's role in the Governor Eyre controversy, see Peart and Levy (2005).

for reform.[20] The question was how best to move society away from one institutional norm that, over time, comes to be regarded as unjust. Even prior to that is the additional question of how Robbins's widely accepted conventions were undermined.

Consider Robbins's challenge and start with a convention that there are indeed unequal capacities for happiness.[21] Suppose that this convention is accepted by master, slave, and an impartial spectator who is neither master nor slave. Then, slavery can be formulated as a dictator game. If master and slave have common sympathetic preferences that specify a sharing parameter, then the master would divide commodities according to their common sharing parameter and the convention of capacity. We can define *fair* this way: were the impartial spectator to become master and the division going to master and slave were to remain constant, then the impartial spectator, who shares the conventional judgment of capacity, would judge the division as fair.

Robbins's point is that conventions are not constant but rather they are shaped by society perhaps through the give and take of discussion. Suppose the convention is first questioned by the impartial spectator who comes to believe that there is no difference in capacity between master and slave. Then, of course, the status quo becomes unfair and the division would need to change. In the British historical record, the spectators (British taxpayers) began to discuss the unfairness of slavery with the masters and the slaves. Emancipation emerged out of discussion. More recently, the institution of marriage has been the subject of discussion – with a growing number of people who have come to believe that it is unjust to preclude some forms of union from the definition of marriage. When economists renounced discussion in order to preserve theoretical coherence, they lost insight into how ordinary people change the status quo.

Among late-twentieth-century economists, it was Knight's student Buchanan who was most interested in the problem of the status quo. For Buchanan, the status quo has normative status because and only because it is actual (Buchanan 1959 and 2004; Buchanan and Samuels 2008). To use the

---

[20]  We examine Mill's statement on compensation (Mill 1965, p. 866) in the context of discussions of reform in Levy and Peart (2008). Richard Whately's proposal for the compensated abolition of slavery is particularly elegant. In Buchanan's defense of real compensation, he suggests that with sympathetic agency the exchange basis of compensation widens considerably (Buchanan 1959).

[21]  We can refine the convention so that capacity is commodity-specific to reflect the actual debates over emancipation. There was, as we read the debates, no claim that the Africans held in American slavery had a lesser capability for happiness from "lower" commodities that humans have in common with other mammals; but many claims that African capability for "higher" commodities was less. See [Carlyle] (1849 and 1866) and Peart and Levy (2005).

phrase that Ken Binmore coined to describe the role of the status quo in contractual theorizing, the status quo is the state of nature (Binmore 1994, p. 14).

The status quo presented Buchanan with a two-directional challenge. First, why ought one start with the actual status quo instead of something that is possible? Here, Buchanan departed from the Kaldor–Hicks tradition in which the mere possibility of exchange via political compensation was sufficient for normative weight. For Buchanan, actual compensation is required to make the reform Pareto preferable (Buchanan 1959).[22] Second, political economists such as F. A. Hayek had argued that the status quo embodies the group's goals and therefore carries stronger normative weight than being simply actual. Buchanan disagreed with Hayek's evolutionary idealization of the status quo; although the status quo was the actual situation from which any reform must proceed through real compensation, it carried for Buchanan no stronger normative weight and was by no means optimal (Peart and Levy 2008b).

In 2010–2012, Buchanan delivered a series of lectures at the University of Richmond in which he differentiated between what he called "Old" and "New" Chicago economics on the basis of the exogeneity of goals, the pursuit of economic efficiency, and a naïve faith in the best of all possible worlds, invisible-hand outcome. The difference between models with exogenous goals and those with endogenous goals came into sharp conflict over the status quo. This became most dramatically clear in the decades-long disagreement between Buchanan and those with whom he was ideologically identified, Hayek and Robert Lucas. The lectures emerged from Buchanan's dissatisfaction with how, in the wake of the financial crisis of 2008, all Chicago School economists were blamed for a hyper-reliance on efficient markets. In Buchanan's view, "New" Chicago was properly associated with such a view: "New" Chicago economics had incorrectly presumed that nonmarket transactions as well as market institutions were efficient.

By contrast, in Buchanan's view "Old" Chicago – the school of Knight and his followers – housed a different sort of economist altogether. Indeed, in Buchanan's mind, "Old" Chicago would never have postulated that institutions, rules, or the status quo might reasonably be conceived of as efficient. In Buchanan's characterization "Old" Chicago economists in fact allowed that institutions might well be inefficient. More than this, they held that as the embodiment of social goals, institutions deserve constant review, discussion, and sometimes reform in the light of the evolving preferences

---

[22] Samuelson's modification of Kaldor–Hicks, which perhaps entailed "possible plus admonition," (note 15) seems to have passed unnoticed in the literature.

of those who are supposed to be both represented and constrained by the institutional framework.

Although we would be more capacious in our characterization of "Chicago" – we include economists who were not physically at Chicago in the group we call "Knightians" (Robbins in particular) – our characterization has much in common with that of Buchanan.[23] Like Buchanan, we have argued earlier that when economists came to impose material efficiency as the norm to judge all economic choices, they closed the door to an examination of the messier but nonetheless important arenas for choice: of the institutional arrangements that constitute the superstructure of our choices. At the same time, they enlarged the scope for the economic expert qua engineer to come into the fray and advise policy makers about how to obtain efficiency.

How does this bear on the role of the economic expert? If norms are exogenous, not to be discussed or changed, then experts might testify "scientifically" about how to obtain larger output or lower costs. The goals themselves fall largely outside the expert's analysis and efficiency rules as metric for analysis. Chapters 5 and 6 examine several instances in which economists assumed the role of economic engineers who specify how to obtain the gains associated exogenously determined goals. If, by contrast, experts recognize that the goals themselves are subject to analysis and discussion, then the expert becomes one of many competing voices talking through a discussion of both the superstructure itself as well as actions within the superstructure. Efficiency no longer can be held up as *the* determinative criteria in this discussion; instead competing and perhaps conflicting goals will be put forward. In a long deliberative process, consensus emerges, but it may not. Beliefs change slowly and perhaps not at all. In such a case continued discussion may be the best possible outcome.

At each and every status quo, a group may well have different goals, if only because people in the group acquire a deeper understanding than previously of goal inconsistency. Evolutionary arguments that combine Hayek and Lucas obtain their power with the explicit supposition that group goals are exogenous. We will consider two sets of such goals in the following section – racial perfection and economic growth – to examine the consequences of the pursuit of exogenously determined goals.

---

[23] In Chapter 9 we return to Rawls's reading and use of *Ethics of Competition* further to document his participation in the Knightian tradition.

# PART III

# WHEN LINEAR MODELS FAIL: TWO CASES

The chapters in this section examine two striking results of supposing that group goals are known without discussion. In terms of our distinction between the linear model of social policy – the goals are exogenously determined and without further discussion experts select the means to implement them – and the cyclical model – the public discusses the experts' proposed means for implementation – the cases that follow are instances of the consequences of linearization.

Charles Darwin's conception of natural selection carried normative weight for him and his early readers. Indeed, natural selection was to be the means by which to perfect the race. For those with such hopes, it was therefore a shock to learn from A. R. Wallace, codiscoverer of natural selection, that natural selection did not apply to humans because of human sympathy and the division of labor. If racial perfection is expressed in terms of bigger, stronger, and faster people, then there is no reason to believe that sympathetic agents will pursue that goal at the expense of the well-being of those who were regarded by the experts as lesser. In Wallace's view, the so-called unfit would then survive, perhaps even flourish, and have children, but that result was immediately challenged by those who argued that people should not sympathize with the unfit. At the heart of the question of eugenics policy, we argue, is thus the question of who chooses goals and means: Are people able to pursue happiness through legal methods (marriage and the birth of children), or do experts impose their goal of human "betterment" and design the means to attain it based on eugenic "science"?

Our second case study examines the role of experts in the direction of American and Soviet economic growth. The authors of US economics textbooks in the 1960s and 1970s maintained that an expert-directed economy, as they characterized the Soviet economy, would outproduce the economy of a democratic capitalism. In a command economy, as it was then called, the experts were not constrained by the need to discuss policy with the public. The name "command economy" speaks to the instantiation of the linear model. Those in charge were able to choose the means by which public goals were pursued. We reproduce the color images by which the textbooks explained the consequences of the empowered experts.

In Chapter 6 we emphasize the puzzle, noted briefly in Chapter 1, that the textbook results demonstrate no obvious ideological bias. Rather, the issue is whether the textbook supposed the Soviet economy to be on the frontier of the production possibility set for the publically announced goals of power and plenty. If the economy were on the frontier, there were no resources devoted to other goods; the public goals are the *only* goals of the group on which resources are spent. The textbook authors failed to rethink their presupposition that experts have no goals other than to implement the group's goals. But this error is precisely the point of analytical egalitarianism: experts who direct an economy may well have and pursue their own goals and may do so at the expense of a group goal.

5

Experts and Eugenics

"Science" Privileges a Social Goal

"They cut me open like I was a hog," she said. "What do you think I'm worth? What do you think I'm worth?"

Elaine Riddick
June 26, 2013

## 5.1 Introduction

As we noted in Chapter 1, the eugenics episode represents one of the most egregious instances in which experts were trusted too uncritically with horrible policy results. This chapter examines the episode with an aim of gleaning clues about how best to avoid such catastrophes. We shall demonstrate, first, that experts endorsed natural selection as the means by which the goal of "racial progress" was to be attained, so much so that they were willing to sacrifice human happiness, indeed human life, in service to this overarching aim. The purported connection between "natural selection" and "racial progress" became an instance of the sort of system that Adam Smith warned about, one to which other considerations might be sacrificed. We provide evidence of how one expert in this context yielded to a temptation to bias, altering his avowed estimation technique in order to produce a result in line with his presupposition on inheritability. All of this drives home the danger of accepting social goals as given and ceding the authority to experts who were then to find the means to obtain the goal. Acceptance of the social goal, without thinking through the implications of how society might attain the goal, led to horrific results.

The conflict between the goals of ordinary people and the goal described by experts was evident at the beginning of the eugenic episode when A. R. Wallace observed in 1864 that humans are sympathetic and they specialize, with the consequence that they do not allow weak or sick people to perish. As individuals pursued their own goals, they interfered with the law of natural selection that Charles Darwin proposed in the *Origin of Species* of 1859. Although Wallace regarded this as a salutary result, others saw it as a bad thing because it impeded racial "progress." This points to a conflict between the goals people set for themselves and the goal presupposed in the model, or, in other words, conflict between sympathy among people as against sympathy for a system. More than this, as experts recommended negative eugenic policies of forced sterilization or immigration restrictions, they willingly acknowledged that harms to one group were for the overall "good" of society, thereby applying an implicit cost-benefit analysis of the sort described in Chapter 4. As they did so, they imposed their own sense of the cost and benefit dressed in a pseudo-scientific garb.[1] Eugenic sterilization programs continued in America well after the horrors of the Hitler era were exposed.[2] In this chapter we focus on the argument advanced by Darwin in the 1871 *Descent of Man*, that sympathy and human morals are simply a development of social instincts of animals (a continuity thesis) so that one principle, natural selection in service of the "general good," ought to be applied to both humans and nonhumans. Darwin's continuity thesis was challenged by his critics on the grounds that he ignored the role of justice in human society, a principle that enforced rights and the requirement of consent. The requirement for consent is not found, they argued, in animals. This is a central moment in the eugenic enterprise since it hints at the butchery of negative eugenics that harmed Elaine Riddick;[3] the principle of the "general good" did not leave room for justice to individuals.

If eugenic proposals presupposed that experts would direct a nation's demography,[4] then in a British context there would be the potential for conflict between eugenicists and the British utilitarians who founded the neo-Malthusian movement. It was Francis Place,[5] friend of Jeremy Bentham

---

[1] One much-neglected point of James Buchanan's discussion of welfare economics (Buchanan 1959) is that sympathetic agency widens the domain for real compensation. This is another aspect of the endogeneity of group goals that Buchanan stressed in his letter to Kermit Gordon (Chapter 3, section 3.5). We know of no eugenic proposal that included compensation to the harmed. In fairness to the Kaldor–Hicks approach, the theory supposed that it would be possible to transfer units to give everyone more if the policy were efficient. One powerful criticism of Kaldor–Hicks approach, however, is that helps and harms are not in comparable units (DeMartino 2015).

[2] See this NPR story about the long history of eugenic sterilization through 1974 in North Carolina, as well as the decision, in 2011, to attempt to recompense sterilization victims: http://www.npr.org/2011/12/28/144375339/a-brutal-chapter-in-north-carolinas-eugenics-past

[3] Elaine Riddick is quoted in the *Wall Street Journal* of June 26, 2013.

[4] For an assessment of the American case, see Leonard (2005 and 2016).

[5] Place (1771–1852) was a tailor whose marvelous library served as meeting grounds for the utilitarian radicals. His political agitation helped repeal the legal restriction on trade

and James and J. S. Mill, who first, in 1822, clearly and publically defended contraception between married people. With contraception a couple pursuing their happiness could marry early in life, in keeping the community's moral standards of chastity, without demanding the community's support for their children. Place's proposal was an alternative institution to allow the self-direction of people.[6] The question of self-direction with discussion or expert direction would come to a head over the issue of contraception in 1877.

Neo-Malthusianism remained primarily an ideological movement until the obscenity trial of Charles Bradlaugh and Annie Besant in 1877 for distributing a manual on contraception. At the trial, Besant contrasted Mill's views on self-directed contraception with those of Darwin. When the obscenity verdict was reversed on appeal in 1878, the neo-Malthusian movement became a viable force in British politics with international connections. The episode illustrates the importance of competitive sources of expertise. Moreover, the Bradlaugh–Besant trial offers a hint that important issues of public policy might be decided in the legal system instead of by regulatory bodies.

In some cases the experts also let their ends drive the means by which they chose their results. In particular, Karl Pearson was willing to violate his professed statistical standards in order to obtain results that would "demonstrate" the inferiority of Jewish immigrants. Those who read the study without knowledge of Pearson's statistical philosophy would fail to see a problem with what he published.

In fact, the entire episode reveals a cascading nontransparency: although some economists were indeed wary of eugenic policies early on, they became convinced by the "experts" on the subject matter, that inherited differences rendered education alone insufficient to obtain lasting progress because poor people supposedly inherit characteristics that cause them to remain poor. Throughout this chapter the clarion message is that the judgments of the experts were accepted too readily, too uncritically and with

---

unions. Later he and a colleague drafted the People's Charter. When Chartism became violent he withdrew and gave his attention to the repeal of the Corn Laws. A young J. S. Mill came to police attention for distributing one of Place's handbills that encouraged contraception.

[6]  William Godwin had originally believed that without the institution of private property, a society of self-directed individuals could flourish. Later, he realized the enormity of the collective-action problem such a system of equality would create (Godwin 1801). Place's proposal is the basis of Mill's discussion of the possibility of a socialism in which selfish behavior is checked by public opinion. See Peart (2009, 2015) for detailed discussions of Mill and socialism.

too much deference: there was no one to speak for those whose lives were irreparably affected by the policy measures that followed.

## 5.2  Experts on Ends: Human Happiness versus Progress

In 1864 A. R. Wallace asked whether the survival principle of "natural selec-tion" applied to humans. In a paper first presented at the Anthropological Society, then presided over by James Hunt[7] and subsequently widely reprinted, Wallace asserted that natural selection stopped at the edge of human civilization because humans are connected by sympathetic bonds and as such they would not let the disabled perish. Moreover, with the divi-sion of labor, people find occupations suited to a wide variety of capacities and thereby support themselves and their children. Wallace emphasized the importance of what was then referred to as sympathy for creating a sphere of rights for individuals in which an ethical claim to pursue their happiness subject to the consent of others was protected by the laws of justice.[8] By contrast, Darwin argued that we should apply the same normative principle to humans as we do to nonhuman animals, because human sympathy and morality were a continued evolution of the social instincts in nonhumans. This position attenuated considerations of justice for humans.

Wallace's demonstration that natural selection is checked by human sympathy marks the beginning of the eugenics movement: W. R. Greg[9] responded that since sympathy blocked the "salutary" effects of natural selection, sympathy should, therefore, be suppressed:

[7]   James Hunt was president of the Anthropological Society and the owner-editor of the *Anthropological Review*. His influential racial views, identifying inferiority with less varia-tion, offered a biological alternative to Adam Smith's explanation of character by occupa-tion. The obituary from the *New York Weekly Day-Book* (November 6, 1869) gives some flavor of contemporary opinions: "beyond doubt the best, or at all events, the most useful man in England, if not, indeed in Europe." See Keith (1917); Curtis (1968); Banton (1977); Lorimer (1978); Rainger (1978); Stepan (1982); Desmond (1994); Young (1995); Levy (2001) and Peart and Levy (2005).

[8]   Wallace closed his 1864 article with a generous acknowledgement of his debt to Herbert Spencer's 1851 *Social Statics*. This note is missing in later reprints, for example, Wallace 1871. *Social Statics* marks an important mid-nineteenth century revival of interest in the sympathetic principle that Smith had developed in his 1759 *Theory of Moral Sentiments* (Peart and Levy 2005). For a recent biography of Spencer see Francis (2007). For a detailed study of the role of sympathy in Darwin and eugenics, see Levy and Peart (2015b).

[9]   Greg was a classmate of Darwin and, in his time, an influential writer on political econ-omy. He opposed J. S. Mill's view of the vulgarity of racial explanations. He was also long associated with *The Economist* whose role in applying biological arguments to political economy has been largely overlooked (Levy and Peart 2009b).

My thesis is this: that the indisputable effect of the state of social progress and culture we have reached, of our high civilization in its present stage and actual form, is to counteract and suspend the operation of that righteous and salutary law of "natural selection" in virtue of which the best specimens of the race – the strongest, the finest, the worthiest – are those which survive ... and propagate an ever improving and perfecting type of humanity. (1875, p. 119)

Thereafter, much of the eugenics rhetoric attempted to show that the "unfit" were a breed apart and, therefore, undeserving of sympathy. Greg described the Irish, as a subhuman relative to their human counterpart, the Scots: "careless, squalid, unaspiring Irishman, fed on potatoes, living in a pig-stye, doting on a superstition, multiply like rabbits or ephemera" (Greg 1868, p. 360). Late in his life, when Wallace remembered Francis Galton's[10] proposals for positive eugenics, subsidizing the marriages of college professors (Wallace 1913, p. 127), he was much more critical of Galton's disciples who proposed negative eugenics, policies to reduce births among the "unfit."

If natural selection serves as an exogenously determined *norm* specifying an ideal trajectory of human "progress" then the failure of natural selection signifies that there is something "wrong" with human beings and their institutions. In this context Darwin worried that natural selection would fail. Wallace described his conversation with Darwin:

In one of my latest conversations with Darwin he expressed himself very gloomily on the future of humanity on the ground that in our modern civilization natural selection had no play, and the fittest did not survive. Those who succeed in the race for wealth are by no means the best or the most intelligent. (1900, p. 509)

In *Origin of Species*, Darwin details his belief that natural selection is superior to human selection:

As man can produce and certainly has produced a great result by his methodical and unconscious means of selection, what may not nature effect? ... Man selects only for his own good; Nature only for that of the being which she tends. Every selected character is fully exercised by her; and the being is placed under well-suited conditions of life. (1964, p. 83)

Humans interfere with what Darwin will later call sexual selection. Moreover, perhaps motivated by sympathy, they refrain from killing lesser creatures for whom they are responsible (pp. 83–84). The question of

---

[10] Galton was an accomplished African explorer, perhaps the most influential statistician of his era, contributor to the use of fingerprints for identification, all in addition to being the chief early investigator to attempt to establish the inheritance of human capacity. See Peart and Levy (2005).

whether humans, with their ability to reason, are a part of nature separate from other animals was central in the debates that followed.

In the *Descent of Man*, the reader is warned as early as the second chapter that an unfortunate characteristic of humans is their unregulated breeding (Darwin 1871, vol.1, p. 112): Humans marry and have children in pursuit of happiness. Darwin proposed a new standard of morality, that of the racial perfection; the "general good" was to replace the greatest happiness principle of utilitarianism. We emphasize Darwin's continuity thesis – "*the social instincts both of man and the lower animals have no doubt been developed by the same steps*" – since it is critical to the debate that followed:

The term, general good, may be defined as the means by which the greatest possible number of individuals can be reared in full vigour and health, with all their faculties perfect, under the conditions to which they are exposed. *As the social instincts both of man and the lower animals have no doubt been developed by the same steps*, it would be advisable, if found practicable, to use the same definition in both cases, and to like as the test of morality, the general good or welfare of the community, rather than the general happiness; but this definition would perhaps require some limitation on account of political ethics. (Darwin 1871, vol. 1, p. 198) [Emphasis added.]

Biological perfection is now offered as the norm. Darwin emphasized this when he asked whether we ought to check sympathy in the section entitled *Natural Selection as affecting Civilised nations* (Darwin 1871, vol. 1, pp. 167ff). There, he asked the Platonic question anew: if we are interested in biological perfection, why do we breed cattle but not men (Plato 1930, p. 459)? The context is the question of vaccinations. If the life of a person is better than her death, as it is for utilitarians, the answer is trivial. But from the standpoint of biological purity the answer differs:

There is reason to believe that vaccination has preserved thousands, who from a weak constitution would formerly have succumbed to small-pox. Thus the weak members of civilised societies propagate their kind. No one who has attended to the breeding of domestic animals will doubt that this must be highly injurious to the race of man. It is surprising how soon a want of care, or care wrongly directed, leads to the degeneration of a domestic race; but excepting in the case of man himself, hardly any one is so ignorant as to allow his worst animals to breed. (Darwin 1871, vol. 1, p. 168)

Darwin was critical of this misdirection of effort but he accepted a good deal of biological imperfection at the cost of allowing moral agents to persist. For him, the hope for racial improvement rested on sexual selection in which better people have more children than the worse people (Darwin 1871, vol. 1, p. 169). As the chapter continues, Darwin cites the arguments of Greg and Galton against the Malthusian recommendation to increase human happiness by delaying marriage (1871, vol. 1, p. 173).

Soon after the publication of *Descent*, Charles Darwin's son, George Darwin proposed negative eugenics in his 1873 "Beneficial restrictions to liberty of marriage."[11] G. Darwin starts with Francis Galton's argument that from a policy point of view, people are similar to cattle (1873, p. 414). In contrast to Galton's positive eugenic proposals – subsidizing the marriage of the highly intelligent – (Darwin 1873, p. 415), G. Darwin offered an early proposal for restricting marriage among the "unfit." His prediction that this would become the future course of eugenic policy was correct. (1873, pp. 415–16)

The motivating fear expressed in the article is the inheritance of insanity. But that is just the beginning of the younger Darwin's plans for the future of mankind. He appeals to his father's book: "There can be no doubt that the health of large numbers in our present highly civilized condition is alarmingly feeble, and that the advance of medical science will, by the preservation of the weak, only aggravate the evil for future generations. The extent to which, in the present age, the weak are placed almost at par with the strong in the struggle for life has been pointed out in the 'Descent of Man.'" (1873, p. 419) In addition to describing Galton's positive eugenics as inefficient, G. Darwin finds Greg's worry about the importance of consent to be defeatism:[12]

It does, however, seem to me reasonable, that just as in the case of the army the country protects itself by causing its would-be recruits to pass a medical examination, so that persons of untainted blood, being convinced of the truth of heredity, should protect themselves and their descendants by debarring the tainted from entering the army of married life. (G. Darwin 1873, p. 421)

## 5.3 Charles Bradlaugh, Annie Besant, and Charles Darwin: Competing Experts

One important aspect of Darwin's continuity thesis is his proposal to change the standard of morality from the greatest happiness principle of utilitarianism to what he called the "general good," a norm based on racial

---

[11] Gruber (1960, pp. 98–110) and Elder (1996, pp. 100–04). George Darwin had previously written the response to Wallace for his father (Vorzimmer 1970, p. 208).

[12] Darwin's "third-party" debating strategy – using others to express his views – is now the subject of a specialist study (Campbell 1989). The episode in which critics of the continuity thesis made it clear that Darwin's new norm excluded considerations of justice is examined in detail in Levy and Peart (2015b).

perfection. We now turn to a challenge to natural selection that emerged from non-Christian utilitarians of that era who promoted contraception among married couples as an instrument to greater happiness. Their challenge occurred somewhat accidentally when in 1877 the flamboyant Charles Bradlaugh and Annie Besant faced the criminal charge of obscenity for reprinting and distributing a forty-year-old manual on contraceptive methods.[13] Besant's testimony at the trial presented the competing views of Darwin and J. S. Mill.[14]

The substantial question debated at the trial concerned the *means* by which Bradlaugh and Besant disseminated contraceptive information. The question for the jury was this. Stipulating that contraceptive information, when presented in medical books at 30 shillings or sold to the wealthy patients of physicians at 2 shillings 6 pence, was entirely legal, did publishing the same information at a much lower price in a 6 pence pamphlet constitute an obscenity? (*Queen v Bradlaugh & Besant*, 1878, pp. 139, 147) The high price and dissemination by physicians had initially served as control mechanisms. Debate at the Trial focused on whether birth-control material constituted something that all people could read and understand on their own or whether it should be dispensed by physicians to those deemed capable of understanding the information.

Two additional questions underscored discussion at the Trial: whether natural selection yielded felicitous results in humans; and, supposing it did not, what might be done to improve the results of unimpeded natural selection? Experts entered into the debate on both sides. Political economists such as Mill found little reason to intervene in the family size decisions of married couples since the private goal of personal happiness was regarded as fully consistent with the goal of the greatest happiness for society. Biologists, who worried that natural selection in humans somehow failed to yield the best outcome for the race, favored policy recommendations to "correct" the "failure" among humans.

We present, in Figures 5.1 and 5.2, a picture of the indictment itself with Bradlaugh's name and the copy of Charles Knowlton's *Fruits of Philosophy* introduced as evidence at the Trial above Besant's written statement. It is

---

[13] The classic study of Charles Bradlaugh is found in Arnstein (1965).

[14] That Mill admired Bradlaugh was well known in their time. Mill's £10 contribution to Bradlaugh's 1868 Parliamentary campaign was an important factor in his own election defeat (Mill 1981, p. 289; Bonner 1895, vol. 1, pp. 274–75; Kinzer, Robson, and Robson 1992). Mill and Bradlaugh are linked in the political cartoons of the time; see Kinzer et al. (1992, pp. 289–90). Mill and Darwin's role at the Trial are noticed in the *Times* (Peart and Levy 2008a).

Figure 5.1. Indictment of Charles Bradlaugh.

tribute to the importance of the Trial that these artifacts are preserved at the National Archives U.K [Public Record Office].

Bradlaugh wrote before the Trial began to ask whether Darwin might support the defendants. Darwin responded that he hoped not to testify because his health was declining. He emphasized that the "principle of Natural Selection" ought *not* to be allowed to fail when it comes to humans and he insisted that, if he were called to testify at the trial, he would *oppose* Bradlaugh and Besant rather than supporting them. As we have seen in section 5.2, Darwin had six years earlier sketched his opposition to contraception in his *Descent of Man*. His response to Bradlaugh contained the passage from *Descent of Man* in which he quoted Galton's concern about the fate of the race when only the "prudent" consciously limit their numbers. Darwin thus reminded Bradlaugh that, in Darwin's view, a goal of racial perfection attained by means of natural selection ought to replace the goal of human happiness attained by means of individuals' conscious choices.

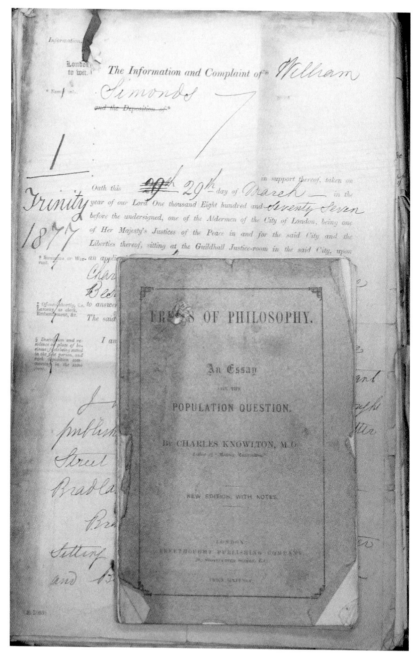

Figure 5.2. Annie Besant's memorabilia.

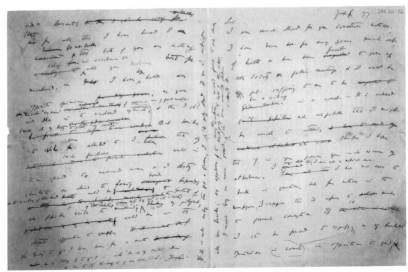

Figure 5.3. Charles Darwin's letter to Charles Bradlaugh. Reproduced by permission of the Cambridge University Library.

The letter in Figure 5.3 with a transcription expresses Darwin's considered opinion on this issue in a serious legal context and helps clarify that Darwin was much troubled by the idea of leaving selection among humans to the unimpeded judgment of individuals.[15]

Darwin's response to Bradlaugh's entreaty for support begins by excusing himself from testifying for health reasons. He continues to state that if he were forced to testify, he would oppose Bradlaugh and Besant's views. Bradlaugh's initial belief to the contrary was apparently misplaced. Darwin provides three reasons in the letter for his opposition to the public dissemination of contraceptive information. An enclosed extract from his *Descent of Man* repeated the case, made by Galton and alluded to previously, that the "prudent" restrain their numbers, whereas the "reckless" do not. Darwin consequently worried about degrading the race in the event that people were left to make these decisions without expert guidance. He also suggested in the letter that wide use of contraception would destroy chastity and the "family bond." The unpublished letter from Darwin to Bradlaugh, as transcribed by the Darwin Correspondence Project at Cambridge University, follows.[16]

[15] Treatments of whether Darwin viewed "natural selection" as progressing toward some exogenous goal have focused on his published work; see Ospovat (1981), Mayr (1991), Richards (1992), Ruse (1999), Gould (2002).

[16] The transcription is at a prepublication stage and the Project cannot be held responsible for any errors of transcription remaining.

June 6 1877

Sir

I am much obliged for your courteous notice. I have been for many years much out of health & have been forced to give up all Society or public meetings, & it would be great suffering to me to be a witness in a court. – It is indeed not improbable that I might be unable to attend.

Therefore I hope that if in your power you will excuse my attendance.

I may add that I am not a medical man. I have not seen the book in question, but from notices in the newspapers, I suppose that it refers to means to prevent conception. If so I sh^d be forced to express in court a very decided opinion in opposition to you & M^rs Besant; though from all that I have heard I do not doubt that both of you are acting solely in accordance to what you believe best for mankind. – I have long held an opposite opinion, as you will see in the enclosed extract, & this I sh^d think it my duty to state in court. When the words "any means" were written I was thinking of artificial means of preventing conception. But besides the evil here alluded to I believe that any such practices would in time spread to unmarried women & w^d destroy chastity on which the family bond depends; & the weakening of this bond would be the greatest of all possible evils to mankind; & this conclusion I sh^d likewise think it my duty to state in Court; so that my judgment, would be in the strongest opposition to yours;

On Friday the 8th I leave home for a month & my address for the 8th to. [...] will be at my sisters house & from the 13th at my sons house, PS. If it is not asking too great a favour, I sh^d be greatly obliged if you w^d inform me what you decide; as apprehension of the coming exertion would prevent the rest which I receive doing me much good.

Apologising for the length of this letter.

Sir your obed.
C. R D.

Besant discussed the letter from Darwin in detail at the trial, and she defended *her* position against that of Darwin by appeal to Mill's *Political Economy*. Although Mill had passed away four years earlier, there could be no doubt that the defendants were able exponents of his political economy. In this reproduction of a remarkable image from the *Cope's Tobacco Plant's* 1878 advertising "card," *In Pursuit of Diva Nicotina*, Figure 5.4, the likeness of Mill is in close proximity to the very book at issue at the Bradlaugh and Besant trial, *Fruits of Philosophy*. Mill is being trampled by a crowd of pleasure seekers.

The jury ultimately decided the sixpence pamphlet was obscene. Bradlaugh and Besant were sentenced to six months in prison and a fine of £200 each (*Queen v Bradlaugh & Besant*, 1878, p. 323). The higher court to which they appealed later reversed the judgment on the basis that the indictment had not spelled out what the particular obscenity was. One of Besant's powerful arguments was that the discussion of contraception

Figure 5.4. J. S. Mill and the Bradlaugh-Besant Trial from John Wallace *In Pursuit of Diva Nicotina*.

could not be *per se* obscene because contraception was defended, albeit delicately, in Mill's *Principles of Political Economy*, a text used at both Oxford and Cambridge.[17] After their convictions were reversed, the publication of contraceptive information in Britain went unhindered. Mailed from a British address, it could then go to any other country, regardless of its laws on the matter, without legal risk to the sender. The "Malthusian League" was soon organized along with its publication, *The Malthusian*.[18] Consequently, the Bradlaugh–Besant trial has deservedly received much attention as a critical moment in the international birth-control movement (see Chandrasekhar 1981). In short, a jury trial played a significant role in reforming British policy. We return to this insight in Chapter 12.

## 5.4 Expert Advice Cascades: Economists Change Course

Expert knowledge sometimes spreads by way of those who read the considered conclusions of the scientists and then pass the conclusions on in other

---

[17] Besant emphasized the importance of Mill's discussion in *Political Economy* (*Queen v Bradlaugh & Besant*, 1878, p. 111): "John Stuart Mill's work on Political Economy – which is regarded everywhere as a standard work, and is accepted as a text-book at the Universities of Oxford and Cambridge for the instruction of young men, and on which young men are examined, and in which they are taught – invites them to restrain their passions, and to limit the number of their families … " As we noticed (Chapter 2, n15) Mill's defense of contraception was very delicate.

[18] The fact that T. Robert Malthus himself publicly disavowed contraception on all occasions when the question arose seems not to have bothered his admirers (Levy 1978, 1999).

contexts. Mid-nineteenth century "science" soon purportedly demonstrated that characteristics vary by race and were at least partly determined by heredity. In this section we provide an example of how the expertise of one group of experts came to be accepted by another group (the economists) writing at the time or somewhat later.

A key example of the cascade entails the post-classical-economists' position, accepted from the biologists' conclusion, that the less fit would tend to have larger families than the more fit. A. C. Pigou provides a case in point, suggesting that the lower classes reproduce at relatively high rates, whereas the "higher classes" delay marriage and have few children (1907, pp. 364–65). The "injurious" effects of such relatively high reproductive rates among the poor might be counteracted by policies designed to improve the well-being of low-income people (as recommended in Webb 1910). But the biological question remained for Pigou: "Is there reason to believe that bad original properties and poverty are closely related?" For the answer to this question, Pigou relied on the research of others, specifically the biologists whose work apparently convinced him to answer affirmatively:

For, if we consider the matter, it is apparent that among the relatively rich are many persons who have risen from a poor environment, which their fellows, who have remained poor, shared with them in childhood. Among the original properties of these relatively rich presumably there are qualities which account for their rise. A relatively high reproductive rate *among those who have remained poor* implies, in a measure, the breeding out of these qualities. It implies, in fact, a form of selection that discriminates against the original properties that promote economic success. (Pigou 1907, p. 365).

From here it was a short step to endorsing the policy recommendations of eugenicists: positive measures to encourage births from the "superior" portion of the distribution; negative measures to sterilize those in the "inferior" portion of the distribution; and immigration restrictions to ensure that the distribution would not be degraded by the "wrong" sort of immigrants. Pigou was joined in his acceptance of biological explanations for poverty by economists including (among others): Irving Fisher, Frank Fetter, J. R. Commons, Sydney Webb, and J. M. Keynes.[19] This view was the background for Milton Friedman's development of a theory of savings, discussed in Chapter 3, which supposed that individuals have no time preference.

---

[19] See Peart and Levy (2005) for a more detailed analysis; Thomas Leonard (2016) for a comprehensive treatment.

## 5.5  Experts Who Pick Results to Support the Ends

In the Bradlaugh–Besant obscenity trial, expert opinion was used on both sides of the case: Mill to support a goal of self-directed happiness and Darwin in opposition to human choice at least among poor women. In the years following the trial, the divided nature of such expertise fell away and the economics profession came overwhelmingly to accept the argument that the capacity to make economic and political decisions was largely inherited with some groups being more capable than others. Nothing in the foregoing suggests that the experts were dishonest in the transmission mechanism. Yet we have argued in our introductory chapter that there is a temptation to bias: supposing a scientist is predisposed to a "system" he or she might be more willing to choose results or techniques that shore up the system and convince his or her colleagues accordingly. That this was the case with eugenic policy will become apparent as we discuss Pearson's study of Jewish inherited characteristics.

The first article in the *Annals of Eugenics*, of which Pearson was the founding editor, is part one of "The Problem of Alien Immigration into Great Britain Illustrated by an Examination of Russian and Polish Jewish Children" by Pearson and Margaret Moul. Pearson and Moul motivate their exercise with a concern over racial quality in densely settled countries. They begin by telling a story of climate and race suitability. The inherent inferiority of the Negro – unsuitable even for Africa! – was said to be obvious (Pearson and Moul 1925, pp. 6–7).

Pearson–Moul then review contending views of the results of immigration. On the one hand, there is the human homogeneity story, whereas, on the other hand, immigrants might overly compete for jobs and resources. In the face of these competing predictions, Pearson and Moul call for disinterested scientific study. They explained why immigration is the central matter in eugenics policy and they remind the reader that "special cases" do not support general conclusions (1925, p. 7).

Pearson and Moul then begin the serious work by testing whether Jewish children were as clean or as well dressed as Gentile children. They conclude that Jewish children were poorly dressed compared to their Gentile counterparts, a result that gives "some ground" for the argument that Jews "undersell natives in the labour market" (1925, p. 49).[20]

---

[20]  The result was challenged in the *Journal of the Royal Statistical Society* in an article that claimed the result contradicted the "common view" of those who dealt with Jewish children: "does not accord with the common view held by social workers and school teachers who labour among Jewish children." (F.S. 1926, p. 148–149).

Assuming that they held income constant across groups – which they attempted to do – Pearson–Moul detected a difference in cultural expenditure patterns, evidence that Jewish parents were spending less on their children's clothing than nonJewish parents. If Jewish parents were saving the rest of their income, or spending it on education, then the results suggest that Jews in their sample have a *lower* rate of time preference than their Christian neighbors. Since eugenicists at the time identified lower time preference with racial superiority,[21] Pearson and Moul would have to conclude that Jews were superior. But Pearson and Moul were silent on where the income went. Instead, they concluded that lower expenditure on clothing was evidence of a racial failing, for which intelligence might compensate. They used the result to argue that Jews should prove they are *superior* in intelligence to make up for their poor physical traits and habits (1925, pp. 124–25).

Pearson–Moul proceed to compare the intelligence of Jewish and Christian children. They find little difference between the intelligence of Jewish boys and their Christian peers, but a significant difference between Jewish boys and girls. Since Jewish boys are not more intelligent than non-Jews, and girls are inferior, Pearson and Moul conclude that Jewish immigration should be curtailed.

Pearson's views on statistical inference were spelled out long before he turned to the question of Jewish immigration. He remains famous for estimating the process at work (the underlying distribution) from the data.[22] The technique has a name – method of moments – in which one estimates a sequence of progressively more complicated properties. One estimates the mean (the first moment) and the variance (the second moment). The third moment tells about the skew and the fourth moment relative to the second tells what portion is in the central part of the distribution and what portion is in the "tails." Not surprisingly, the Pearson–Moul study made its case in terms of average intelligence, the first moment of the distribution. The study turned next to the question of the occasional extremely capable Jew, a Spinoza or an Einstein (Pearson and Moul, 1925, p. 127). Acknowledging that the occasional immigrant will be exceptionally talented, Pearson–Moul dismiss the need to consider such outliers.

As is well known, elsewhere Pearson strenuously defended method of moments-estimation procedures against both maximum-likelihood

---

[21] Peart and Levy 2005, chapter 4, provide evidence that this was the overwhelming presumption among eugenicists at the time. One of the most important aspects of James Heckman's research has been the demonstration that what he calls "noncognitive" skills are acquired at an early age (Heckman 2005).

[22] For an overview of Pearson's achievements in this regard, see Stigler (1999).

methods, in which the underlying distribution is often assumed, and procedures that discard "outliers" (Pearson 1936; Stigler 1986, p. 338; Levy and Peart 2005, pp. 98–99). But when Pearson and Moul claim that information about characteristics of exceptional Jews is not important, they have thrown out information that is critical to the estimation of the higher-order moments of the distribution. The Pearson–Moul study, therefore, violated Pearson's own statistical principles.

The sequence of Pearson–Moul papers, laying out the data and the procedures, seems perfectly transparent. Nonetheless, the reader who does not know Pearson's statistical principles cannot accurately judge how much Pearson is willing to give up to obtain these results. Thus, the nontransparency is itself nontransparent.

We pause to note here that we have no reason to believe that other researchers in the field followed suit. In point of fact we have noted elsewhere that Galton provides an interesting counterexample to Pearson. In stark contrast to Pearson, Galton acknowledged in print that he sought and failed to obtain a particular result in line with his prior suppositions.[23] Our point here is that as consumers of expert advice we should keep in mind the temptation to bias and the nontransparency that may follow when a result is presented without divulging the prior commitment or the full array of estimation techniques. As we have stated, the benefits flow more readily from experts when we take precautions against believing their wisdom uncritically.

## 5.6 Conclusion

We have deliberately attempted in the previous sections to keep our focus narrow, to come to some conclusions about the roles of experts in eugenics.[24] We draw three lessons from the foregoing: first, we take Smith's advice about being wary of the commitment to systems to heart. In the move from asking how the race evolves to how it *should* evolve, from a description to a policy prescription, some experts were so committed to improvement of the race as to neglect considerations for the actual well-being of people who make up the race. This represents an extreme example of how experts need to be aware of the ethical implications of moving from expert analysis

---

[23] We discuss Galton's composite photography in Peart and Levy 2005. He informs the reader (Galton 1883) that he anticipated using composite photography to identify criminals but he was unable to do this. The only success he reported – this is also Pearson's judgment – was his composite photographs of Jews.

[24] Allen Buchanan has asked, what we can learn from the eugenic episode (Buchanan 2002, 2007).

to policy prescriptions. Second, we have pointed to the messy but perhaps salutary effects of competition in expertise, when a type of discussion emerged between surrogates for Mill and Darwin himself. For the case in which expert judgment was unquestioned, by contrast, it cascaded through the economics profession with widespread policy implications.

There are wider lessons to be learned. First, in the context of the family size decision, the foregoing reveals that experts had two sets of views about the results of human decision making. On the one hand, Besant, Bradlaugh, and Mill trusted that individuals could make the family size choice using information about how to prevent births. More information was seen as better than less, and such information need not be kept away from poor people or filtered through the intermediary of a physician. On the other side of this divide – and recognized as such at the time – Charles Darwin's views were used to make a case for controlling access to information. Widely available information might, he urged, dilute the effects of natural selection and weaken the institution of the family. Experts who followed, like George Darwin and other eugenicists took this farther and showed a remarkable willingness to lay aside the happiness of some for the progress of the race.

Our treatment has deliberately been restricted to the significant situation that prevailed until the 1970s, in which eugenic policy imposed the exogenous goal of racial perfection on individuals. Such state-imposed eugenic policies are unlikely to return, at least in democratic societies. But although states now struggle to overcome the long shadow of top-down imposed sterilizations, scientific knowledge related to genetic defects has proceeded at a rapid pace and individuals can acquire knowledge about precise genetic markers for unborn children. This opens an entirely new set of ethical questions related to a "New Eugenics" in which individuals, relying on the advice of physicians, make choices to abort or not in the attempt to influence the genetic quality of their offspring.[25] The science of heredity and the influence of scientific knowledge on policy remains a lightning rod in American politics. Although "Jensenism," the idea that IQ varies irrevocably by race, has been discredited,[26] debates continue over the best mix of policies to help young people attain their full potential in cognitive and noncognitive skills.[27]

[25] See the October 30, 2014, *Huffington Post* blog: www.huffingtonpost.com/jon-entine/lets-cautiously-celebrate_b_6070462.html
[26] See *The New York Times* 2012, Gould 1981; for a favorable account, see Herrnstein and Murray 1994.
[27] See Heckman (2005, pp. 5–7): "The people who favor genetic explanations of social phenomena need to be careful about two things. The methods they use for determining

All this will generate new ethical questions about the role of experts, discussion, and goal formation. Some of these will be less controversial than others. So, for instance, if science demonstrates that cognition is unaffected after a specific age, then policies that target cognitive skills are best aimed at young individuals. More controversially, perhaps, what is the role of the expert when his or her advice seemingly clashes with individual happiness? Does the expert advocate policies that restrict the choices by humans, knowing that these constraints would not be chosen by individuals? Finally, what is the expert's role in shaping institutions, such as marriage, adoption, and legislation that influences family formation choices? We shall touch briefly on these questions in our next chapter, which looks at how economists evaluated economic growth under very different institutional arrangements – capitalism and communism – and then shall return to consider them more fully when we examine institutional arrangements governing experts and expertise.

Behind the controversy over sources of human differences, the question of the expert's authority to direct choice for the betterment of the group remains. Our skepticism is hardly novel. We noted in an earlier chapter that Paul Samuelson saw and appreciated Lionel Robbins's skepticism about whether the expert has more scientific warrant to advocate for policies than a voter does. For the technical issues raised in eugenics, we can do no better than quote James Heckman, who has done much to address the actual sources of human differences. His remark is taken from an interview in which he let go of his formidable technical tools to ask the question: what is the marginal product of an economic expert:

We tell stories in nursery school, such as the story of the tortoise and the hare and the story of the little train that could. I read these to my kids, and they were read to me. All these folk tales, all these pieces of wisdom, the fact that a mother's love matters and all this stuff, we tend to dismiss them in our formal models of education policy. We economists like to write down specific technologies and make things very precise. That's a useful discipline, and that's what I am doing with various coauthors. We are making this subject precise. But sometimes I have my doubts. Some of what economists do is to explain to fellow economists what most intelligent people already know. A lot of what economists do is explain to themselves what the rest of the world already knows. There's a real risk of being caught up in that. (Heckman 2005)

heritability assume additivity. They don't allow for interaction [of genetic and environmental factors]. Secondly, when one does the standard additive analysis for different socioeconomics groups, one finds that socioeconomic status critically affects the so-called heritability coefficient" (p. 6).

# 6

# Expert Judgment and Soviet Growth

We take pleasure in beholding the perfection of so beautiful and grand a *system*, and we are uneasy till we remove any obstruction that can in the least disturb or encumber the regularity of its motions. All constitutions of government, however, are valued only in proportion as they tend to promote the happiness of those who live under them.

This is their sole use and end.

From a certain spirit of *system*, however, from a certain *love* of art and contrivance, we sometimes seem to value the means more than the end, and to be eager to promote the happiness of our fellow–creatures, rather from a view to perfect and improve a certain beautiful and orderly *system*, than from any immediate sense or feeling of what they either suffer or enjoy.

Adam Smith (1790)

## 6.1 Introduction

*Department of State*
*22 October 1963*
*Dear Warren,*

*Many thanks for your kind invitation of September 24th. This autumn is too tied up for me to take the trip to Charlottesville. Could we fix it for the spring? Your name and your work are very much on my mind these days. Our loyalty to the notion that key Soviet sectors were subject to deceleration, a loyalty we both pursue against the views of the intellectual establishment appears increasingly to be vindicated. Should you come this way I should very much like to chat with you.*

*All the best.*
*Walt Rostow.*

We begin this chapter with the letter from W. W. Rostow, acclaimed economist and Kennedy-appointed State Department expert, to Warren Nutter, author of *The Growth of Industrial Production in the Soviet Union* (Nutter 1962), the culmination of years of research sponsored by the National Bureau of Economic Research [NBER]. Nutter was one of the principals of the Knightian Thomas Jefferson Center whose proposal to the Ford Foundation we discussed in Chapter 3, section 3.5. We reprint the letter to illustrate that, despite a fairly strong consensus among experts about the potential threat to US hegemony offered by the Soviet Union, even at the level of the State Department there was some disagreement about the rate of growth in the Soviet Union.

Interestingly, Rostow's letter refers to the "intellectual establishment" as the opposition to the Nutter–Rostow doubts about Soviet growth. In this chapter we examine the fairly tight consensus among the establishment, academic economists who reported on Soviet growth and who educated generations of American students in economics classes across the country. We consider the treatment of Soviet growth in multiple editions of US economics textbooks published after the launch of Sputnik in October 1957, between 1960–1980.[1] We report first on those textbooks that contained the consensus view of the Soviet Union, that it was growing faster than the United States, and would consequently eclipse the United States as an economic power. These textbooks relied on and applied standard neoclassical economic thinking, in particular the production possibility frontier (PPF), which describes the economy in purely physical terms, to the Soviets.[2] Of particular interest is their treatment of the problem of Soviet relative growth over time and whether and how revisions were made to the forecasts once authors came to realize they had been overly optimistic about Soviet prospects. A few textbooks took a more catholic view, contending instead that communist economies were different from that of the United States and taking no position about economic growth in the Soviet Union relative to the United States.

The question of how one analyzes different economies at the level of first-year college textbooks raises the additional issue of where the observing

---

[1]  Full documentation of the treatment of Soviet growth and the use of the production possibility frontier (PPF) in all principles textbooks catalogued in the Library of Congress under HB 171.5 between 1948 and 1970 is available on request. The catalog contains many texts that were "missing in inventory" but with Internet shopping tools we acquired copies of all the textbooks we describe.

[2]  In the article from which this chapter is derived, we discuss the history of the production possibility frontier, and the concerns expressed by Frank Knight's colleague, Jacob Viner, about when it is plausible to believe society is on the frontier (Levy and Peart 2011).

economist is supposed to be located.[3] In the textbooks used until the post-World War II era, the economist was inside the economy. The economist included him or herself in the analysis, using introspection and observation to make sense of economic activity. We label this as a "thick" treatment. One of the first textbooks to break this tradition was Paul Samuelson's 1948 *Economics* in which, by means of the production possibility frontier, he situated the observing economist outside of all economies. We label this a "thin" treatment. The older method took it for granted that an economy was grounded in a set of institutions that required thick description; the newer method presumed that for many problems institutional differences among economies could be neglected so thin descriptions would serve the problem better.

The distinction became important in the late 1940s when the first generation of economics textbooks influenced by J. M. Keynes's teaching were subject to a political attack by public intellectuals of the individualist tradition who disapproved of *both* government involvement in the economy and democratic decision making (Levy, Peart, and Albert 2012). The first significant Keynes-influenced textbook was Lorie Tarshis's 1947 *Elements of Economics*. Tarshis situates his economist inside the American economy and urges his fellow-citizens toward political action to reform. Perhaps because his reform orientation and his candor about reform made him vulnerable, Tarshis's book was attacked by critics and the alternative to a Samuelsonian treatment was thereby destroyed by a political campaign.[4] The use of the PPF, on the other hand, put Samuelson's economist above the fray.

Unfortunately, the textbook controversy has since been collapsed into a one-dimensional debate over the scope of government in stabilizing the economy. What has been missing in these accounts is the democratic dimension. The individualists were as unhappy with the democratic commitment of Ludwig von Mises as they were with Tarshis (Levy et al. 2012).[5] The destruction of the market for Tarshis's textbook in turn dramatically reduced competing points of view in principles of economics textbooks.

---

[3]  By the late nineteenth century, economists such as William Stanley Jevons increasingly placed themselves outside the model as an all-knowing theorist who wrote of a perfectly informed consumer. See Peart (1995).

[4]  Historians as well as the participants have long been puzzled by this outcome (Elzinga 1992; Colander and Landreth 1996, 1998; Samuelson 1997).

[5]  This in turn explains why one of von Mises's students, F. A. Hayek, declined to endorse William Buckley's *God and Man at Yale*, the last of the major statements against the new economics textbooks (Peart and Levy 2013).

The episode documented in what follows reveals, first, just how strong the consensus subsequently became among academic specialists. Second, we review a few textbooks that did contain different views. We argue that, although ideology may have played a role in any given position of an expert, the tools used by the experts were more important than ideology. Economists who developed or used one set of tools for market economies and then used the same tools to analyze the Soviet Union were more likely to overstate economic growth in the Soviet Union than those who recognized the institutionally determined limitations associated with models.

The difference between thick and thin accounts in the textbooks was replicated in the specialist controversy over Soviet-American growth. Nutter (1957, 1962) insisted that growth comparisons preserve institutional information and he asked whether the Soviet Union was catching up with America. His many critics, including Rendigs Fels,[6] saw no need for institutional details to enter into the accounts.

In section 6.4 we explore how economics at a textbook level might have incorporated institutional detail. Here, we suggest that economics of the second best provides a helpful framework.[7] This approach regards an institution as imposing constraints on what is physically possible and then allows the use of standard mathematical tools while preserving institutional embeddedness. The textbook of the period that was written in the second-best tradition contains no overstatement of Soviet growth.

In the interests of transparency applied to ourselves, the reader should know how this last result made a difference in our thinking. Without the second-best insight, one faces an unhappy choice. One alternative is to ignore the constraint and offer advice from a model without a constraint. That practice is hard to distinguish from ideology. The other alternative is to remain silent, to offer no advice whatsoever. When we asked ourselves what can we do in a world in which nontransparency cannot be removed, the second-best formulation seemed to offer a preferable alternative to both of these. We shall consequently return to the second-best approach in Chapters 9 and 11.

---

[6]   Rendigs Fels was a President of the Southern Economic Association and for many years, the Treasurer of the American Economic Association. It was under his guidance that the AEA launched its main vehicle for popularizing technical ideas, the *Journal of Economic Perspectives*. One of us (DML) was introduced to economics through Fels's textbook although Andreas Papandreou changed to Samuelson's textbook for the second semester.

[7]   Richard Lipsey and Kelvin Lancaster's general theory of the second best was first published in Lipsey and Lancaster (1956–1957).

During the passage of time between the completion and publication of the article on which this chapter draws (Levy and Peart 2011) and as we write this, we have offered an interpretation of economic models that require society to be on the frontier of the production possibility set and those that allow them to fall into the interior (Levy and Peart 2015a). This interpretation distinguishes between exogenous and endogenous group goals, the central distinction of the Knightian approach described in Part II.

## 6.2 Soviet Growth in US Economics Textbooks

The collapse of the Soviet Union surprised many western students of economics in part because its economy had long been portrayed in textbooks as a viable alternative to democratic capitalism. For years, textbooks had shown that the Soviet economy was growing faster than the economy of the United States, and many concluded that Soviet citizens would soon enjoy a higher standard of living than Americans. In this chapter we systematically examine the treatment of Soviet growth in American economics textbooks from 1960–1980. These textbooks report that Soviet growth was faster than that of the United States, whereas the ratio of Soviet-US output remained constant. The most successful textbooks published during this period overstated Soviet growth and understated the range of uncertainty associated with the estimates. The treatment in successive editions of American economics textbooks remains overconfident in the estimates of Soviet growth and reveals an asymmetric response to past forecast errors.

Of course, it is now well known that the Soviet economy was growing less quickly than once thought. Yet far less appreciated is the fact that accounts of Soviet "growth" emerged and changed over time in successive editions of American economics textbooks. This trust in the future and skepticism about the past formed the basis of a standard Soviet-era joke: "Under Communism, the Poles are fond of saying, only the future is certain; the past is always changing" (Nutter 1969).

Why were the authors of important textbooks of the 1960s and 1970s so confident about Soviet economic growth that evidence of model failure was repeatedly blamed on events outside the model's control? We offer at least a partial answer in the tools used by the experts involved. Those who we now know to have been overly optimistic, whose textbook predictions were repeatedly falsified over time, adopted as a starting point the presumption that the Soviet and the US economies were essentially the same. That assumption that economic analysis applied across wide institutional differences meant that the country that invested more as a share of national income would also grow more quickly.

Samuelson's textbook pioneered the use of the PPF as the means by which to compare different economies. The PPF bought elegance by abstraction and collapsed each society into a two-dimension production possibility set. Of course, if an omitted variable was important in only one of the societies being compared, the model's predictions would be incorrect.

The textbooks discussed in most detail in the following subsections were selected for attention in Kenneth Elzinga's study of market leaders (Elzinga 1992). The first two constitute the most successful multiedition textbooks, Campbell McConnell's *Economics: Principles, Problems and Policies*, first published in 1960, and Samuelson's *Economics: An Introductory Analysis*, first published in 1948. The other successful textbook noted by Elzinga is George Bach's *Economics*. Elzinga also offers a careful discussion of Tarshis's 1947 *Elements of Economics*. We use Tarshis's little-known 1967 *Modern Economics* to address the counter-factual question of how a Tarshis-influenced textbook market might have considered Soviet growth. Two others are selected to illustrate related issues. Robert Heilbroner's influential book speaks to the question of ideology and institutional thickness. Royall Brandis's textbook suggests that the PPF gained popularity because of its use in United States-Soviet comparisons.

### 6.2.1 McConnell

McConnell published the first edition of his textbook, *Elementary Economics*, in 1960. There, apologizing to the reader for the brevity of the "survey of a very complex economy" (1960, p. 718), he offered a snapshot view of the US and the Soviet economies. He did so using a pie chart that appeared with only minor variations in McConnell's chapter on the Soviet economy through the 1990 edition. The pie chart (Figure 6.1) is presented as if the ratios were true parameters, with no indication that they were estimates with associated errors of various sorts.

McConnell's second edition (1963), now entitled *Economics: Principles, Problems and Policies*, added a discussion of "the growth record of Soviet Russian controlled economy" (1963, p. vi). The 50 percent Soviet-US output ratio reappeared in most of the editions that followed and thirty years later, in the 1990 version, McConnell and his co-author presented the same Soviet-US output ratio of 50 percent (Figure 6.2). Twenty-seven years had passed in which the Soviet economy was characterized by

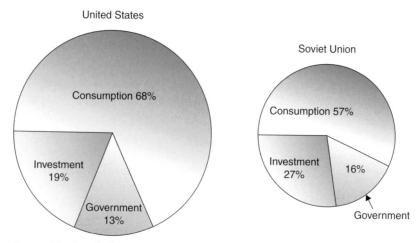

Figure 6.1. Campbell McConnell's pie chart comparing US and USSR investment 1963. Reproduced by permission of McGraw-Hill Education Material from Campbell R. McConnell, *Economics: Principles, Problems, and Policies*, Second edition, 1963, p. 751.

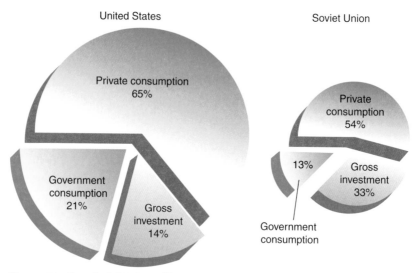

Figure 6.2. Campbell McConnell's pie chart comparing US and USSR investment 1990. Reproduced by permission of McGraw-Hill Education Material from Campbell R. McConnell and Stanley L. Brue, *Economics: Principles, Problems, and Policies*, Eleventh edition, 1990, p. 857.

greater investment and faster growth, yet the Soviet economy remained at half the size of the US economy throughout the period (1990, p. 857).

The pie chart comparison is a staple of McConnell's textbook. It always appears in the last chapter. From 1975 onward, US investment is said to be

Table 6.1. *The sequence of McConnell's comparisons of US and USSR 1960–1990*

| Edition | Figure | US Investment (% of GNP) | USSR Investment (% of GNP) | GNP Ratio US to USSR |
|---------|--------|--------------------------|----------------------------|----------------------|
| 1960 | 38.1 | 19 | 27 | 5:2 |
| 1963 | 40.1 | 19 | 27 | 2:1 |
| 1966 | 42.1 | 20 | 33 | 2:1 |
| 1969 | 44.1 | 19 | 31 | 2:1 |
| 1972 | 46.1 | 19 | 31 | 2:1 |
| 1975 | 45.1 | 15 | 30 | 2:1 |
| 1978 | 45.1 | 15 | 30 | 2:1 |
| 1981 | 45.1 | 15 | 28 | 2:1 |
| 1984 | 46.1 | 15 | 33 | 2:1 |
| 1987 | 44.1 | 14 | 33 | 5:3 |
| 1990 | 42.1 | 14 | 33 | 2:1 |

about half that of the Soviet Union as a share of GNP and yet the ratio of Soviet to US GNP is usually 50 percent. Table 6.1 summarizes the contents of the McConnell pie chart over the sequence of editions of the textbook.[8]

In McConnell's pie chart, consumption and investment always sum to 100 percent of GNP; there is no room for inefficiency. Consequently, investment in the two countries is equally effective and, without some disturbing cause from outside the economic system, higher investment in one country manifests itself in higher growth. Yet the pie charts never indicate that the Soviet economy is catching up with the United States.[9]

It is important to emphasize that the reader of McConnell's textbook would not see Table 6.1 detailing the history of US–Soviet comparisons. There was no discussion that we could find about the past projections. At a point in time, the textbook seems completely transparent; only when one considers the *sequence* of texts, as reconstructed by us, does the

---

[8] Our pie chart reproduction (Figure 6.1) is from the 1963 edition. McConnell cited the same sources for the pie charts in 1960 and 1963. However the reported ratio of Soviet to US output changed from 40 percent to 50 percent in the three-year period.

[9] McConnell's explanations in the textbook also refer to higher Soviet investment and growth without catching up. In 1963 he writes that "Soviet GNP is roughly one-half that of the United States." (1963, p. 754) and "the rate of economic growth is two or three times as great as that of the United States." In 1975 we read: "Although the Soviet GNP is only one-half as large as that of the United States, the Soviet GNP has grown more rapidly than ours" (1975, p. 905). In 1984, "Although the Soviet GNP is only one-half as large as that of the United States, the Soviet GNP has grown more rapidly than ours" (1984, p. 837). In 1987 the text notes that "Although the Soviet GNP is only about 60 percent as large …" (1987, p. 911). The sentence is removed from the 1990 edition, leaving a statement about the "high historical growth rates in the Soviet Union" (1990, p. 865).

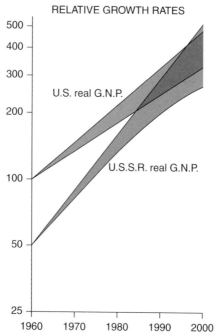

Figure 6.3. Paul Samuelson's growth forecasts of US and USSR 1961. Reproduced by permission of McGraw-Hill Education Material from Paul A. Samuelson, *Economics: An Introductory Analysis*, Fifth edition, 1961, p. 830.

nontransparency itself become transparent. Thus, our Bibliography lists the sequence of editions as the unit of reference.

### 6.2.2 Samuelson

In 1961, Paul Samuelson took a step beyond McConnell and devised a graph that provides a rough and ready forecast of Soviet and American growth trajectories. Using different assumptions about Soviet and American growth rates, Samuelson projects when the Soviet economy will overtake the US economy. His first projection (which we call a max-min overtaking point) is based on the maximum respectable Soviet growth assumption and the minimum respectable American growth assumption. The second date, which we call a max-max prediction, is more cautious about when the overtaking will occur: it uses the maximum Soviet growth assumption and the maximum American growth assumption. The graph inspires confidence because it presents a range of growth estimates as opposed to just one.

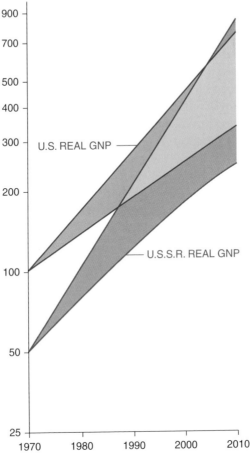

RELATIVE GROWTH RATES, U.S.A. AND U.S.S.R.

Figure 6.4. Paul Samuelson's growth forecasts of US and USSR 1970. Reproduced by permission of McGraw-Hill Education Material from Paul A. Samuelson, *Economics*, Eighth edition, 1970, p. 3.

In the 1961 graph, reproduced as Figure 6.3, the max-min year seems to be 1984; the max-max year is about 1997. The optimistic forecast of time before the Soviet overtaking is twenty-three years; the more pessimistic time to overtaking in the max-max world is thirty-six years. The nonovertaking trajectory supposes an exogenous shock outside the scope of the theory.

Like McConnell's pie chart, Samuelson's overtaking graph is always the first graph in the last chapter of the book. There are, however, two editions – the seventh of 1967 and the eighth of 1970 (reproduced here as Figure 6.4) – in which the projection is the first graph that students see. Perhaps the projection is offered as a key motivation to study economics.[10]

Table 6.2 presents the Samuelson edition year, the placement of the graph, the two forecasts obtained from reading the graphs, and the ratio of US to USSR starting points. There are two regimes in the history of the graph. One – which is in bold type – preserves the 1960 starting point. The second regime rebases the forecast to the year of the edition, thus implicitly revising the US-Soviet output ratio in 1960 to something well below 100:50.

The table also presents the starting ratio of American and Soviet real outputs used in each graphical representation. From 1961 through the 1973 edition, this is constant at 100:50. Only in the last two graphs does the ratio change. The claim of considerably faster Soviet growth made *by the graph* is juxtaposed with an unchanging ratio of real output levels, notwithstanding the obvious fact that sustained faster growth would have to imply a change in the ratio.

As we noted, the graphs appeared twice in Samuelson's 1967 and 1970 editions. The following information accompanied the second appearance of the graph in the text:

In the decade preceding 1970, the United States grew toward the top of its projected range of growth rates. But the U.S.S.R., because of bad weather and crops and short-ening of the workweek, seems to have moved lower down on its projected range of growth rates. (Samuelson 1970, p. 831)

Exogenous elements such as bad weather and unforeseen political decisions are said to have intervened to throw the forecast off.

The numbers in Table 6.2 are derived from the graphics in the textbooks. Samuelson also provides commentary about Soviet productivity and bad weather. In the fifth edition (1961) he offers the following discussion:

The decision of how to combine various productive factors – land and labor, degree of mechanization – appears to depend on a mixture of purely technical consider-ations and adaptions to the scarcity of various economic resources. A continual pro-cess of trial and error goes on. The observer finds operations curiously uneven: on the one hand, he may see a military ballistic plant which has achieved a precision of ball bearings and gyroscopes rivaling the best in the world; on the other hand, he may find things being done an almost unbelievably primitive way, with the quality of output practically worthless. (Example: A Soviet farmwoman may be assigned one cow to take care of; on a Wisconsin dairy farm, a man and wife may take care of 30 cows, in addition to performing countless other daily chores. (Samuelson 1961, p. 826)

---

[10]   From the sixth through the tenth editions Samuelson has line graphs comparing many dif-ferent countries on the inner lining. McConnell has a table of National Income Accounts.

The same paragraph appears in the sixth edition (1964, p. 803). The graph in the 1964 edition is accompanied by this additional information:

From 1960 to 1964 it would appear that the United States has moved at the very top of its projected range. But the U.S.S.R., because of bad weather and crops and shortening of the work week, may have moved at the bottom of her projected range. (Samuelson 1964, p. 807)

The productivity paragraph appears in the seventh edition (Samuelson 1967, p. 786). In 1967 it accompanies Figure 40–1, but not Figure 1–1, with the ending date changed from 1964 to 1967.

Samuelson rewrote the productivity paragraph in the eighth edition, updating the example from 30 to 50 cows and bringing mechanization to Wisconsin:

Example: A Soviet farmwoman may be assigned one cow to take care of; on a mechanized Wisconsin dairy farm, a man and wife may take care of 50 cows, in addition to performing countless other daily chores. (Samuelson 1970, p. 827)

In the ninth edition, the productivity paragraph is unchanged (Samuelson 1973, p. 879). Unlike the graph in the 1964 edition, this edition's graph (1973, p. 883) is not qualified by bad weather although a footnote on the page before remarks "In the last dozen years both growth records were comparable" (Samuelson 1973, p. 882).

In the tenth edition, the ratio of US to USSR output changed to 100:57 (1973, p. 883). The productivity paragraph contained a new piece of information:

Private allotments of land on the collective farm often have much higher, not lower productivity than the collectivized sectors. (Samuelson 1976, p. 879)

The text mentions bad weather in a footnote and offers a prediction about future efficiency:

Despite unfavorable weather, much-improved efficiency would seem technically feasible in the future. (Samuelson 1976, p. 881)

In the eleventh edition, the productivity paragraph italicizes "higher" (Samuelson 1980, p. 822); the ratio of US to USSR output now falls to 100:55. (1980, p. 825). The edition drops the "bad weather" explanation and now simply refers to the "unfavorable past":

Despite this unfavorable past, much-improved efficiency would be technically feasible in the future. (Samuelson 1980, p. 824)

As we pointed out, the graphs comparing the Soviet Union to the United States appeared twice in Samuelson's 1967 and 1970 editions. Their placement as the first figure the student encountered suggests how important this issue was.

Table 6.2. *The sequence of Samuelson's growth forecasts 1961–1980*

| Year | Figure | Max-Min Overtaking Time | Max-Max Overtaking Time | Start GNP Ratio: US to USSR |
|------|--------|-------------------------|-------------------------|------------------------------|
| **1961** | **37.1** | **23** | **36** | **100/50** |
| **1964** | **38.1** | **20** | **33** | **100/50** |
| **1967** | **1.1 & 40.1** | **10** | **28** | **100/50** |
| 1970 | 1.1 & 42.1 | 18 | 35 | 100/50 |
| 1973 | 43.1 | 17 | 35 | 100/50 |
| 1976 | 43.1 | 16 | 32 | 100/57 |
| 1980 | 43.1 | 22 | 32 | 100/55 |

Table 6.2 allows us to compare the information in editions over time; the numbers in the chart are taken from the graphics in the textbooks.

### 6.2.3  Bach

Not all the textbooks in the period assumed efficiency in the same manner that Samuelson and McConnell did. Instead of opening his discussion of Soviet-American growth with a PPF, Bach discussed the details of the American economy. In contrast with McConnell and Samuelson, Bach acknowledged (1960, p. 841) dissenting voices in the profession, noting that the NBER studies by Nutter and Gregory Grossman "suggest that the spread between Soviet and American growth rates may not be as wide as has been commonly supposed." In the sixth edition, he reported that Soviet growth had in the last decade "just about equaled that of the U.S.A." (1968, p. 572). He noted: "Comparing U.S. and U.S.S.R. growth rates is one of the favorite statistical games of the generation … " (1968, p. 573). Per capita gross national product, however, solidly indicated a discrepancy (1968, p. 573).

As a partial explanation, Bach pointed to unemployment caused by a failure of planning in the Soviet Union (1968, p. 571). In 1968, Bach added a new table of hypothetical growth rates (1968, p. 574), beginning with a base of 100 for the United States and 50 for the Soviet Union. Over the 1965–1995 period, he specified the US growth numbers at 2, 3, and 4 percent and the Soviet numbers at 4, 5, 6, 7 percent. The table of hypothetical growth rates was removed from the seventh edition (1971) and replaced by a table showing's Japan's growth rate at more than 10 percent, Soviet growth at 4.1 percent and US growth at 3.1 percent (Bach 1971, p. 691).

In the ninth edition Soviet growth is said to have slowed even more (Bach 1977, p. 650) and black markets have arisen (1977, p. 651). Bach again noted differences of opinion on this matter: "Some observers put Russian per capita incomes as high as half ours, but not more" (1977, p. 651). The hypothetical growth table stays missing. Comparisons of American-Soviet per capita income become more complicated by 1980: "$9,600 in the United States, $3,500–$4,500 in the USSR" (Bach 1980, p. 675). In this edition, a new piece of information is added, a Soviet cartoon showing a planning confusion and an anecdote – "a standard Russian joke" – about incentives:

The accompanying cartoon shows the Russian wryly observing the problem. In a market system, the profit incentive continually pushes managers to avoid such inefficiencies. Under quotas and physical planning, the manager's goal is to meet the quotas, not to question why. A standard Russian joke has a factory turning out one huge one-ton nail as the cheapest way to meet its quota of one ton of steel nails. (Bach 1980, p. 676).

The textbook no longer predicted the Soviet Union overtaking the United States and the fixed ratio of Soviet–US output disappeared.

Bach's table of hypothetical growth rates that showed Soviet growth exceeding US growth appeared in only one edition. He provided no explanation to accompany the specification; this would have required a PPF, which his textbook did not contain.

### 6.2.4 Tarshis

Tarshis began his 1947 *Elements of Economics* with a clear statement that an unguided economy will be inefficient: "If doctors had designed the human body, there would probably be no diseases. Likewise, if economists had designed the economy, the chances are that there would be no economic problems to worry about. As it is, the economist believes his job is to understand the existing economy in order that he can properly guide efforts to make it work efficiently" (Tarshis 1947, pp. 4–5). This provoked some controversy. Rose Wilder Lane[11] (1947) read the book as advocating political solutions in lieu of voluntary solutions, and for that reason she was highly critical. Yet Tarshis's reformist point of view may have immunized his analysis from an assumption of economic efficiency.[12] Indeed, the Soviet

---

[11] Rose Wilder Lane (1886–1968) was a self-described "individualist," a journalist, novelist, and political theorist. She was the daughter of Laura Ingalls Wilder. For a study of her attack on interventionist economics textbooks, see Levy et al. (2012). Her reaction to Milton Friedman and George Stigler's removing the stigma from "rationing" is reported in Chapter 3, section 3.3.

[12] Harcourt (1995) emphasizes the importance of Tarshis's assumption of imperfect competition. Tarshis focused, for instance, on price rigidities associated with oligopoly (1947, pp. 182–84). Samuelson's chapter on the firm treats perfect and imperfect competition together (1948, p. 491–97) and does not consider the possibility of oligopoly-induced price rigidity.

Table 6.3. *Lorie Tarshis's 1967 comparison of US and USSR*

| | USSR GNP as % of US GNP (1958) | Growth Rates (1950–1958) | |
|---|---|---|---|
| | | US | USSR |
| Weights correspond to US prices | 65 | 2.9 | 6.0 |
| Weights correspond to USSR prices | 33 | 2.9 | 7.5 |

section in his much-ignored *Modern Economics* of 1967 contained no such assumption. Tarshis's brief discussion there addressed the implicit assumptions behind the "perennial issue" of the relative growth rates of the United States and the Soviet Union (Tarshis 1967, p. 663). He began by asking what index we ought to use to compare growth rates. Output per capita was problematical, he argued, because it assumed a roughly constant and equal labor input across countries (1967, p. 661).

Tarshis's table (1967, p. 663), reproduced as Table 6.3, illustrates the problem with all US and Soviet comparisons. Since labor inputs were relatively poorly paid in the USSR, prices there were lower than in the United States and a simple switch of weights from US to USSR prices would then reduce the resulting measured size of the Soviet economy.[13]

Tarshis then considered how to select time periods for the purposes of comparison, pointing out that a short period analysis makes the choice of end points critical (1967, pp. 661–62). Relying on Simon Kuznets's work, he compared growth rates of nineteen countries. The time period (1870–1954) spanned both Russian and Soviet history and Tarshis chose to treat them as one country (1967, pp. 666). Nutter had also followed this convention and was widely and strenuously criticized for doing so (Gordon Brady 2008). Tarshis's conclusion again emphasized the economist's role as reformer:

It is noticeable that most of these countries showed a decline in growth rate, comparing the two periods. The exceptions were Italy and the Soviet Union, to which industrialization came late; Sweden which succeeded in maintaining a high rate throughout … an economist cannot refrain from pointing out that Sweden; more than any other country in the group studied, has followed the advice of its economists – who incidentally have been exceptionally able. (Tarshis 1967, pp. 666–67)

[13] This consideration is noted in Samuelson as "a technical index number problem involved that need only be indicated," which gets solved by simply splitting the difference in all the editions; (1961, p. 828); (1964, p. 806); (1967, p. 790); (1970, p. 830); (1973, p. 881); (1976, p. 882); (1980; p. 824).

The treatment of Soviet-American growth in Tarshis's 1967 textbook suggests that the comparisons depend very much on one's point of view. Indeed, this is one of Tarshis's key points in the textbook. He offers no guidance for the future of US-Soviet competition. The textbook, one notes with some regret, disappeared without a trace soon after it appeared.

### 6.2.5 Heilbroner

Heilbroner's 1968 textbook positions itself farther than any other from Samuelson's "neoclassical synthesis."[14] Heilbroner presupposed that market economies require a culture of self-reliance, free of direction either by tradition or command. He divided the world into regions of command, markets, and tradition in a map (Figure 6.5) shown here from the first edition inner liner (Heilbroner 1968). For Heilbroner the economy of the Soviet Union must be studied in the context of the evolution of its institutions (1968, p. 599). He questioned the assumptions of constant growth and of fixed institutions, remarking that growth was decelerating (1968, p. 628) and the Soviet Union was moving toward markets (1968, p. 599). Heilbroner predicted "a convergence of systems" (pp. 629–30) as institutions developed toward some "advanced" form.

Samuelson had elegantly captured the key features of economies using tradeoffs of guns and butter. By contrast, Heilbroner discussed tradition, markets, and command before he turned to guns and butter. For him, it was no easy matter to compare economic activity in America with economic activity in the Soviet Union since one model failed adequately to encompass both economies.

Heilbroner occupies a distinct ideological position among textbook writers of the time.[15] Yet, interestingly, from the other side of the ideological perspective, Armen Alchian and William Allen shared Heilbroner's reluctance to present an encompassing model for all economies. Their *University Economics* comprised the Chicago-school alternative to Samuelson at this

---

[14] Blanchard (2008) describes "neoclassical synthesis" as "the blend of Keynesian theory with a theory of market coined by Paul Samuelson to denote the consensus view of macroeconomics which emerged in the mid-1950s in the United States" with "important contributions, by Hicks, Modigliani, Solow, Tobin and others"

[15] Heilbroner (1968, p. 3): "no other branch of study holds such possibilities for the improvement of the human condition in a world that is, in the main, still brutally poor. I do not mean that the rescuers of mankind must be economists, although I myself believe that the appeal of economics is greatest to those who feel affronted at the miseries and inequities of the human spectacle." Without minimizing "Stalinist" horrors, he asked students to reflect on the brutalities of capitalistic development (1968, p. 595).

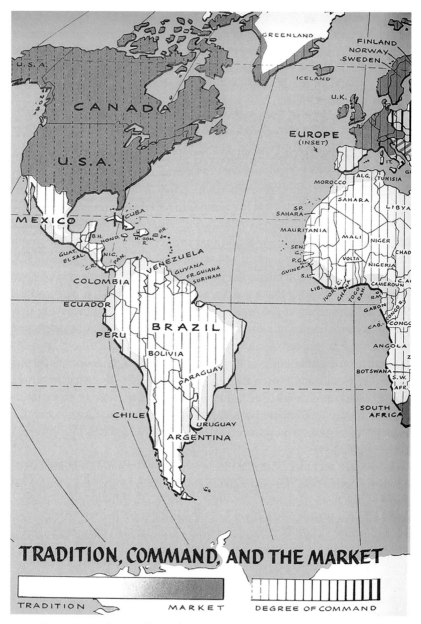

Figure 6.5.  Robert Heilbroner's 1968 comparison of the world economies.

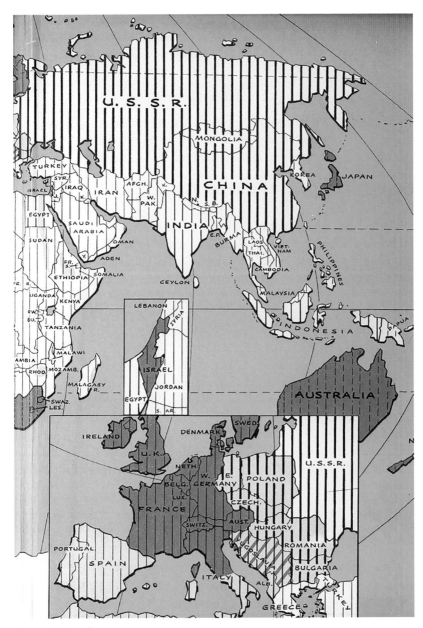

Figure 6.5 (*cont.*)

time. Alchian and Allen explain why their book does not analyze any form of socialist economy: neoclassical theory failed to characterize the Soviet economic system.[16]

## 6.3　Poor Forecasts: Ideology or Model Failure?

Some accounts of this period's textbooks have emphasized an ideologically inspired romanticization of planned economies (Skousen 1997). There was, perhaps, some hopefulness on the part of reform-minded textbook writers. Yet our account suggests that the treatment of Soviet-US growth was not driven by ideology alone. Tarshis's ideology was similar to that of Samuelson. Yet his view of the Soviet economy in 1967 was very nonromantic indeed.

Ideological explanations of the different treatments also cannot account for how specialist researchers who differed greatly on ideological terms, such as Nutter and Rostow, united across their political differences to oppose the CIA's use of the Soviet–US growth estimates (Nutter 1983a, pp. 231–32, and 1983b, Lipsey 2008). In his letter to Nutter, reproduced at the beginning of the chapter, Rostow referred to the "intellectual establishment" against which they were united (Rostow to Nutter, October 22, 1963).

What other explanation might account for the very different treatments of Soviet relative growth rates by American economists? An alternative explanation is to be found in the modeling approach of the authors. Samuelson pioneered the textbook use of the PPF, reproduced here from his first edition (Figure 6.6), to conceptualize production in different societies. In Samuelson's formulation, abstracting from the possibility of involuntary unemployment (Keynes's concern), all economies are efficient. Thus, Samuelson wrote about the Soviet economy in terms of the production possibility frontier in his first edition:

The Russians, having no unemployment before the war, were already on their Production-possibility curve. They had no choice but to substitute war goods for civilian production–with consequent privation. (Samuelson 1948, p. 20)

Both Tarshis and Samuelson believed in activist government policy to counteract what they saw as the inherent instability and inefficiency in

---

[16] "The portion of economics comprising the theory of exchange is applicable to a wider class of problems in a capitalistic private-property economy than it is in a socialist society. This does not mean there is no exchange in the latter; there is, of course, a great deal of it … In a socialist system… political power and exchange of *non* private-property rights are used much more widely to solve the economic questions. If we were to devote primary attention to the socialist system, we would investigate much more fully the processes of political exchange and political decision making" (Alchian and Allen 1964, p. 6).

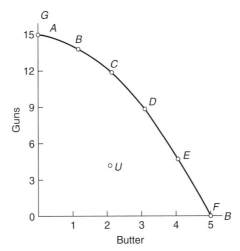

Figure 6.6. Paul Samuelson's 1948 production possibility set. Reproduced by permission of McGraw-Hill Education Material from Paul A. Samuelson, *Economics: An Introductory Analysis*, First edition, 1948, p. 20.

democratic capitalism; as a result, their books were attacked for being liberal and antimarket.[17] They differed, however, on whether the economy might be represented by a PPF as a thin model or whether they required a thick description. For Tarshis, the institutional framework of the Soviet Union was too different from that of the United States to be captured by the same model; for Samuelson, the similarities between the two economies were enough to warrant the use of one PPF to describe them both.

The following matrix (Table 6.4) captures the differences in textbooks. It shows that the reformist attitude was neither necessary nor sufficient for overstating Soviet growth.

If the overstatement of Soviet growth was *mainly* driven by the expert's viewpoint (ideology), we would expect Samuelson, Tarshis, and Heilbroner to overstate Soviet growth more dramatically than McConnell and Bach. They did not. If the problem arose primarily because of the tools used by the expert (the modeling devices), Samuelson and McConnell would overstate Soviet growth more dramatically than the other authors. This is what we have observed. The lesson we take from this is that, although the beliefs or

---

[17] As noted in Chapter 3 section 3.3, Lane vigorously attacked Tarshis's textbook; Buckley was critical of the apparent homogeneity of approach to economics on college campuses in *God and Man at Yale* (Buckley 1951).

Table 6.4. *Expert ideology or model fragility?*

|              | Liberal              | Neutral   |
|--------------|----------------------|-----------|
| Thin model   | Samuelson            | McConnell |
| Thick model  | Tarshis, Heilbroner  | Bach      |

viewpoint of the expert may indeed influence results, so, too, do the analytical devices used by experts.

We also noted that Bach drew his students' attention to the Nutter–Grossman research. Their approach (Nutter 1957, 1962; Rostow 1960), measured the years by which Soviet industry lagged behind American industry. This required a belief that when Russia became the Soviet Union, its fundamental institutions did not change. Tarshis's skepticism about Soviet growth followed from a similar belief that institutions in the Soviet Union remained much as they had been in Russia and very different from those in the United States.

As an additional indication of this contrast, consider Fels's 1961 purely empirical textbook, which contained no PPF, and Brandis's theoretical treatment, which relied heavily on the PPF. Fels's *The Challenge to the American Economy*, whose very title refers to Khrushchev's boast that the Soviet Union will bury Americans economically, dismissed Nutter and those who relied on Nutter's research. After quoting Khrushchev and presenting standard growth comparisons, Fels turned to Henry Hazlitt's use of Nutter's data:

The table appears to justify amply Hazlitt's conclusion that "the evidence has been unmistakable that, far from there being any 'miracle' of Communist production, the lands behind the Iron Curtain are going through an economic crisis." These results are in striking contradiction to the figures cited in the previous section. There it was proved that Communist output grows twice as fast as American. Here it is proved that under Communism output lags farther behind. Plainly it cannot do both at once. (Fels 1961, p. 11)

Fels (1961, pp. 11–12) criticized Nutter for using figures based in 1913 to discuss Soviet growth and Hazlitt for his blind faith in the goodness of capitalism, a belief that reportedly biased his analysis:

Popular writing on economics is strewn with errors. Although it is perhaps unfair to expose Hazlitt in one, since he generally maintains a high standard, nevertheless for educational purposes it is valuable to do so. The fact that one of the best has fallen into a trap is a warning to read everything – including his book – with a healthy degree of skepticism. The probable cause for his going astray is likely to

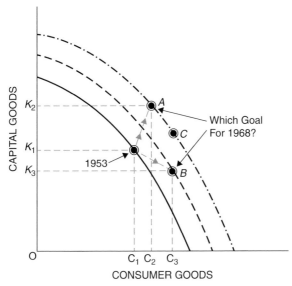

Figure 6.7. Royall Brandis's analysis of the Soviet economy. Reproduced by permission of McGraw-Hill Education Material from Royall Brandis, *Principles of Economics*, 1968, p. 34.

infect anyone. Hazlitt is a stronger believer in capitalism and a vigorous critic of any other economic system. (Fels 1961, p. 12)

Nutter's data disappear from the second edition (Fels 1966).

Fels's textbook was in some respect thick; it contained no PPF and in other ways it was less abstract than Samuelson's textbook. But as a thick textbook, it contained no abstract model to predict continued rapid Soviet growth. What we observe in Fels' textbook is the dismissing of evidence because the authors had a point of view. After the Ford Foundation's treatment of Nutter and his fellow Knightians of the Thomas Jefferson Center (Chapter 3, section 3.5) for their point of view, this would not have come as a surprise.

To illustrate why the PPF was so attractive at this time to textbook writers, consider how Brandis adopted the PPF midway through his textbook run as a way to model the Soviet economy. His was perhaps the most elegant use of the PPF in the period (Figure 6.7).

In the "note to the instructor" Brandis explained the addition: "the production-possibility curve technique is developed and then used to explore briefly a number of economic problems generally familiar to the student. These questions are not only important in their own right but serve to fix the analytical tool in the student's mind …" (Brandis 1968, p. vii). Brandis's analysis is remarkable for making explicit the supposition that investment goods will shift the production possibility frontier for the future more than consumer goods. Thus, higher investment brings about faster growth (Brandis 1968, p. 34). The assumption of efficiency is critical here and is often viewed as the default assumption in the absence of "involuntary unemployment."

## 6.4  A Second-Best Test

Our focus on the PPF as the source of the problem sends us back to consider whether there were any textbook treatments that explored the possibility of an interior solution. Constraints that forced inefficiency and thus interior solutions came into general equilibrium theory in 1956–1957 with Lipsey's and Lancaster's "General Theory of the Second Best." As Lipsey wrote an important British principles textbook (Lipsey 1963–1966) that was imported to America in a coauthored version (Lipsey and Steiner 1966–1981), we use his second-best insight to test our larger account. We should expect Lipsey's textbooks to be careful about supposing a society is producing the maximum conceivable output and consequently to contain less systematic overstatement of Soviet growth.[18]

Lipsey authored a pair of textbooks, the British edition and the coauthored American edition (1963–1966).[19] He begins the economics section proper with a detailed discussion of the need to distinguish between movements along the PPF and movements from the interior to the frontier. Although one source of interior positions is idle resources, other sources are presented as inefficiency, a concept to be explored as the text unfolds. Lipsey (1963) contains nothing on the Soviet Union and the revised edition has only a sentence that links Stalin with Hitler and Mao (Lipsey 1966, p. 810).

The American edition starts in 1966 with a production possibility set for defense and consumer goods and the separation between regions of attainable and unattainable combinations (Lipsey and Steiner 1966, p. 6).

---

[18] One of us (SJP) was introduced to economics through the Canadian counterpart, Lipsey, Gordon Sparks, and Peter Steiner (1978).

[19] Samuelson's textbook was changed in important but gradual ways when it was exported to Canada. The first edition has the overtaking graph in the final chapter "Alternative Economic Systems" (Samuelson and Scott 1966, p. 867). The next two editions put the overtaking graph at the front of the book (Samuelson and Scott 1968, p. 3; 1971, p. 4). This preserves the US editions' structure. The fourth edition however removes the "Alternative Economic Systems" chapter and with it the overtaking graph. Some material from the American "Alternative Economic Systems" chapter appears as an appendix to chapter 3 (Samuelson and Scott 1971, pp. 57–63).

Table 6.5. *Richard Lipsey and Peter Steiner's*
*hypothetical growth comparisons*

Number of years until Soviet level of income reaches U.S. Level*

| Soviet Growth | US Growth Rates (%) | | | |
|---|---|---|---|---|
| Rate (%) | 2 | 3 | 4 | 5 |
| 5 | 23 | 34½ | 69 | ∞ |
| 6 | 17½ | 23 | 34½ | 69 |
| 7 | 14 | 17½ | 23 | 34½ |
| 8 | 11½ | 14 | 17½ | 23 |

*Assumes present Soviet level is one-half US level.

The text next to the second figure of the possibility set tells the student, "Unemployment of resources is similar to an inefficient use of them … in that they both lead to production inside the production-possibility boundary. They are not the same problem … " (Lipsey and Steiner 1966, p. 10). The new Soviet material from Lipsey (1966) is carried over (Lipsey and Steiner 1966, p. 688). Lipsey and Steiner (1966) remains very similar to Lipsey (1966) in that the Soviet economy is simply not of much interest.

The year 1969 brings a US–USSR growth comparison. The comparison is similar to that in Bach, with computations of the years until the Soviet level of income would increase from one-half that of the United States to attain equality (Table 6.5). One of the table's sixteen cells contains equal growth rates; one other cell requires sixty-nine years to equality and so on (Bach 1969, p. 812). The table is small, three inches wide by two inches tall.

There is, following the table of hypothetical growth rates, a quite substantial discussion of the reality of frictional, structural, and disguised unemployment and a striking two paragraphs on what inflationary taxation looks like in a command economy. Then follows a two-paragraph section on the "economic shortcomings of the Soviet economic experience" in which shortages, gluts, and mis-shipments are detailed (Lipsey and Steiner 1969, p. 814). The economic cost of planning activity, in terms of the highly trained workers who are pulled from production to direction, is discussed in a paragraph that speculates about how computers may eventually reduce this in the future (1969, pp. 814–15). The benefits of planning are also mentioned: the goals can be whatever the planners want (1969, p. 815).

The same table of hypothetical years to equality appears in the third edition (Lipsey and Steiner 1972, p. 782) along with the discussions. We find the table and discussion again in the fourth edition (Lipsey and Steiner 1975, p. 899) although "never" replaces "∞" in one cell.

The fifth edition, of 1978, marks another dramatic change. The time to income equalization table is now removed and replaced by a report from the CIA's *Soviet Economy* publication that contains estimated growth by sectors in the Soviet Union for two periods, 1966–1970 and 1971–1975 (Lipsey and Steiner 1978, p. 844). In the second period, Soviet growth in agriculture turns negative. In addition to the previously discussed "sources and costs of the achievement," Solzhenitsyn's reports are mentioned, prompting Lipsey and Steiner to ask why such tyranny is found in the Soviet Union but not in other command economies? Their answer appeals to the reality of institutions.[20] In the next edition, the CIA seems to have revised its numbers and so Soviet agricultural growth is now positive over the 1971–1975 period (Lipsey and Steiner 1981, p. 859).

The focus on constraints in general equilibrium theory also characterizes Lipsey and Steiner's textbook. Even as they had the same *hypothetical* time to equality table, with its no-slower growth and unchanging relative levels for three editions, the text described *real* sources of inefficiency and the *fact* of various sorts of unemployment. There is good reason to believe that the Soviet economy was not on the frontier of the possible and, from that, there was no good theoretical warrant to believe that lower Soviet consumption would lead to an overtaking growth rate. That question required examining the evidence.

The Lipsey and Steiner textbook offers an opportunity to consider how a thin model of the economy, augmented by second-best insights that take institutional constraints seriously, performs in competition with thick institutional models. The same PPF could not be used to describe both societies since what is possible depends on institutions.

## 6.5 Conclusion

Authors of the most successful principles textbooks in the 1960–1980 decades were so confident of the superior prospects for Soviet growth relative to the United States that they persisted in their forecasts even though

---

[20] "It is not necessary to assume, however, that this degree of tyranny *must* accompany any command economy. After, all, the tradition of political tyranny in Russia stretches well back into the time of the Czars ... " (Lipsey and Steiner 1978, p. 846). In point of comparison, Nutter's pessimism about the possibility of Soviet reform, points to the old "dilemma of the Czars," reforming the system without giving up the autocratic political order (Nutter 1969, pp. 131–32).

doing so meant rewriting the past. This overconfidence did not character-ize less successful textbooks, even those whose authors shared Samuelson's political views. We conclude from this historical episode that an expert's viewpoints matter, but so, too, might the tools. If an expert chooses aver-age income or full employment as characteristics of the devices by which to measure growth, then already much has been sorted as relevant to the picture, or not.

The natural question is whether there was something that made for a suc-cessful textbook that contributed to the overconfidence. One candidate is the institutional-free model of the economy, pioneered at the textbook level by Samuelson's employment of the PPF, to analyze the potential for growth. In this two-dimensional representation, as long as the involuntary employ-ment that so worried Keynes was precluded, a society that consumed less, as the Soviets surely did, would grow faster. This of course assumed away rent seeking, the de facto barter system, and the disguised unemployment that long characterized the Soviet economy. By supposing such institutional details were epiphenomenal, the model yielded crisp implications.

The full implication of the negative reviews and the political campaign against the use of Tarshis's textbook becomes clear when we consider his much-overlooked 1967 textbook attempt. Here, we find a reform-minded textbook that denies social efficiency. More than this, Tarshis's account of Soviet growth in the 1967 text might have been written by Nutter or Rostow. Had the market for principles textbooks found space for such a set of argu-ments and discussion, Tarshis's textbook might have helped those who did not share Nutter or Rostow's ideology to see more deeply into the chal-lenges facing the Soviet economy. The consequences of the destruction of competition among experts was a dramatic loss of a point of view through which to view the Soviet Union.

The foregoing historical account reveals that many economists got eco-nomic growth badly wrong and failed to recognize over decades of mal-performance that they were getting it badly wrong. Therefore, one warning about economic experts is to be wary of the (monopoly) model. The expert may become so enamored with a model and the supposed consensus that he or she uses it even when the expert knows its assumptions have been violated and the model simply does not fit the data.

This is the problem with economic experts that so preoccupied Adam Smith. In the passage quoted at the beginning of this chapter, Smith warned his readers that we can be so beholden to the system that we come to value the system itself more than the end that the system is supposed to promote. In the case of analyzing growth in the Soviet Union, the system relied on a model that was a simple and elegant one: the production possibility frontier. This is all well and good as long as one recognizes that incentives are required before an economy attains a position on the frontier. If we are so blinded by the elegance of the model that we fail to do a full check when it seems to be malperforming, we have fallen into Smith's trap. So while the model was apparently consistent at a point in time, it was inconsistent over time and the economists who were so committed to its use failed to give it up. This is the power of system that Smith described.

In this context, it is important to reflect on why Lipsey's very theoretical textbook avoided the trap. Although there may be many reasons for this, the fact that second-best theory prompts us to check whether there are institutional constraints that impede first-best efficiency considerations suggests that we place our confidence in this approach. We shall return to second-best thinking in Chapter 11.

In the textbooks we have studied, the production set specifies what is available to society in terms of two exogenous goals, power and plenty. That seems unexceptionable. When the society is supposed to be on the frontier, the model tells us that all society's resources are going to satisfy these goals. There is, as consequence, nothing left for other goals. When the society is located on the interior of the production possibility set, there may be other goals that are being pursued. Thus, the distinction between exogenous and endogenous goals discussed in Parts I and II is recreated in the textbooks examined here. This provides a good reason to take the distinction seriously.

# PART IV

# AN END TO DISCUSSION: SECRECY
# AND THE TEMPTATION TO BIAS

The two cases studied in this part of the book are financial reforms undertaken in two very different contexts. Characteristically, accounts of these episodes offer a linear model as history. John Law's monetary reform was said to reduce the social cost of the monetary unit, and the rating agencies in the days before their use in regulations were supposed to have provided impartial advice to investors. Although many experts who have studied these episodes have argued that the problems occurred in the details or were the fault of the ordinary people who participated in the reformed markets, we shall depart from that approach. We point instead to the secrecy that allowed the experts to pursue their private goals.

Instead of blaming the problems on delicate technical issues, let alone the incapacity of the public, we shall document that the problems were recognized in the course of the reforms but those voices were ignored. In the first case that follows, the public was taken in by what many contemporaries regarded as a con – John Law's Mississippi Bubble. Here we offer a rereading of evidence that has been available for almost three centuries. In the second case, the public was taken in by a willingness to believe that the opinion of any one expert rating agency was as good as that of any other rating agency, even if the rating came from a procedure likely to produce an upward bias in the rating. The problem of agency difference and attendant differential upward bias was documented in the first academic study of rating agencies as a guide to investment. Here we offer new archival evidence of how the contractual relation between the rating agencies and the experts who carefully examined the possible role of ratings in regulation suppressed discussion. The lesson we take from these examples is that we benefit most from expertise when we check the advice of experts. This insight will help us develop suggestions for obtaining trustworthy advice from experts in Part V.

The examples that follow share some structure. Both relate to the world of finance in which secrecy has played a significant role over the centuries. We consider these cases of expert monetary management because they are instances of two types of nontransparency. In addition to that described earlier, there is potentially a nontransparency in motivation. Although experts articulate a goal for reform, saving resources for all, they may also be motivated by private goals, achieving fame and fortune. Or perhaps simply there was a sympathy for the client. As we have noted in Chapter 1, if people neglect the private goals of experts, they may fail fully to question the experts' recommendations; whereas, if they keep private motivations in mind, they can take steps to reduce the experts' temptation to bias.

In Chapter 7 we examine John Law's attempt to create a bank that used land as its asset base. The bank collapsed in 1720 in what is referred to as the Mississippi Bubble, a disaster so complete that it has served as a warning against the movement from gold and silver to paper for close to two centuries. We survey the warnings that were offered by contemporaries as they help us understand the nontransparency. Our second case resulted from the collapse of the fractional reserve US banking system in the 1930s. To answer the question of how to determine the soundness of the asset base for deposits, investors relied on the experts in four extant security-rating firms. This system of expert-guided deposit insurance was widely applauded until the collapse of highly rated securities in 2007. After the collapse, fingers were pointed at the rating firms for offering biased ratings. In Chapter 8 we demonstrate that this bias was nothing new. Specialists in the 1930s realized that the ratings were biased. The regulating experts knew this, too, and they found a way to mitigate against the temptation to bias. What changed was that over time this wisdom decayed. This, we believe, was a consequence of the suppression of discussion. What is not controversial is that the precautionary mechanisms went by the wayside until the surprise in 2007.

7

# Experts and the Philosopher's Stone

## John Law's Secret Financial Alchemy

*Has half the nation found the philosopher's stone in the paper-mills?*

Is Law a god, a rogue, or a quack, who poisons himself with the drugs he administers to all the world?

Voltaire 1719
Quoted in Wilson (1881)

## 7.1 Introduction

When an expert fails, where does the fault rest? The approach of many, certainly the one to which we are attracted, is to ask whether the expert's program was discussed widely enough before its implementation, whether a sufficient number of distinct points of view were consulted to be able to spot the problems that would arise? A variation on this is to question whether the supposed goal of the policy was the real goal, and to consider whether wider discussion would have shed light on the discrepancy. In this chapter we turn our focus to the financial collapse in 1720 (the Mississippi Bubble) associated with John Law. In 1841 Charles Mackay opened his *Extraordinary Population Delusions and the Madness of Crowds* with a discussion of Law's monetary reform and the market collapse. Mackay accepts that the goal of Law's reform program was to replace a costly monetary unit with one that was not. Mackay tells his reader that blame for the collapse rests on the inherent inability of the masses to control themselves, something that Law had failed to appreciate.[1] Mackay's view is that the failings

---

[1] "John Law was neither knave nor madman, but one more deceived than deceiving, more sinned against than sinning. He was thoroughly acquainted with the philosophy and the true principles of credit. He understood the monetary question better than any man of his day, and if his system fell with a crash so tremendous, it was not so much his fault as that

of ordinary people led to Law's downfall. As evidence of such incapacity, he points to the demand for such "pretended sciences" as alchemy that comprised "erring philosophers, or the willful cheats, who have encouraged and preyed upon the credulity of mankind" (p. 99).[2] From this point of view, questions of transparency and discussion, and certainly experts' discussions with ordinary people, have little to commend themselves.

Not only has Mackay's thesis – the madness of crowds – become a catch phrase encapsulating an attitude toward the incapacity of ordinary people for collective action, but also his use of contemporary Dutch images of Law found in a volume whose title is often translated as the *Great Mirror of Folly* opened an entire branch of scholarship, the leading lights of which gathered together for a 2008 conference at the Yale School of Management to discuss the current financial crisis in historical context.[3] In what follows we explore what Law's contemporaries thought about his financial reforms. We argue that the words and images in the *Great Mirror of Folly* accuse Law of alchemy. Indeed, as will become clear below, one of the two images from the *Great Mirror of Folly* that Mackay had reengraved for *Madness of Crowds* is decisive.

Supposing we recognize images that associate Law with alchemy, what are we to make of this? We shall connect these images in what follows with Desiderius Erasmus's celebrated account of alchemical fraud, in which the scam works because discussion is suppressed; the victim is isolated and unable to speak with others.[4] These images make the case that there are private goals at work in Law's system. Alchemy is traditionally classified as "occult" – Latin for "hidden" – for reasons that Adam Smith explained to his students in the 1760s. Successful alchemy would be felonious private coinage.[5] One hundred and fifty years earlier, one of the characters in

---

  of the people amongst whom he had erected it. He did not calculate upon the avaricious frenzy of a whole nation ... " (Mackay 1932, p. 1).

[2] "Three causes have excited the discontent of mankind; and, by impelling us in a maze of madness and error. These are death, toil, and ignorance of the future ... From the second sprang the search for the philosopher's stone, which was to create plenty by changing all metals into gold" Mackay (1932, p. 99).

[3] Papers from the conference are published in a work of considerable scholarship from which we have benefited. Mackay's role in drawing attention to the *Great Mirror of Folly* is widely noted; see De Bruyn (2013, p. 31n4); Frehen, Goetzmann, Rouwenhorst (2013, p. 86n25); Hochstrasser (2013, p. 205n66); Spieth (2013, p. 233n16).

[4] If indeed there is an opposition between John Law and Desiderius Erasmus in the *Great Mirror of Folly*, perhaps the very title is a tribute to the 1511 *In Praise of Folly* and those who seek the "fifth element" whom Erasmus singles out (1979, p. 61).

[5] "All attempts to increase the kings coin are accounted felony, as the seeking to find out the philosophers stone." This, from the 1762–63 lecture notes, Smith (1982, p. 301); also see the 1766 lecture notes, Smith (1982, p. 430).

Ben Jonson's *Alchemist*, the very well-informed Subtle, offered an ingenious excuse against a charge of coinage to his gulls.[6] This interpretation is consistent with the 1811 diagnosis by Henry Thornton. What puzzled Thornton, the nontransparency of Law's system, is for us, and we argue his contemporaries, the heart of the matter.

Our first theme in what follows is thus that secrecy can induce strange pathologies, in this case the apparent attribution of alchemical properties to the procedure and supernatural qualities to the expert. We make no claim that secrecy always induces such odd results; but we do find this to be one piece of evidence that nonexperts ought to be wary of nontransparency. Second, the chapter provides telling evidence of self-interested behavior on the part of the expert. No one should find this startling: as we said in Chapter 1, we are all at least partly self-interested. But should we trust an expert with our money when the expert is unwilling to reveal how extra-normal returns are earned? If the expert is a benevolent God, perhaps we should; if the expert is a self-interested human, we may wish to know more about the secret process used to obtain the returns rather than simply trusting the expert to look out for us. Experts are more likely to act in a nontransparent way and perhaps to make ethical missteps when all is based on blind trust between the expert and the client.

## 7.2 John Law and the Mississippi Bubble

The Mississippi Bubble story begins with John Law's 1705 *Money and Trade Considered* in which he proposed the creation of a national bank to issue paper money backed by land. In 1716, after many adventures, Law convinced the French government to allow him to form a French private bank that would issue paper money. The paper notes were to be supported by the bank's assets of gold and silver and government securities, and would serve to increase the money in circulation, thereby stimulating commerce. Government securities served as some three–quarters of the bank's capital. The next year, Law acquired controlling interest in a French trading company based in Louisiana, the Compagnie d'Occident, soon to be known as the Mississippi Company. In Louisiana, the Company was to trade in

---

[6]    "It is no coining, sir. It is but casting" (Jonson 1974, III.3.153–154). The editor of the Yale edition of *The Alchemists*, Alvin Kernan, offers this judgment: "While Face and Subtle may use the language of alchemy only as a spiel to take in the gullible, Jonson saw to it that the terms and the theories they used were authentic" (Kernan in Jonson 1974, p. 228). Erasmus's discussion of the alchemical fraud was on Jonson's reading list (Kernan in Jonson 1974, p. 227).

precious metals; in Canada it would trade in beaver skins. The Company absorbed the Compagnie des Indes Orientales and the Compagnie de Chine, and it obtained a monopoly of French trade with North America and the West Indies. Law's private bank became the Banque Royale, whose issue was guaranteed by the King, in 1718. By then, Law controlled all trade with France as well as the right to mint new coins for France and to collect most French taxes.[7]

The scheme to finance the Mississippi Company was simple. Law sold shares in the Company for cash or, more likely, state bonds. He exaggerated the wealth of Louisiana, and shares in the Company became wildly popular. When shares generated profits, investors were paid out of paper bank notes issued by Law's bank. The Company and the bank were united in 1720 and Law was named Controller General of Finances. The same year, offering the rapidly appreciating shares in exchange – a thirty-fold increase in the year – Law's company acquired all the French government's debt. When share prices in the Company began to depreciate in January 1720, a sell-off began. Investors sought to convert their shares into specie and Law attempted to stop the sell-off by restricting payments in gold and rendering the paper notes at the Banque Royale as legal tender to be used to pay off debts or taxes. As a consequence, the money supply in France suddenly increased and with it followed inflation. Law devalued shares in the Company in several stages. The scheme unwound very quickly, Law was dismissed from his positions, and he soon fled to Venice.

The collapse in share prices and the attendant wealth transfers discredited Law's theory of managed money for generations.[8] In 1811 Thornton diagnosed the fundamental problem that Law's system would face:

Mr. Law considered security as every thing, and quantity as nothing. He proposed that paper money should be supplied (he did not specify in his book at what rate of interest) to as many borrowers as should think fit to apply, and should offer the security of land, estimated at two thirds of its value. This paper, though not convertible into the precious metals, could not, as Mr. Law assumed, be depredated ... He forgot that there might be no bounds to the demand for paper; that the increasing

[7]   For more detail on these events see Backhouse (1988) and White (2013). Voth (2013) discusses the Bubble in terms of modern finance.

[8]   Pronouncements from this century are mixed; some historians of economics, notably Schumpeter 1954; Kindleberger 2000; Murphy 1997, pp. 331–32; and White 2013, have argued that Law's system would have been successful had not some details gone wrong. Murphy stresses that Law's vast holdings in what would become the United States would have served as security (Murphy 2012). None of these arguments confronts Thornton's analysis. In any event Law himself is widely regarded as a gambler who took enormous risks with other people's money and discredited paper money for generations (White 2013).

quantity would contribute to the rise of commodities: and the rise of commodities require, and seem to justify, a still further increase. (Thornton 1939, pp. 341–42)

Thornton's diagnosis points to the possibility of an increase in the money supply by manipulation of the value of security. We return to this in section 7.4. Earlier, in his 1802 *Paper Credit*, Thornton explained why such a scheme's temporary impact on the demand for labor could make it appear to be successful.[9] Thornton was particularly troubled by the lack of transparency in the relationship between the Banque Royale and the Mississippi Company.[10]

Consistent with our thesis that discussion of expert plans is important, we propose to pay attention to what engaged spectators had to say. As the Mississippi speculations themselves were unfolding, a young Voltaire described Law's activities as a search for the philosopher's stone and he asked whether Law was a god or a charlatan. This widely noted remark is taken as a joke by some, but it conveys a message of the dark side of alchemy. It bears emphasizing that Bernard Madoff was widely described as a hedge fund manager with a "Midas touch." Elie Wiesel's "We thought he was God" suggests the danger of losing touch with Voltaire's skepticism (Levy and Peart 2013b).

The most significant source of contemporary views on Law and his financial schemes is the Dutch portfolio, The *Great Mirror of Folly [Het Groote Tafereel der Dwaasheid]* whose publication date is claimed as 1720. The *Great Mirror of Folly* has been called the emblem book about the early eighteenth-century speculations (De Bruyn 2000a). A central image in the *Great Mirror of Folly* is a cartoon that depicts Law in a cart that flies through the air. The cart is drawn by a pair of creatures.

Voltaire expressed his views in ordinary French, the meaning of which has not altered much in only three centuries. Emblems are quite another issue.

---

[9]  Thornton (1939, p. 239): "That an encrease of the circulating medium tends to afford temporary encouragement to industry, seems also to be proved by the effects of the Mississippi scheme in France; for it is affirmed by French writers, that the notes of Mr. Law's bank appeared for a time to have a very powerful influence in extending the demand for labour, and in augmenting the visible and *bonâ fide* property of the kingdom."

[10]  "In the progress of the scheme, the Bank became confounded with the Mississippi Company, for whose actions the bank notes were interchangeable; so that it was not easy to trace causes and effects through the whole progress of those extraordinary speculations." Thornton (1939, p. 342). Thornton's 1811 speech on the Bullion Report, from which this is quoted, is included in Hayek's edition (Thornton 1939). Judging by the indices Thornton's analysis is not cited in Murphy (1997) or Goetzmann, Labio, Rouwenhorst, and Young (2013). Viner (1937, pp. 149–50) calls attention to Thornton's analysis of Law's error.

They, too, serve as means by which to carry on a discussion but their meaning is clouded by both a separation in geographical space and the passing of time. What does this image tell us about contemporary views of Law's role in the Mississippi Bubble? As we read it, the image warns about the dangers of nontransparency, and in so doing it attempts to make the nontransparency itself transparent. Although we agree with many commentators that the creatures pulling the cart appear to be roosters, we suggest that they have an additional Biblical interpretation, that of a beast whose forefathers spoke to Eve about the consequences of eating from the tree of knowledge. The religious image signifies the danger associated with knowledge.

So, as the Mississippi Bubble unfolded, images about Law's role in the speculations focused on the hierarchy of knowledge induced by nontransparency. Specifically, the images portray a sort of madness caused by alchemy. Alchemy, as J. M. Keynes's research showed, survived and flourished well into the age of Isaac Newton (Keynes 1972; Dobbs 1975 and 1990a; Newman 2004). More recently specialists argue that alchemy is distinguished from chemistry because alchemy is characterized by secrecy, by institutions that support nontransparency (Dobbs 1975 and1990b).[11]

### 7.3 The Hidden: Alchemy in the *Great Mirror of Folly*

Today, economic historians stipulate that asset bubbles occur when the asset's price is temporarily in excess of its fundamental value. Modern explanations revolve around contagion of expectations. Mackay's "madness of crowds" has entered the language as shorthand for this sort of contagion. By contrast, the images of the Mississippi crisis provide a different explanation for an economic crisis, that alchemy induces madness, a disconnect from reality. In alchemical fraud, as explained by Erasmus in 1524, there is no fundamental value; someone is instead tricked into believing an investment has value when it has none. Erasmus's explanation depends on an individual being *isolated* from common opinion or information. The isolation and consequent lack of information are the keys to fooling individual investors.

In Erasmus's story, the longer the fraud lasts, the more incredible are the claims the victim is willing to believe. It seems as if the contagion becomes

[11] When important chemists such as Robert Boyle hide their "alchemy," the distinction between alchemy and chemistry becomes subtle (Newman and Principe, 1999). Erasmus and the stock figure of the alchemist-as-fraud are discussed at length in Nummedal (2007 and 2009).

intrapersonal across time.[12] Since the madness in Erasmus's story depends on isolation, it is perhaps not surprising that when the victim finally realizes the folly and understands the trick, he is willing to pay to have the episode hushed up and avoid disapprobation.

Erasmus, perhaps alchemy's greatest enemy, often referred to the alchemist's "fifth essence" as giving the power of life itself.[13] The fifth element, the spiritual essence of the four Aristotlian elements, is the philosopher's stone. The strange claim, gambling to become a god, can be appreciated in two linked accounts that specialists have offered of the alchemist's world view.[14] In recent scholarship, Dobbs describes a particularly interesting manuscript:

> The alchemist writ large who broods over the egg is the Second Person of the Trinity, the cosmic Christ, so often identified with the final achievement of the philosopher's stone, and who will bring the entire course of history to a beatific end at the end of time. (Dobbs 1990a, p. 23)

Alchemical madness occurs because the gambler sees things that are invisible to everyone else.

With this in mind, we turn to commentary on the Mississippi Bubble and along with those who have studied Law's role in the Mississippi Bubble, we proceed to a widely available reproduction of a plate in the *Great Mirror of Folly*,[15] Mackay's commissioned reengraving and interpretation in the second edition of *Extraordinary Popular Delusions*. The image in Figure 7.1 is copied from the plate entitled (in Arthur Cole's reproduction of George Stephens's translation): "The inventor of stock-jobbery in his triumphal car" (Arthur Cole 1949, p. 31 #46; [Stephens]

---

[12] This might suggest what Maurice Allais (Allais 1966) described as the changing perception of time in a hyperinflation. Erasmus himself used the analogy of intoxication so perhaps a closer analogy is George Stigler and Gary Becker's model of addiction, where the change in current utility is induced by past consumption of an addictive commodity (Stigler and Becker 1977).

[13] "There is a doctor here from my country who by the aid of the Fifth Essence proposes to work miracles, makes old men young, and brings the dead to life, so that I have some hope of becoming young again, if I can only get a taste of the quintessence." Erasmus (1904, volume 2, p. 19)

[14] Jung reads alchemy as offering a psychic truth, which is, of course, foreign to our purpose (Principe and Newman 2001, pp. 401–15). For us, alchemy is, instead, a model in which beliefs are described. Newman helps explain the model; he writes about the alchemist who challenges God (Newman 2004).

[15] Bibliographical complications follow because this is a portfolio bound to order, rather than a book in a modern sense, so the concepts of "original" and "copy" and "edition" are ill-defined. Cole (1949) summarizes and extends an older literature, which established that no two instances were exactly the same. De Bruyn (2000b) and Forrer (2013, p. 35) discuss the printing history.

LAW IN A CAR DRAWN BY COCKS

Figure 7.1.  John Law in a car drawn by cocks (Mackay reproduction).

1873 #1671).[16] Mackay's interpretation is found in the caption he added below the image: "Law in a car drawn by cocks" (1932, facing p. 42).

---

[16]   We provide the "Muller number," which is useful for cross-referencing to the Yale conference volume. We also reproduce from Cole the number in the British Museum catalogue adding Stephens's name as cataloguer. [Stephens] (1873) includes substantial amounts of translations. The Prints and Photographs room of the Library of Congress holds a copy of Stephens's *Catalogue* in which one can determine which of the Library of Congress's holdings is a duplicate of or differs from that in the British Museum. This is not available online. Cole states (1949, p. 25) that "translations of the Dutch titles taken wherever

At first glance the image appears to be a whimsical portrayal of magic: Law is, after all, being drawn through the air by creatures. The definitive *British Museum Catalogue of Prints and Drawings* ([Stephens] 1873, p. 523) augments Mackay's interpretation, describing Law's cart as "drawn by two French cocks who have lost nearly all their feathers." Simon Schama provides a photographic reproduction of the image; he suggests that Law's chariot is drawn by a "pair of Gallic roosters."[17] The importance of Schama's study of the Dutch context in which the *Great Mirror of Folly* appeared is evident from the fact that his reproduction of the image and his interpretations are reprinted in an authoritative collection of source material on financial bubbles (Schama (2000, p. 156).

The plate itself, (Muller #31, [Stephens] 1873, #1671) has a title and text that borders the image. A close examination of the image and the text reveals that the "roosters" have a second meaning. A section of the image is reproduced next (Figure 7.2).[18]

The tails of the "roosters" resemble snake or dragon tails. The puzzle becomes, what sort of a creature has the body of a chicken and the tail of a snake or dragon? K. J. S. Bostoen provided both a strict translation and also help with the meaning of the critical words that accompany the image.[19] First the translation:

> Door Bazelisken, die hy toomd,
> En dwingt met goude dwanggarélen,
>
> Basilisks he bridles
> With golden force constraining horsecollars

Stephens's *British Museum Catalog* translates the words (1873, p. 524): "drawn by basilisks." His interpretation of the image by contrast says "drawn by two French cocks" (1873, p. 523). This may be correct but he provides no reason to distrust the words that accompany the image nor to discount the strange "rooster" tails. Mackay and Schama give the same interpretation of the image, but there is no evidence that they paid attention to the words that

---

possible from [George Stephens] 'Catalogue of the prints and drawings in the British Museum.' " Goetzman et al. (2013, p. xiii) state that his translations are "often inaccurate."

[17] Schama (1987, pp. 367–68). H. Spencer Banzhaf offered the suggestion that the rooster-like qualities of the image represent the French state.

[18] The image is contained in Goetzmann, et al. (2013, p. 296). The wider problem of interpreting alchemical imagery is discussed by Warlick (2006, p. 105) who points to a "relative neglect of alchemical images by art historians." In the images that Warlick discusses, it is difficult even to identify the gender of those represented.

[19] We are grateful to Professor Bostoen, a specialist in Early Modern Dutch at Leiden University, for his assistance.

Figure 7.2. Section of the original.

accompany the image. Professor Bostoen helped us with this suggestion: "Basilisks [=cockatrices, see Isaiah 11:8]."

The question then is what is a basilisk/cockatrice and why would they be included in an image of Law? Basilisk/cockatrice came into existence largely as a result of St. Jerome's Latin mistranslation of the Hebrew for a venomous snake (Breiner 1979a). It survived in four verses of the King James Bible, in the books of Isaiah and Jeremiah, neither of which could be based on William Tyndale's celebrated translation of the Hebrew into English (Tyndale 1992; Daniell 2003). The King James translators, lacking a Tyndale starting point, seem to have reverted to the Wycliffe translation of the Vulgate's Latin.[20]

---

[20]  The verses are Isaiah 11:8, 14:29, 59:5, Jeremiah 8:17 (Breiner 1979a, p. 34). The basilisk's corruption of Eve is noted by Jung (1967, p. 143). Debates over the basilisk's properties can be traced by considering the two-dozen references to "basilisk" in Lynn Thorndike's seventeenth-century volumes of *History of Magic and Experimental Science* (1958).

The standard account links a cockatrice with immortality (Breiner 1979b, p. 10). The link between the English cockatrice and the continental basilisk follows:[21]

The term was adopted by George Ripley, the great fifteenth-century pioneer of English alchemy, as a native synonym for the "basilisk" of continental alchemy, where the word indicated the final stage in the procedure by which the Philosopher's Stone was achieved (Breiner 1979b).

So, the appearance of the basilisk signifies that Law has created the philosopher's stone in the course of the Mississippi Bubble. If Law successfully created the philosopher's stone, as the image suggests, then he has acquired properties of the divine.

If this were the only reference to alchemy in the *Folly*, it might be a simple eccentricity. But there are others. The title of one image is translated by Stephens as *The controller of the fortunate and miserable lapis seekers, or searchers for the philosopher's stone* (1949, p. 29 #29; [Stephens] 1873, #1670). Stephens translates the final Dutch sentence that comes under the image as "He who melts precious stones can transform nature and make wonderful stocks, outwitting all the tricks of Law" ([Stephens] 1873, p. 522). Lapis is also mentioned in the subtitle of one of the plates (Cole 1949, p. 26, #4; [Stephens] 1873, #1646). Stephens's translation (1873, p. 481) provides: "Whoever reasons errs. You will find the Philosopher's Stone by guessing." The identification of lapis with the philosopher's stone was noted earlier. Outside the *Great Mirror of Folly* portfolio, "lapis" is found in the words that border Pieter Bruegel's print, "The alchemist" that graces the cover of our book (Sellink 2007, p. 121; Principe and DeWitt 2002, p. 11) as well as in the title of one of the Southey lots of Newton's alchemical papers (Dobbs 1975, p. 242, lot 70).

## 7.4  Uncovering the Fraud: Desiderius Erasmus on Alchemy in the *Great Mirror of Folly*

Recent scholarship has demonstrated the importance of Erasmus's writing on alchemical fraud – "Colloquia on Alchemy" – for contemporaries.[22]

---

[21] Subtle, "mistaking" Ananias for a "brother," asks about his philosophy; only Lull precedes Ripley: "What's that? A Lullianist? A Ripley?" Jonson 1974, II.5.77–8. "Cockatrice" is used as a synonym for "whore" at V.3.35, perhaps suggesting the corruption of Eve.

[22] As noted previously, Erasmus linked alchemy and madness in his advertisement for his *Colloquies*. "By no means the slightest of human afflictions is alchemy, a disorder so intoxicating, once it strikes a man, that it beguiles even the learned and the prudent" (Erasmus 1999, vol. 40, p. 1103).

Everyone read it. Princes who dealt with "alchemical entrepreneurs" were warned on its basis to write precise contracts for the delivery of gold (Nummedal 2009, pp. 178–80). Failure was discouraged by the occasional public execution, sometimes, amusingly enough, on iron gallows (Nummedal 2009, p. 148). This witty response suggests that the authorities had a working understanding of the pretense of the alchemist to speed the natural growth of iron into gold.[23]

An image of the *Great Mirror of Folly* also portrays Erasmus's opposition to alchemy. In it (Cole 1949, p. 27 #15; [Stephens] 1873, #1654), his ghost appears in opposition to Law. This complicated plate titled "The active bellows and the spirit of Erasmus … " is discussed at length by Darius Spieth who calls attention to the bellows as the means to inflate the value of shares, an interpretation that ties in with the theme of "wind" in the *Great Mirror of Folly* portfolio.[24] Bellows are a traditional alchemical image since alchemy as a discipline revolves around the forge.[25] Many of the images in the *Great Mirror of Folly* contain bellows, some very obvious and some less so.[26]

The plate is reproduced in Goetzmann et al. (2013, p. 283). Given Erasmus's long dispute with the alchemists, its message is "John Law, Alchemist. Beware." The messages make the nontransparency of alchemy itself transparent.

Erasmus's story involves a priest who purports to be an alchemist. The priest approaches his victim, Balbinus and confesses his "failure" to understand the alchemical path of "curtation" because he has had the misfortune of studying only "lognation" (Erasmus 1999, vol. 39, p. 547).[27] Flattered

---

[23] The growth of metals was explained by Subtle: "we say of lead and other metals, which would be gold if they had time" (Jonson 1974, II.3.135–136). Quoted in Eliade 1972, p. 51.

[24] Spieth's discussion is in a preliminary version of Spieth (2013).

[25] See Eliade 1972, p. 29. Not surprisingly bellows are also found prominently in Bruegel's alchemist (Sellink 2007, pp. 120–21). Principe and DeWitt (2002, p. 11) parse the images this way: "a squinting fool apes the alchemist pumping bellows at the coals." Newman (2004, pp. 301–02) reprints an illustration of *Faust* from the mid-nineteenth century that shows a bellows involved in bringing Homunculus to life. Mackay's image of an alchemist features a bellows (Mackay 1932, facing p. 100). Subtle's associate Face is renamed "Lungs" by one of the gulls: "That's his fire-drake, his Lungs, His Zephrus, that puffs his coals Till he firk nature up in her own center" (Jonson 1974, II.1.27–28).

[26] Using the Library of Congress's copy of the first state (*Het Groote Tafereel Der Dwaasheid &c.* LC HG 6006 G82; Cole 1949, pp. 23–24) we find bellows in the following Muller numbered plates: 4, 9, 11, 12, 15, 20, 33, 36, 40, 53, 62. As bellows are not discussed in the Yale volume, we cannot explain why they seem to be more frequent in the earlier plates than the later. Because the Library of Congress's Rare Book Room now allows digital photos, we can provide photographs of bellows on request.

[27] Thompson explains the unusual words: "Erasmus evidently fashioned them from *longo* or *elongo* and *curto* or like forms for his rhetorical purpose of enabling the wily priest

to be included with the knowledgeable elite, someone presumed to know the short, fast way of alchemy, Balbinus believes that the priest knows the obvious long, slow way and he agrees to finance the priest's venture.[28] There follows a wilder and wilder collection of excuses for failure, including a narrow escape from the wrong bedroom. Balbinus persists in believing all these excuses and he continues to add to the amount already paid. Finally, when an acquaintance explains the scam, Balbinus pays the priest to run away and keep quiet. Wonderfully enough, the story continues.

If the Mississippi adventures are similar to an alchemical fraud along Erasmus's lines of secret "knowledge," then we can trace how this works and fits into Law's plan to demonetize gold.[29] Rumors were circulated that gold and silver were to be found in Mississippi (Gleeson 1999, p. 122). This seemed plausible since there were gold mines in South America. The additional rumor of an emerald mountain suggests that someone knew the Spanish adventures rather well since indeed emeralds had been discovered in Colombia. If the rumors raised the values of shares, then the debt-equity swap by which the French government got rid of its debt would seem to be a reasonable investment. Spieth (2013, pp. 228–29) correlates the rumors of the marvelous wealth of Mississippi with the images. The imagery and explanations in the *Great Mirror of Folly* warn people against believing in the economic equivalent of alchemy. This is also Voltaire's judgment, and that is why we have quoted as epigram to the chapter.

What about the immense value of the American holdings that secured Law's bank (Murphy 1997 and 2012)? A pair of images in the *Folly* portfolio speaks directly to the difference between the "fundamental value" of Mississippi, as "Fancy" makes it, and what is really there. First, a section of the image (Figure 7.3) depicts "Fancy" painting a picture of what exists in Mississippi.[30] Stephens's translation of the title provides a warning (Cole 1949, p. 23 #59; [Stephens] 1873 #1657): "Fancy, the ruler of the guild of smoke-sellers, paints here Mississippi, which wastes France's treasures." The

---

to impress Balbinus with them, and Balbinus swallows the bait" Thompson in (Erasmus 1999, vol. 39, p. 554).

[28] Subtle's "mistaking" Ananias as a "brother" alchemist (Jonson 1974, II.5) is a variation on Erasmus's plot line.

[29] Murphy (1997, p. 275) describes Law's plan to demonetize gold: "He further argued that while it was in the interests of nations such as Spain, Portugal and China to sustain the value of gold, France, which did not produce gold, had a vested interest in developing and maintaining its own 'money' in the form of Mississippi Company shares rather than gold."

[30] "Mississippi, or the world-famous Goldland in the fancy of the wind-trade" (Cole 1949, p. 28, #59; [Stephens] 1873] #1683).

Figure 7.3.  Mississippi painted by Fancy.

image shows a ship nearing a port in Mississippi, pictured as cityscape to rival one of the great European harbors.

That is the representation of the asset base of the Mississippi adventures. Spieth (2013, p. 229) describes the section of a print (Cole 1949, #23; [Stephens] 1873 #1657) that "portray[s] investors (and not potential colonists) as the target audience for the deceptive stories about gold mines, agricultural riches, and emerald mountains to be found in Louisiana." Several images depict what actually exists in Mississippi. What seems to be a very late print entitled "The King and Queen of the Mississippi" gives one such view (Cole 1949, p. 34, #71).[31] Here (Figure 7.4) there are no buildings or cityscape; all that exists is a fire and some real Mississippians.

---

[31] There is no copy in the British Museum collection. Complications related to this print are discussed extensively in Forrer (2013). The chart provided (pp. 44–45) tells how infrequently it is encountered.

KONING en KONINGIN van de MISSISIPPI.

Figure 7.4. Mississippi actual.

Frehen, Goetzmann, and Rouwenhorst who reprint a much reduced copy of "The king and queen of the Mississippi" provide the following description of the profits of the entire Atlantic trade in 1720:

> In reality, in 1720 profits from the Atlantic trade by firms such as the Mississippi Company, the South Sea Company, and the Dutch West India Company were minimal. The Mississippi Company had a tiny colony in New Orleans … Thus share prices could not have been driven by news about actual profitability of the current Atlantic trade. Rather the skyrocketing valuations would necessarily have been based on extrapolations of future potential profits: long-term hopes as opposed to short-term concrete profits. (Frehen, Goetzman, and Rouwenhorst, 2013, p. 72)

Extrapolations resulting from the manipulation of information, rumors of gold mines, and the like suggest the alchemical disconnect from the underlying value of the security is complete.

If this is correct, we have a way to fill in the missing piece in Smith's account – why was the "company [Law] erected seeming[ly] in a very flourishing condition."[32] Everything else in Smith's discussion is straightforward, society becoming richer by trading its metal for paper, but the valuation of Mississippi Company stock is somewhat mysterious.

Nor was Voltaire the only commentator to portray Law as an alchemist. The *British Museum Catalogue* contains a broadside ([Stephens] 1873, p. 587, #1718) that is a printed version of what was read on October 27, 1721 as the epilogue to a performance of Jonson's *Alchemyst*. Readers of Jonson would have had many things about alchemy explained to them. Here, too, Law is identified with the philosopher's stone:

> Our Knaves Sin higher Now then those of Old,
> Kingdoms, not Private Men, are Bought & Sold,
> Witness the South-sea Project, which hath shown
> How far Phylosophers may be out done
> By Modern-men that have found ye Stone.
> …

---

[32] Smith (1982, p. 517). Smith's extensive discussion of the Mississippi Bubble is found in the later of the two student reports, which comprise the *Lectures on Jurisprudence*. The argument in *Wealth of Nations* that paper money can enrich a country ought to be read in the context of Smith's discussion of Law's project. Indeed, the oft-quoted passage might be read against the images in the *Great Mirror of Folly*. Smith 1904 II.ii.86: "The commerce and industry of the country, however, it must be acknowledged, though they may be somewhat augmented, cannot be altogether so secure when they are thus, as it were, suspended upon the Dædalian wings of paper money as when they travel about upon the solid ground of gold and silver. Over and above the accidents to which they are exposed from the unskillfulness of the conductors of this paper money, they are liable to several others, from which no prudence or skill of those conductors can guard them." Recent scholarship (Newman, 2004, p. 11) also suggests that Icarus is used to show the problem of man challenging nature.

Figure 7.5. Icarus descending.

Well! Since wee've Learn'd Experience at our Cost
Let us preserve the Remnant not yet Lost,
Though L – w from France, be landed on the Coast,
By Sober Arts Aspire to Guiltless Fame,
And Prove that Virtues is not an Empty Name.

## 7.5 Conclusion

The Mississippi Bubble generated a rich set of texts and images that reinforce one major theme: the dangers associated with experts who lay claim to secret financial knowledge. Images and texts in the Dutch 1720 *Great Mirror of Folly* warn that Law was engaged in a type of financial alchemy. In Law's own time, some people believed he was perpetrating a fraud based on pretensions to hidden knowledge and supernatural properties. This reading helps explain why Voltaire immediately concluded that Law was either a god or a charlatan. The images warn about something that people do not understand. In the context of their time, the occult "science" of alchemy was an exemplar of such hidden knowledge. Today, we rarely regard images of alchemy as warnings. The fact that we have difficulty making sense of such images is evident when we consider that authoritative accounts have failed to recognize that the image of roosters was also given characteristics of the serpent that tempted Eve. To the informational content in a message of "Here be symbols of France," the images also warned "Here be The Serpent Himself. We will not understand Its ways but we know that It is dangerous."

Images have a life of their own. When Smith worried about the fragility of paper money, he used an elegant classical reference, "Dædalian wings," to describe the danger. He was not the first to do so. The *Great Mirror of Folly* contains two images of Icarus. Figure 7.5 shows the first (Cole 1949, p. 28, #20; [Stephens] 1873, #1660), warning of dangers for all.

8

# The Consequence of Suppressing Discussion

## Imprudence with Biased Experts

The difficulty is that [Palyi's] article is very critical of the bank supervisory and rating agencies. I cannot find it possible to say much about his article without appearing to put the memorandum of the Corporate Bond Study in the position of criticizing the cooperating agencies which were responsible for it.

Letter from Harold Fraine to Donald S. Thompson, March 18, 1943

## 8.1 Introduction

The damage caused by the belief that AAA-rated investments were as secure as those offered by the US government is still being tallied.[1] It is not surprising, then, that the transformation of the rating agencies from purely market participants to significant players in the regulatory framework in the United States has become central in the search for explanations of what went wrong with American capitalism in the financial crisis of 2007–2008. One widely accepted partial explanation for the crisis is the organizational transformation of the industry early in the twentieth century that changed the incentives of the rating agencies. In the days before the rating agencies were merely market participants, they sold their advice in book form (manuals) to the buyers of securities. Their expertise was valued, not because the agencies had any particular gift for forecasting, but instead because they were disinterested. Over time, the industry evolved and ratings were provided to the sellers of securities. The change brought with it increased incentives to bias the ratings upwards.[2] This widely disseminated history

---

[1] The upward bias in ratings of recent history is no longer a matter of speculation; see Kolchinsky (2010).

[2] Flandreau, Gaillard, and Packer (2009, p. 18): "In conclusion, the agencies' new role in the 1930s did not result from any evidence of the superior forecasting qualities of the ratings. They became important because *they were perceived as being free of conflict of interest.*"

contains a variation on what we have seen in the previous chapters. The rating agencies earlier on were supposed to instantiate the linear model of policy we described in Chapter 1. The public wanted disinterested advice; the experts at the rating agencies provided this. Just how powerful the linear view of policy was can be gauged by the persuasive power of the narrative.

But the foregoing explanation does not speak to the "rating shopping" that was evident leading up to the 2007–2008 crisis. For that practice to be effective, consumers of the ratings must have believed that one rating is as good as any other rating. We shall demonstrate in this chapter that discussion of differences among rating agencies was suppressed in the arrangements between those who relied on the ratings and the rating agencies. What followed was a decay in prudence as those who first took precautionary measures to deal with biased ratings let the precautions fall away.

We shall examine the resulting transition from caution to imprudence in what follows. We demonstrate that, early on, people knew about the nontransparency of the ratings procedure and they did not believe that any one rating was as good as any other rating. When the regulatory use of the ratings was first implemented, the nontransparency of the rating procedure was the basis of a blistering attack in 1938 by a former student of Max Weber who was then teaching monetary economics at the University of Chicago, Melchior Palyi. Palyi also pointed out how poorly the agencies' ratings had predicted defaults (Palyi 1938).

The year 1938 also saw the publication of the first academic study of bond ratings as a guide to investment (Harold 1938). In his study of the preregulatory period, Gilbert Harold described a completely nontransparent procedure by which the sellers of securities could appeal an "undeserved" low rating – he pointed out that no one ever complained about an undeserved high rating! – by communicating their displeasure with the rating agencies. Harold took for granted what the literature discussed in Chapter 2 was at pains to document: language encourages cooperation. He documented the differences among the rating agencies using a small sample. He also described and tested a prudential use of the ratings in the event that they are differentially biased upward. As a consequence, the nontransparency of the ratings was itself made transparent in the process of public discussion; consequently, prudential methods for dealing with bias were developed.

[Emphasis added.] The picture of an unbiased, impartial era is found in the "facts" stipulated in Judge Scheindlin's opinion and order in Adu Dhabi Commercial Bank et al. versus Morgan Stanley et al. (08 Civ. 7508 (SAS)) of September 2, 2009. Also, Morgenson and Rosner 2011; Mehrling 2011.

When such discussion makes the nontransparency itself transparent, acceptable solutions emerge to counteract the temptation to bias. After the ratings became part of regulation, the Federal Deposit Insurance Corporation [FDIC], operating through the National Bureau of Economic Research [NBER], conducted a massive study to determine how well the ratings predicted performance. In section 8.4 we present archival evidence that the economists and statisticians conducting the FDIC/NBER study helped to make the nontransparency of the agency ratings itself nontransparent. First, under the agreement with the rating agencies, the economists and statisticians of the FDIC/NBER were forbidden to reveal the differences among the rating agencies. We know this because this is precisely what the published documentation says. Although we believe they improved on Harold's procedure for statistical use, they did not publicly discuss what worried Palyi and Harold. We know this because there is archived correspondence in which they discuss how they might respond to Palyi without actually mentioning his criticism. They provided no rationale for their Harold-like procedure. As long as institutional memory held, the prudential methods developed by the FDIC/NBER were employed. But without public discussion of the differences among rating agencies, consumers failed to appreciate the significance of these methods and they adopted instead the practice of shopping for ratings.

Every history of rating agencies begins with a discussion of the Corporate Bond Project [CBP] and the sequence of NBER volumes published by Braddock Hickman in the 1950s (Hickman 1952, 1953, 1958; Hickman and Simpson 1960). The CBP occurred in two phases, the first, federally funded from 1938–1944; the second resumed after the war with private funding.[3] Less frequently discussed, however, is the earlier, unsponsored Columbia dissertation by Harold, published in 1938. Unlike the NBER study, which had the resources provided by the FDIC operating through the Works Progress Administration [WPA] to study the *universe* of large bonds plus 10 percent of the less interesting small bonds, Harold worked with a sample of 363 bonds.[4] Such a small study was apparently overshadowed by one that utilized (almost) all the information in the market.

Even with vast resources at its disposal, the NBER research effort is treated in the literature as *manna* from heaven, as if economic research

---

[3]  The relationship between the two phases of the study is sketched in the short papers collected as "Corporate Bond Experience Re-Examined" in an unidentified periodical of December 1952 found in the Arthur Burns Papers, Box 146, "Corporate Bond Project – NBER." We will make copies available on request. The online NBER collection turns up nothing when searched.

[4]  The agency that began as the "Works Progress Administration" became the "Works Projects Administration" in 1939.

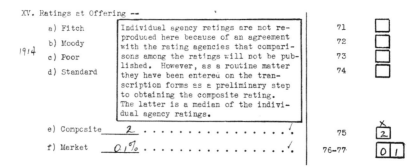

Figure 8.1. Suppression of individual ratings in NBER / FDIC documentation.

were outside economics itself.[5] The NBER Corporate Bond Project was pre-cluded from revealing the ratings given by individual agencies *even* in the illustrative documentation.[6] Figure 8.1 is an example of the censored documentation in the Corporate Bond Project. The boxes on the right edge indicate missing information: the real cards had information in those columns.

In what follows, we begin with Palyi's fundamental challenge to the use of nontransparent ratings for public policy. Palyi's critique is particularly important for its emphasis on nontransparency as well as its demonstration of how poorly the individual ratings performed. In section 8.3, we consider Harold's discussion of the differences among rating agencies, his estimator of investment quality and his documentation of the incentives to bias and

---

[5] "We are fortunate the research projects of the National Bureau of Economic Research studied US corporate bond quality, including the performance of bond rating agencies, during a long period … " (Sylla 2002, p. 25). There is nothing in his helpful three-page discussion of the NBER project that suggests how the project was financed. Who would be willing to pay as many as 200 full-time workers for a multiyear project? The mimeo-graphed history of the first phase of the project was produced and distributed. The title page answers the question for whom the study was produced: *The Corporate Bond Project, A History and Description, A Work Projects Administration Study Sponsored by the Federal Deposit Insurance Corporation, Supervised by the National Bureau of Economic Research.*

[6] A hint of the contractual arrangements between the FDIC /NBER and the rating agencies is provided in the letter from the NBER to the FDIC when the first phase of the project was completed in September 1944: "The cooperating agencies entitled to punched cards under the original project arrangements have received the cards for the latter three records. Upon completion of the punching of a master set of cards from the Periodic and Annual Records, duplicate sets may be reproduced for the files of such agencies. The National Bureau is custodian, on behalf of the FDIC, for the files and records of the Corporate Bond Study, and these are now deposited at the Hillside quarters of the National Bureau, where they are available to the cooperating agencies" (Folder 9 of Box 108 in the GMU Clark Warburton collection). Jerome Fons has informed us that the NBER card set was found years ago, decomposed.

the face-to-face nature of transactions between raters and rated. Section 8.4 presents the response to Palyi's criticisms in the final report of the first phase of the CBP. Section 8.5 documents how the FDIC/NBER composite was constructed.

## 8.2 The Early Criticism of Rating Agencies in Regulation

Following the collapse of 1929–1933, two options emerged as possible corrective measures for the banking system. One, often referred to as the Chicago banking plan, would attempt to make banks run-proof by turning them into monetary warehouses. This had the merit of minimizing the uncertainty induced by political discretion. The winning alternative, however, became law in the Glass-Steagall Act, which separated the banking system into a commercial banking sector that offered deposits insured by the Federal government and an investment banking sector. For many years, the country's experience with deposit insurance was offered as evidence that economists had been overly pessimistic about the role of discretion.[7]

At his first Presidential news conference, Franklin Roosevelt pointed out the problem with Federal insurance: "The general underlying thought behind the use of the word 'guarantee' with respect to bank deposits is that you guarantee bad banks as well as good banks" (quoted by Phillips, 1995, p. 38). A solution to Roosevelt's worry about insuring both sound and unsound banks was adopted shortly thereafter. It appealed to the rating agencies to specify the difference between speculative and prudent investments.

Almost as soon as this arrangement was proposed, Palyi attacked the role of the rating agencies in the University of Chicago's *Journal of Business*. Palyi's stature as one of Max Weber's last students, a public intellectual who had been the chief economist of a large German bank in the days before Hitler, and the professor who taught the monetary theory course at Chicago in the days of Frank Knight, Jacob Viner, and Henry Simons, was such that the attack demanded a response.[8] Palyi wrote that the Banking Act of

---

[7] Laidler (1993) stresses the importance of the integration of liberal norms into economic theory by Henry Simons (1934) and Milton Friedman (1962b) for understanding the Chicago monetary contribution. Putting Palyi back into the picture strengthens Laidler's findings. An expression of confidence from the prevailing side is found in Viner (1962); see also Luca Fiorito and Sebastiano Nerozzi (2009, p. 117) for Viner's opposition to the Chicago banking plan.

[8] Palyi does not fit neatly into any of the Weberless modern retellings of the Chicago story. A study of his economic writings begins with Warren Samuels (2005). The fact that Rose Director [Friedman] was both a Palyi student and an NBER staff member on the

1935 gave the rating agencies the effective authority to determine whether a security was of investment quality (1938, p. 70). He called their work "extremely secretive," thereby calling attention to their lack of transparency. Another of his criticisms focused on the lack of market-based valuations for securities (1938, p. 76). But all that was preliminary to what seems to have been viewed as his main attack, the empirical point. Palyi checked to see how well Moody's did. His "astonishing" results suggest the ratings performed poorly relative to the revealed investment quality of the securities:

> What, then, has been the past experience with the rating standards of the current manuals? No field study of this kind has been published, and the volume of material prohibits a comprehensive survey. The tables in the Appendix are based on random samples taken from major railroad and public utility securities issued before 1930 and rated in 1929 as in one of the four high grades. Three of the forty selected issues have maintained their grades for five years or longer without interruption; two succeeded in rising on the quality scale of the eight-year period. All others fluctuated in rating with the net outcome of a substantial decline. Not less than twenty-two issues became ineligible, among them four which were rated Aaa in 1929 and three of which have defaulted. There appear seven more subsequent defaults of eligible bonds of lower than Aaa rating in 1929. (Palyi 1938, p. 78)
>
> Perhaps the most astonishing single result is that 70 percent of the volume of railroad bonds which defaulted in 1924 were rated Baa or better in the same year. Of course, 1924 was a recession year, hard on railway finance; but the interesting fact is that a minor recession is sufficient to cause an enormous percentage of error in the rating agency's foresight. (1938, p. 79)

More than this, all the agency ratings performed just as miserably (Palyi 1938, p. 78 note 10).

### 8.3  Gilbert Harold's Prudent Estimator of Investment Quality

In 1938 Harold published his Columbia dissertation, *Bond Ratings as an Investment Guide: An Appraisal of Their Effectiveness.*[9] Although his book

---

Corporate Bond Project has not been noted, although her connection to Palyi is mentioned in Friedman and Friedman (1998, pp. 16, 305).

[9]   Harold Fraine and Melvin Brethouwer summarize the literature: "Melchior Palyi had expressed concern early in 1938 that there were no adequate field studies of past experience with the rating standards of the current investment manuals. He raised a number of questions regarding the use of ratings in determining the eligibility of bonds for investment by commercial banks. Gilbert Harold's research on bond ratings reached the public in the same year. His tests of the accuracy of bond ratings, however, consisted mainly of comparisons of number of defaults and changes in market values" (Fraine and Brethouwer 1944, p. 3). Palyi is not mentioned in Hickman (1958). Harold's work is cited twice (1958, pp. 144, 190) in contexts in which one can recover neither Harold's concern about bias nor his worst-case estimation.

continues to be cited as the first major academic study of bond ratings, a point that was made by contemporary reviewers, it has been relatively neglected in recent times.[10] In his preface, Harold notes that bond ratings have become part of the financial regulations, a point that helps explain why the NBER Corporate Bond Project was funded (Harold 1938, p. v). He raises the question of investigator impartiality:

> Since the author has worked entirely as an individual, subsidized by no person, group of persons, corporations, or organization of any kind whatever, he alone is responsible for any statement that may appear to be critical. (Harold 1938, p. v–vi)

One critical distinction between Harold's work and the more famous Corporate Bond Project is that Harold, without the involvement of the rating agencies, was freed from the need to disguise the properties of any individual agency's estimates.

Another remarkable difference between Harold's work and the later NBER study is that Harold explicitly considered how the experts at the rating agencies are tempted to bias their ratings upwards. Ratings bias, the temptation that results from shopping for ratings and negotiation is now at the center of discussion of the financial crisis.[11] In Harold's account, the temptation to bias always exists and, for the rating agencies, the temptations are not symmetrical; in the face of an unfavorable judgment, sellers of securities "typically" offered to present a more sympathetic reading of the evidence in a face-to-face meeting:

> The development of ratings in the securities field, especially in bonds, was not greatly dissimilar. Corporations were opposed to it, and many of them still are, especially among those whose issues are assigned low or mediocre ratings. Some indeed exert their forces to the point of protesting, through the person of an officer or in writing, to the rating agency. A typical statement by corporate officers is summed up in the challenge, "*Send your man around, and we'll show him a few things that will cause you to raise your rating.*" (1938, p. 16) [Emphasis added.]

---

[10] Harold's study is cited by Frank Partnoy (2002) who reproduces the distribution of agency ratings (p. 69) and notes "a certain amount of rating 'inflation' evident in each of the agency's scales." Harold's finding that the skew disappeared when the minimum of the ratings was selected is not mentioned. Sylla (2002, pp. 25–30) discusses the NBER Corporate Bond Project but he does not consider how the NBER's use of the downward-rounded median adjusts for the skew that Harold reported in the individual ratings.

[11] White (2010, pp. 220–21) sketches the dimension of the problem. The importance of transactions in language for encouraging cooperation is stressed in Chapter 2 although it is not clear how widely diffused these empirical regularities have been. We develop a model of sympathetic bias in Chapter 11.

Table 8.1. *Bond ratings: distribution of issues by ratings, July 15, 1929*

| Rating | Fitch | Moody | Poor | Standard |
|---|---|---|---|---|
| A+ | 147 | 97 | 68 | 78 |
| A | 64 | 63 | 89 | 93 |
| A- | 80 | 99 | 110 | 104 |
| B+ | 40 | 59 | 61 | 40 |
| B | 17 | 25 | 22 | 26 |
| B- | 4 | 2 | 7 | 16 |
| C+ | 3 | – | – | 4 |
| C | – | – | – | – |
| C- | – | – | – | – |
| D+ | – | – | – | 1 |
| Unrated | 8 | 18 | 6 | 1 |
| Total | 363 | 363 | 363 | 363 |

In two critical paragraphs quoted here, Harold recounts how investment bankers attempted to influence the ratings:

**Attitude of Investment Bankers.** – In no circles has the attitude toward bond ratings been more hostile than among the investment bankers. Such hostility is, of course, easily understood. For not only does the existence of ratings tend to narrow the price spread between trading points, but it also affects the resale of bonds that have come back to their original sponsors, as well as the original sale of new issues of the same corporation. If the rating is high, sales are easily effected; if low, sales are made only with great difficulty. When the rating is high it is often mentioned in lists of bonds for sale, issued to customers by the bond house. When the rating is low, it is rarely so mentioned.

No complaint is ever made by a bond house that an issue which it is sponsoring is rated too high. Other bond houses, however, owing to the pressure of competition, have been known to make such complaints. So vital are the ratings to investment bankers that extreme steps have been taken in some cases to influence those ratings. (Harold 1938, pp. 16–17)

Harold, who worked without formal cooperation from the rating agencies, was able to discuss the agencies on an individual basis. He discovered that the distribution of ranks varied across agencies. Moreover, the distributions appeared to be far from symmetrical in the chart he prints (1938, p. 90).

As one might expect, given when he conducted his research, Harold did not conduct a formal test of the hypothesis about whether the distributions were the same or not but the suggestion conveyed by the table is that there is no reason to believe in a common distribution.[12] Fitch certainly appears

---

[12] Using a two-sample Kolmogorov–Smirnov test on the empirical distribution in Harold's table we can reject at the one tenth of one percent level the hypothesis that the distributions

to have given significantly more *A+*'s than the others. Harold's twofold conclusion is that, on average, the ratings are a good prediction but the averages hide a problem:

**Recapitulation** – Considering averages only, there can be little doubt that both the record of market action ... and the yield record of bonds by ratings indicate that the system of ratings is an effective guide to investment values. Although an average is an important summary measure of the performance or standing of any group of economic data, it may represent the movement of individual items comprising the average rather inadequately. It is small comfort to the investor who has been led to believe that any bond of a specific rating is even the approximate equivalent of any other bond of the same rating when averages are considered, if he happens to own a security the market behavior of which departs radically from the average. Taking account of such variations from averages, the findings of this chapter cast considerable doubt upon the validity of rating agencies' claims that the ratings have been "perfected," that they are "scientific," that they are "conservative," that they are "accurate," or that they "do not rest on opinion." (Harold 1938, pp. 126–27)

What to do? A decade before Abraham Wald's minimax (Wald 1950; Good 1983) and two decades before John Tukey's robust revolution (Tukey 1986; Stigler 2010), Harold considers the possibility of an estimator that avoids disaster:

**The Pessimistic Theory.** – One of these would be to adopt as the proper rating of a bond that rating which is the lowest assigned by any agency. In other words, one would accept the most "pessimistic" rating. Assuming that the investor harbors the "calamity point of view" – and most bond rating users do – this would seem to be a reasonable procedure. It rests upon the assumption that four "minds" are better than one, and on this basis the feasibility of using the most conservative appraisal of all the rating agencies to greater advantage than could be done for any one agency appears both reasonable and attractive. Indeed, it appears entirely possible that the greatest protection would be obtained by accepting only the lowest rating assigned. On this plan, then, the investor would accept as the proper rating for a bond that rating, of all four organizations, which was the lowest assigned. Thus a bond rated A-, A-, A, and A by the respective agencies would be regarded by the investor as an A- bond. (Harold 1938, p. 150)[13]

The term *composite-rating* being popular among specialists, Harold considered an averaging procedure but he concluded in a heuristic fashion that the average failed to protect against disaster. Instead, he formed his

---

of Fitch's and Standard's are the same. Likewise for Fitch and Poor's. The equality of Fitch's and Moody's could not be rejected at that level, nor even at the one percent level. Details are available on request from the authors.

[13] Burtchett (1939, p. 223): "By using a 'pessimistic' rating, i.e. the lowest rating assigned by the several rating agencies, a more dependable guide to investment can be obtained than by using any individual agency rating."

Table 8.2.  *Gilbert Harold's distribution
of pessimistic rating*

| Rating | Number |
|---|---|
| A+ | 48 |
| A | 83 |
| A– | 106 |
| B+ | 64 |
| B | 36 |
| B– | 19 |
| C+ | 5 |
| C | – |
| C– | – |
| D+ | 1 |
| Unrated | 1 |
| All | 363 |

Table 8.3.  *Gilbert Harold's distribution of default ratios by agency ratings*

| 1929 Rating | Fitch | Moody | Poor | Standard |
|---|---|---|---|---|
| A+ | 3 | 1 | 3 | 5 |
| A | 22 | 8 | 7 | 9 |
| A–– | 8 | 18 | 14 | 15 |
| B+ | 20 | 14 | 15 | 13 |
| B | 35 | 28 | 32 | 12 |
| B–– | 50 | 50 | 43 | 19 |
| C+ | 33 | – | – | 50 |
| C | – | – | – | – |
| C–– | – | – | – | – |
| D+ | – | – | – | 100 |
| Unrated | 13 | 17 | 17 | 100 |
| All | 12 | 12 | 12 | 12 |

composite estimate of investment quality on the basis of the *minimum* of
the four ratings. He reported his resulting table of the distribution of ranks
in his sample of 363 bonds.

Comparing Harold's proposed estimate (Table 8.2) with his table of bond
ratings (Table 8.1), it is evident that the distribution of the minimum of the
four ratings is a good deal more symmetrical than the ratings themselves.

One of the reasons to use Harold's "pessimistic rating" is to avoid default.
Harold provides tables that compare the default rates on a single agency
basis with his "pessimistic" composite. We reprint two of the tables. First, in

Table 8.4. *Gilbert Harold's distribution of default ratios by pessimistic rating*

| Pessimistic Rating | July 18 1932 | July 17 1933 | July 16 1934 | July 15 1935 |
|---|---|---|---|---|
| A+ | 0 | 2 | 2 | 2 |
| A | 0 | 1 | 1 | 5 |
| A− | 0 | 8 | 13 | 13 |
| B+ | 5 | 10 | 20 | 16 |
| B | 3 | 8 | 11 | 17 |
| B− | 11 | 16 | 21 | 21 |
| C+ | 0 | 20 | 40 | 40 |
| C | – | – | – | – |
| C− | – | – | – | – |
| D+ | 100 | 100 | 100 | 100 |
| Unrated | 100 | 100 | 100 | 100 |
| All | 2 | 7 | 10 | 12 |

Table 8.3, he presents the experience cumulated through 1935 on a single agency basis, percentage defaulting by 1929 ratings. The second (Table 8.4) presents the 1935 cumulative and compares it to the default rate by the composite pessimistic rating for the four years.

Of course, disasters such as 1933 happen rarely. The point, though, is that they do happen and this is one of the reasons for working with uncertainty instead of risk.[14] With risk, we suppose we know the probability distribution; with uncertainty, we make no such claims.

As noted earlier, Harold's independence from the rating agencies' procedure allowed him to report the distribution of ratings by agency, something precluded by the NBER agreements since, as we have seen, even the worksheets printed as depository documentation suppresses the individual ratings.

## 8.4 The Corporate Bond Study Responds to a Critic

The NBER statisticians responded to Palyi's attack on the fragility of single-agency ratings by proposing to use a "composite" rating.[15] This is clear from private correspondence reproduced on the following pages between Harold Fraine of the Securities and Exchange Commission (SEC) who served as the Associate [Technical] Director of the CBP (NBER 1941 p. iv; Fraine and Brethouwer 1944, p. v), and Donald Thompson, Director of Research

---

[14] For more on this distinction see Knight 1933 and Chapter 4.
[15] We have not found an acknowledgment to Harold's use of a composite.

and Statistics of the FDIC.[16] It is also clear that Fraine worried about how to respond to Palyi's criticism honestly and prudently:

The difficulty is that the article is very critical of the bank supervisory and rating agencies. I cannot find it possible to say much about his article without appearing to put the memorandum of the Corporate Bond Study in the position of criticizing the cooperating agencies which were responsible for it.

Fraine proposed this solution:

I have finally hit on the attached as a sufficiently innocuous recognition of his contribution. I am also attaching a copy of the latest draft …

The draft shows both Fraine's original thoughts and what he concluded it was prudent to publish. The reference to the "composite" in the preliminary draft was crossed out. Next is the first version of a critical passage that is found in Figure 8.2:[17]

The Corporate Bond Study has provided "composite" agency ratings which for practical purposes can be used to indicate the eligibility for commercial bank investment of the bonds under the rules in effect.

This was changed, after some strikeouts, to a sentence that omitted any reference to the composite:

The Corporate Bond Study has provided comprehensive data to test the effectiveness of ratings as a guide to the eligibility for commercial bank investment of the bonds under the rules now in effect.

Both versions stressed the importance of the "rules in effect." The omission of any reference to a "composite" measure means that the reader of the published Hickman study may miss how the composite was designed to address the incentives under existing regulations – "the rules now in effect." The published version reads:

The Corporate Bond Project provides comprehensive data designed to test the effectiveness of current supervisory rules which employ ratings as a guide to the eligibility of bonds for commercial bank investment. (Fraine and Brethouwer 1944, p. 5)

A reader unaware that the "current supervisory rules" required a composite would not, indeed could not, guess at that aspect of the study. Moreover,

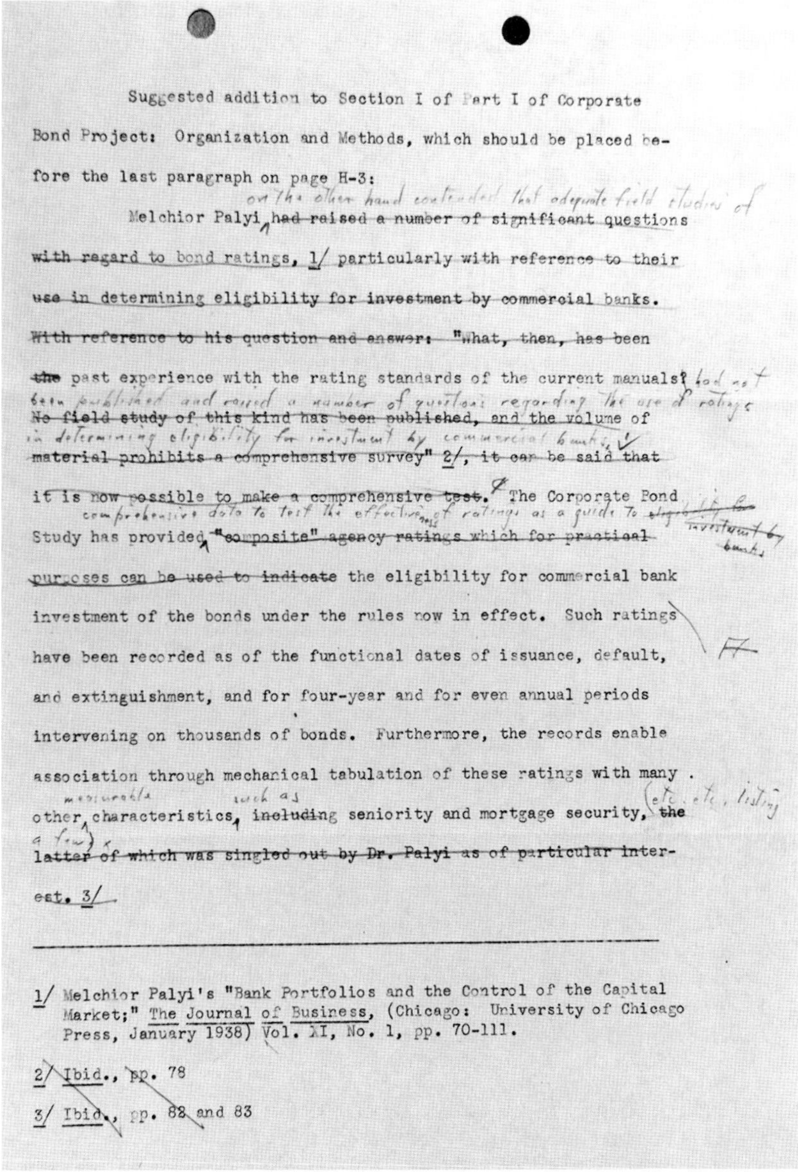

Suggested addition to Section I of Part I of Corporate
Bond Project: Organization and Methods, which should be placed before the last paragraph on page H-3:

Melchior Palyi ~~had raised a number of significant~~ questions [*on the other hand contended that adequate field studies of*]
~~with regard to bond ratings,~~ 1/ particularly with reference to their
~~use in determining eligibility for investment by commercial banks.~~
~~With reference to his question and answer:~~ "What, then, has been
~~the~~ past experience with the rating standards of the current manuals? [*had not*]
~~No field study of this kind has been published, and the volume of~~ [*been published and raised a number of questions regarding the use of ratings*]
~~material prohibits a comprehensive survey"~~ 2/, ~~it can be said that~~ [*in determining eligibility for investment by commercial banks.*]
~~it is now possible to make a comprehensive test.~~  The Corporate Bond [*comprehensive data to test the effect of ratings as a guide to eligibility for investment by banks.*]
Study has provided "composite" agency ratings ~~which for practical~~
~~purposes can be used to indicate~~ the eligibility for commercial bank
investment of the bonds under the rules now in effect.  Such ratings [*FF*]
have been recorded as of the functional dates of issuance, default,
and extinguishment, and for four-year and for even annual periods
intervening on thousands of bonds.  Furthermore, the records enable
association through mechanical tabulation of these ratings with many [*etc. etc. listing*]
other characteristics, ~~including~~ [*measurable such as*] seniority and mortgage security, ~~the~~ [*a few*]
~~latter of which was singled out by Dr. Palyi as of particular inter-~~
~~est. 3/~~

---

1/ Melchior Palyi's "Bank Portfolios and the Control of the Capital
   Market;" The Journal of Business, (Chicago:  University of Chicago
   Press, January 1938) Vol. XI, No. 1, pp. 70-111.

2/ Ibid., pp. 78

3/ Ibid., pp. 82 and 83

Figure 8.2.  Revision of text referring to Melchior Palyi.

since Palyi's study is not included in the index of the published NBER volume on bond quality (Hickman 1958), the reader will not understand his role in the NBER study.[18] Nor, perhaps more importantly, will they understand how the composite responds to Palyi's public challenge. We reproduce Fraine's letter to Thompson with the corrected version of his draft response.

830 Homestead Road
Beechwood Park
Upper Darby, Pa
March 18, 1943

Mr. Donald S. Thompson,
Director Division of Research and Statistics
Federal Deposit Insurance Corporation
Washington, D. C.

Dear Don:

One of the critical comments made on the preliminary draft of my section of the introductory background memorandum was that I had not in describing other research preceding the Corporate Bond Study made mention of Melchior Palyi's article in the <u>Journal of Business</u>. (Chicago: University of Chicago Press, January 1938) Vol. XI, No. 1, pp. 70–111. While I feel it should be mentioned, I have found myself a little embarrassed to know just what to say about this article. The difficulty is that the article is very critical of the bank supervisory and rating agencies. I cannot find it possible to say much about his article without appearing to put the memorandum of the Corporate Bond Study in the position of criticizing the cooperating agencies which were responsible for it.

I have finally hit on the attached as a sufficiently innocuous recognition of his contribution. I am also attaching a copy of the latest draft of my section of the introduction. I thought I had better check with you before including the recognition of Palyi's article. Do you have any serious objection to it being mentioned? Do you think the text I propose is fair to all parties concerned? If not, I would appreciate very much any suggestions for improvement.

Please remember Mary and myself to your family and to Harry.

Cordially,
Harold G. Fraine
Attachments

The archival records of the FDIC response to the questionnaire from Senator Wagner's Senate Banking Committee in 1939 ("National

---

[18]  A search on the NBER web site for Palyi turns up several references to his work on the international gold standard but nothing on ratings.

The basis of the uniform classification is:

(a) A security rated by one service only will be designated as of banking quality if rated within the first four grades by that service;

(b) A security rated by two services only will be designated as of banking quality if rated within the first four grades by both services;

(c) A security rated by three services only will be designated as of banking quality if rated within the first four grades by two of those services;

(d) A security rated by all four services will be designated as of banking quality if rated within the first four grades by three of those services.

Figure 8.3.  Memo responding to Congress about rating.

Monetary and Banking Policy") provides additional insight. The Banking Committee asked:

6. What use is made of the securities ratings of the recognized rating agencies in your examination and supervision of banks? By what means do you ascertain that the ratings are made in a manner appropriate to the use to which you put them?

All the published research, as well as the working documentation which we print, describes the composite as a "median." A worksheet of the response is reproduced as Figure 8.3.[19] We quote the critical case in which all four agency ratings are available:

(d) A security rated by all four services will be designated of banking quality if rated within the first four grades by three of those services.

The banking regulations, therefore, stipulated that banking quality required three of the four ratings to be investment grade. The conventional median of four observations, in which the inner two observations are averaged, supposes that there is no more reason to worry about an error high than to worry about an error low. Choosing to base the grade quality on the third highest rating, rather than the average of the second and the third, suggests a realization that the ratings were biased upward.

The manuscript is reproduced in Figure 8.3.

Hickman's 1958 *Corporate Bond Quality* offers a guide to the regulatory record. In the 1936 regulation, the Comptroller of the Currency, J. F. T. O'Connor, who also served as a director of the FDIC, defined an

[19]  Clark Warburton Archive Box 90, folder 9b.

"investment security" that a commercial bank could purchase for its own account. The passage from the *Federal Reserve Bulletin* allowed that the bank was permitted to purchase "investment securities" for its own purposes of investment under the provisions of R. S. 5136. Under this regulation, the bank was not permitted otherwise to participate as a principal in the marketing of securities.

(2)  The statutory limitation on the amount of the investment securities of any one obligor or maker which may be held by the bank is to be determined on the basis of the par or face value of the securities, and not on their market value.

(3)  The purchase of "investment securities" in which the investment characteristics are distinctly or predominantly speculative, or "investment securities" of a lower designated standard than those which are distinctly or predominantly speculative, is prohibited.[1] The purchase of securities which are in default, either as to principal or interest, is also prohibited. (O'Connor, 1936, p. 195)

The "recognized rating manuals" appeared in a footnote:

[1] The terms employed herein may be found in recognized rating manuals, and where there is doubt as to the eligibility of a security for purchase, such eligibility must be supported by not less than two rating manuals. (O'Connor, 1936, p. 195)

Thus, in a case in which all four rating agencies offered an opinion, the *minimum* requirement for "investment security" for a commercial bank holding was that the upper co-median of the agency rankings be of "investment grade." If there were only three agencies, the terms required the median rating to be investment grade. With two ratings, the terms required the minimum to be investment grade.

As Hickman informs the reader, the footnote did not appear in the 1938 regulations published by the Federal Reserve System. He points the reader to an article in an issue of the 1936 *American Banker*, subtitled "Ratings Services only Advisory" that explains why. The banks evidently found the constraints onerous:

Inquiry has been made as to whether member banks are confined to the purchase of securities which have a rating classification in one of the four groups according to rating services. The responsibility for proper investment of bank funds, now, as in the past, rests with the directors of the institution, and there has been and is no intention on the part of this office to delegate this responsibility to the rating-services, or in any-way to intimate that this responsibility may be considered as having been fully performed by the mere ascertaining that a particular security falls within a particular rating classification. (*American Banker*, 1936, p. 2)

The *American Banker's* report states that the "strictness of the regulation" was contested:

The Comptroller's office has had very few complaints or requests for change: from the banks themselves, it is learned. On the other hand, broker interests have now and then, sought for an easement of the regulation. It has occasionally happened that broker-minded bankers have desired a loosening of the strictness of the regulation. It is pointed out; however, that it is the desire of the Comptroller that the purpose and spirit of the law be maintained; that banks themselves be protected from possible unwise purchase and that they be not subject to pressure from brokerage interests or speculative trends. (p. 2)

Based on conversations with bank examiners, Hickman reports that although the "minimum of two" rule had been formally removed as a matter of regulation, it continued to be enforced as a matter of practice. Indeed, the 1940 FDIC response to the Wagner Committee, which we reproduced as Figure 8.3, insisted upon the lower co-median, a somewhat stiffer requirement.[20]

In summary, recent discussions of trust and the rating agencies fail to mention that for a long time regulations ensured that the ratings were used in such a way as to correct for upward bias. Ratings were said to reflect a "composite" of judgment rather than the judgment of a single agency. All that changed in the 1970s when the evaluations of single agencies themselves became trusted.[21] Harold tells us that bribery was not a problem. Attempts were made and repulsed. He gives no hint of collusion among agencies. If we suppose instead that to the extent that bias existed, it came from something more subtle, a sympathetic connection between the raters and clients that arose and was given weight because of the possibility of face-to-face discussion, then the outcome is not simple falsification or fabrication, but something we have called "sympathetic bias." If this is a correct reconstruction, then there is no reason to believe that this biasing factor will be the same across all agencies. The history of transactions would likely influence how receptive the agency would be to any such appeal.

---

[20]  Hickman (1958, p. 145): "Unofficial discussions with bank examiners indicate, however, that bonds rated in the first four grades by two or more agencies are still generally conceded to meet the Comptroller's requirements."

[21]  White (2002, p. 44) mentions "the presence of a *growing regulatory demand* for rating services …" without emphasizing the critical role of the Comptroller's regulation of 1936, which takes center stage in White (2010, p. 213).

But estimation shopping, as we noted, depends on the supposition that one rating is as useful as any other rating and that supposition depends on us not paying attention to individual differences as Harold did. To use Harold's sample, if we believed that Standard or Poor's gave less optimistic forecasts than Fitch, we would have no basis to treat their ratings as perfect substitutes.

### 8.5 The Corporate Bond Project of the National Bureau of Economic Research

Palyi and Harold published their concerns about relying on the judgment of individual rating agencies in 1938. Even before these public challenges, the topic of rating experience was discussed by the technical staff of the regulating agencies. Clark Warburton, the monetary theorist who was an economist for the FDIC,[22] passed on one such discussion to the chief of research at the FDIC in October 1937.[23]

In addition to a 1941 *History and Description of the Corporate Bond Project*, there is also a history provided in the first part of the 1944 *Organization and Administration of the Corporate Bond Project* by Fraine and Brethouwer. We quote at length from the foreword by Winfield W. Riffler to give some feel for the magnitude of the study:

In May 1938, Chairman Crowley of the Federal Deposit Insurance Corporation suggested to the National Bureau that since this study would deal with subjects of broad implications and develop materials of great importance to the study of the economic and financial system generally, it could best be conducted as an independent scientific inquiry under the supervisory auspices of the National Bureau's Program of Research in Finance. Chairman Crowley also stated that the Federal Deposit Insurance Corporation was prepared to sponsor a Work Projects Administration project in New York City to provide the necessary clerical help, and would cooperate in assembling the data, if the National Bureau would provide technical supervision and work out arrangements for other government

---

[22] The FDIC/NBER documents were given by the FDIC to the Clark Warburton collection at the George Mason University Library.

[23] Memo to Mr. Thompson from Clark Warburton, October 26, 1937 in Box 12 of the Clark Warburton Archive. "Yesterday I saw Mr. Harold Roelse … The problem in which he is interested that of bank holding of securities, particularly the behavior of unlisted securities. He says that Moody's has recently undertaken a study of all of the bonds which they rated in 1929, to see what has happened to them, whether paid on maturity, etc., as a sort of test of the goodness of their ratings. Mr. Roelse thinks a somewhat similar type of study might be made of unrated securities held by banks. This problem is of so much interest to the Corporation that I wonder if some plan of cooperation on the project might be worked out."

agencies and private financial advisory services to participate in the study. (Fraine and Brethouwer 1944, p. i)

The public record further reveals that the FDIC, the Federal Reserve System, the Federal Reserve Bank of New York, the Comptroller of the Currency, the four rating agencies (Moody's, Standard Statistics, Poor's, and Fitch) and the WPA were involved in financing the clerical help for the project, with the NBER in charge. Resources, basically, were of no object.

In 1941, the *History* asked about the *average* rating performance (NBER 1941, p. 14). By 1944, the questions sharpened considerably. Now, four questions asked explicitly about the rating agencies' rankings:

What has been the relative performance of bonds in different agency rating groups, as measured by the number of bonds defaulting in each group, the amount of loss (difference between expected and realized yield), and the realized yield to the investor? How effective have legal lists been as indicators of bond quality? Have legal bonds had a lower realized yield than nonlegal bonds of the same agency and market rating groups?

Has market rating at time of offering (i.e., the difference between the prospective yield on a given bond and that on the highest grade corporate bonds outstanding at that time) been a good indication future performance?

To what extent have the rating agencies differed with the market appraising relative bond quality at the time of offering?

Where [they] have differed, have the agencies rated more accurately than the market? (Hitchens 1944, p. 30).

Harold's dissertation had reported on a sample of 363 bonds. With the resources of the Federal government at its disposal, the NBER CBP collected everything in the universe of interest and 10 percent of the uninteresting.

When the NBER report, *Corporate Bond Quality*, was published in 1958, Hickman reported on the experience of the period by means of a dramatic table (Hickman 1958, p. 10) that featured an "Agency Rating".

Table 8.5 reveals, first, that high-rated bonds defaulted less frequently than low-rated bonds, so high-rated bonds were indeed prudent investments that delivered more than they promised.[24] Second, the realized return from low-rated bonds was very high, although not as high as promised. The finding that attracted the most attention was the performance of "junk

---

[24] "Even the highest grades of corporate bonds, it is shown, were not entirely free of the risk of default; but virtually all of the prospective measures of quality provided reliable rankings in regard to such risk. In other words, the retrospective quality of bond offerings as measured by default rates declines as we move down the scale of each of the major prospective measures of quality." Hickman (1958, p. 12).

Table 8.5. *Braddock Hickman's composite rating*

|  | Default Rate | Promised Yield | Realized Yield | Loss Rate |
|---|---|---|---|---|
| All Industries | 17.3% | 5.3% | 5.4% | –0.1% |
| Railroads | 28.1 | 5.5 | 5.2 | 0.3 |
| Public Utilities | 10.6 | 5.0 | 5.4 | –0.4 |
| Industrials | 14.8 | 5.4 | 5.8 | –0.4 |
| Agency Rating |  |  |  |  |
| I | 5.9 | 4.5 | 5.1 | –0.6 |
| II | 6.0 | 4.6 | 5.0 | –0.4 |
| III | 13.4 | 4.9 | 5.0 | –0.1 |
| IV | 19.1 | 5.4 | 5.7 | –0.3 |
| V-IX | 42.4 | 9.5 | 8.6 | 0.9 |
| No rating | 28.6 | 4.8 | 4.6 | 0.2 |

bonds." Less apparent is how the composite "Agency rating" was computed. Hickman later explains:

When only one rating could be obtained for an issue, the coded value of that rating was used as the composite rating. If two ratings were available, the composite is the arithmetic mean of the coded values of the two, *rounded downward* in the event of a fractional value to the next lower rating (i.e. grade II is the composite rating assigned an issue rated Aaa by Moody's and A1 by Standard). For three ratings, the composite is the middle value of the array of coded ratings; for four values, it is the arithmetic mean of the middle two *(rounded downward in the event of a split rating).* Hickman (1958, p. 143) [Emphasis added.]

This is a subtle variation on how the FDIC responded to the Wagner Committee's questionnaire. Just as Harold's use of the *minimum* as a prudent estimator has fallen out of memory, so, too, has the fact that the NBER used a median, rounded *downward* for an even number of observations.[25]

## 8.6 Conclusion

Harold was emphatic that experts who rate securities are tempted to bias their estimates upward and he offered a subtle statistical procedure to address the bias that took into account how different agencies dealt with temptation. The NBER's use of a downward-rounded median that mimics regulatory practice was also apparently designed to reduce the upward bias in the ratings. But unlike Harold's modest study, the NBER experts could

[25] When Richard Sylla reports the results of Hickman's study, he writes of "a composite average" (Sylla 2002, p. 26) instead of a downward-rounded median as the correction for bias.

not reveal the differences among the rating agencies. The temptation for the agencies to bias any certification of soundness had been well understood and sophisticated steps were taken to attenuate the bias. Nonetheless, over time, the constraints went slack. At the center of the recent financial scandal, the rating agencies were relied upon as experts, without such prudential measures to certify what bonds were secure holdings for the federally insured commercial banks. The results are now well known.

For our purposes, what needs to be emphasized is that the first two important statistical studies of the rating agencies employed estimation procedures to reduce the influence of any single optimistic rating. Harold's minimum traded accuracy for protection from calamity. It proved unattractive for regulatory purposes perhaps because it offered to a single agency an unchecked blackmail ability.[26] The FDIC-financed NBER estimate also attenuated the influence of any single optimistic rating without creating the blackmail temptation.

This history suggests that it is not sufficient to start with a deep understanding of the temptations offered by expertise. One must also create institutions in which such temptations are constrained. In this instance, such institutions existed – there was, as we have seen, a practice of using prudential estimates – and then it decayed. What failed over time was professional memory. The illusion that "this time is different" (Reinhart and Rogoff 2009) happens when people forget the long history of experts who have succumbed to the temptation to bias their results. Economists forgot that the trade that financed the research precluded a public discussion about the need to avoid bias, that was not constant across the agencies. This is not to pass judgment on the working statisticians and economists who, in fact, developed ways to deal with expert bias: they documented the need to write carefully and they preserved the correspondence in which they discussed constraints on what they might say in public. Doubtless they could have said a great deal more about agency differences. But because of the contracts their employers made with the agencies, they were unable to discuss such things and the evidence in the present chapter became obscured.

---

[26] Hugh Rockoff pointed this out in correspondence.

PART V

GETTING THE BEST FROM EXPERTS

The foregoing has focused on the negative, what might go wrong when we too readily trust experts. We have encountered two linked problems – lack of discussion and imposition of exogenous goals. In turn, we have seen that when discussion is lacking or goals are imposed on ordinary people, biased expert judgment may prevail. In the next chapters we turn to the positive, how we might obtain the best possible outcomes from experts, how to minimize the incentive to bias, and how to avoid situations where experts have the power and authority to impose goals without some additional discussion along the way. Our goal is to use the insights we have gained from the negative case studies to begin to conceptualize institutions that will allow us to enjoy the benefits of expertise.

Specifically in the chapters that follow, we consider experts inside institutional constraints that serve to better direct their interests toward the public good. We open by discussing the challenges associated with factionalized economics in which there are no institutional constraints. To set the stage for that discussion we briefly review the closely related positions of two economists who are all too often read only in opposition, Frank Knight and A. C. Pigou. Although they apparently came to their positions independently, it is remarkable that both Knight and Pigou point to a collective-action problem within economics, both have a London School of Economics [LSE] context, and their contributions are only a year apart. Knight's neglected contribution is contained in the new introduction to the LSE reprint of *Risk, Uncertainty and Profit* but it is not included in *Ethics of Competition*. Pigou's contribution is rather better known but it seems to have been read only in the immediate context – his unhappiness with his Cambridge colleague J. M. Keynes's behavior toward F. A. Hayek's criticisms.

Suppose that we think about how and why an economist might pursue his or her self-interest. The examples we have considered suggest an answer to the "how." The pursuit of self-interest will not be transparent to the reader. That provides the how, but what about the why? The American Economic Association [AEA] has recently required that authors in AEA journals reveal their sources of support. However, what Pigou worried about is ideology, a sympathy for a system of governance, not financial inducement. Perhaps that provides an answer to the why. Consequently, we propose an addendum to the AEA that we believe would help the reader infer ideological biases. We do not put an enormous trust in unenforced codes of ethics for improving conduct but nonetheless codes of ethics *can* inform the reader to beware of incentives to bias since that is where personal motivation enters the argument. Making that nontransparency itself transparent offers a second-best solution.

Next, we consider institutions in a pair of contexts. The first, to use a phrase that Michael Polanyi coined in the early 1960s, is "the Republic of Science." Polanyi argued for a truly remarkable result, that of the uniformity of scientific opinion. Gordon Tullock, whose work was inspired by Karl Popper's philosophy of science, found the gap in Polanyi's argument and provided an institutional constraint that might resolve the problem. Without knowing the Knight–Pigou discussion, Tullock pointed out that such a constraint is lacking in economics; consequently, he labeled economics as more of a "racket" than a science. Although Tullock's phrase is delightfully pungent, we prefer the ancient political term *faction* since it fits better within Polanyi's view of science as a self-governing society.

As far as we can tell, Tullock's book had almost no public impact. It did, however, prompt a fascinating letter from Popper who wrote that he was well aware of factionalized science. This raises all sorts of questions since we can think about Thomas Kuhn's "paradigm" as evidence of a factionalized science but Popper's response to Kuhn's criticism did not explicitly deal with the problem of faction. A possible Popper–Tullock response to Kuhn might have developed the sort of institutional framework that replaced faction with an agreement to keep the critical questions open to discussion.

The second context in which we appeal to institutions is that of expert witnesses in the American legal system. The standard literature uses these constraining institutions to allow ordinary jurors to rely on competing expert witnesses to good advantage. We take an idea from Gordon Tullock, that of a court-appointed expert, and provide a rule that improves the incentives for expert candor.

In the American legal system, where contending parties hire their own expert witness, it will surprise no one that the experts' work will be biased in their clients' favor. With the institution of discovery, we can rule out the cruder sorts of falsification or fabrication: neither will resist discovery procedures. So, we have a structure that makes the experts' work replicable in the narrow sense in which economists use the term. We have a jury system in which citizens selected randomly make a decision with full awareness that they do not understand how the experts arrive at their results. Under existing legal rules, ordinary people, who can be assured by the discovery procedure that experts are doing replicable work and who are aware that contending experts are biased, can make perfectly sensible decisions by splitting the difference between the experts. This result shows the power of institutions that allow decision making when the nontransparency is itself transparent. Can we even improve on this result? A split-the-difference process encourages an arms race of wilder and wilder evidence. Our reform changes the incentives so that providing the most plausible evidence is prudent. This allows us to appreciate what is possible if institutional reform changes the incentives to induce a more complete transparency.

# 9

# A Proposal for a Revised Code of Ethics for Experts

The first and main suggestion, looking towards a more relevant economics, is that the inquiry into motives might well, like charity, begin at home, with a glance at the reasons why economists write books and articles.

Frank Knight (1933, p. xxvi)

## 9.1  Introduction

A major theme of this book is that experts are subject to private and public interests that do not always fully overlap. This is the long-recognized problem of partiality. In older days, it was referred to as the problem of "faction." Political economists who worked in the tradition of Adam Smith fully understood that individuals are connected by bonds of sympathy and they exchange not only goods and services but also something more subtle and harder to assess, what we might refer to as approbation. When sympathy is partial and extends only or more fully to those like ourselves, the desire for approval is warped by the desire for within-group – faction – approval. In this case one may act so as to cooperate with those in our group at the expense of those outside the group. Hence arises a collective action problem associated with group action and direction. This chapter and the next two attempt to provide some suggestions by which the private and public interests of experts and citizens might be more fully aligned.

The first step is to recognize the problem; the next is to think about what sort of institutions might attenuate the problem. This approach is in line with the cyclical model of expertise we set out in Chapter 1: We point to the problem and suggest an institutional reform to attenuate the difficulty. At no time do we suppose that the motives of experts differ from those of anyone else.

The key problem we confront in the following pages is that experts may be tempted by sympathetic connections with their clients, like-minded experts, or some other group, to provide biased advice. Although it is in the interest of society to obtain disinterested advice from experts, there may be strong private incentives for any one expert to offer biased advice. In recognition of this temptation, the American Economic Association (AEA) has recently implemented new publication guidelines (AEA 2012) that ask for disclosure of any financial rewards associated with research conducted by economists. This is, of course, quite typical; most codes of ethics require disclosure of financial incentives to bias.[1] As will become clear in what follows, we cautiously applaud the new disclosure requirements that successfully do some of the work required to more fully constrain experts from giving biased advice. Might we do better? On the occasion of a discussion of the new AEA publication guidelines, we asked whether the disclosure rules are sufficient to constrain experts from pushing their point of view onto their consumers and the public. We suggested then, and continue to maintain, that the guidelines might be strengthened more fully to solve the collective action problem associated with expertise.

To explain our caution, we call attention to the remarkable results that Daylian M. Cain, George Loewenstein, and Don A. Moore published some years ago with the delightful title "The dirt on coming clean" (Cain, Loewenstein, and Moore 2005). They find that when researchers are obligated to detail their financial "conflict of interests," they take this as a ticket to engage in *additional* distressing behavior at the expense of their clients. This seems a completely plausible result if the expert is asympathetic with the concerns of the client but sensitive to disapprobation. If part of the cost of dishonesty is being called dishonest, then the cost of actual dishonesty falls with disclosure. As the authors suggest, the downside of conflict of financial interest statements is the "moral licensing" such rules convey (Cain et al. 2005). We will return to their results in the conclusion of the chapter in which we begin to think about sympathetic experts.

In what follows, we approach the problem from the point of view of the consumer of expert advice. In a world of fully aligned group and private interests – a state of affairs that presupposes full transparency – the sensible rule would be always to trust the experts. We would make the same decision as they recommend had we spent our resources on obtaining their knowledge. However, when transparency fails and the misalignment of expert and consumer goals is unknown, that trust can be catastrophic. We accept that full transparency and fully overlapping goals may be a pipedream. So, we

---

[1] Some examples of conflict of interest disclosures are www.councilofnonprofits.org/conflict-of-interest www.idealist.org/info/Nonprofits/Gov5 https://www.aeaweb.org/journals/policies/disclosure-policy

propose to think in terms of the general theory of the second best in which we accept the existence of constraints, in this case partiality, which cannot be removed (Lipsey and Lancaster 1956–1957). In this second-best world, full transparency is unattainable but what *is* possible is to make that non-transparency itself transparent to the public. A code of ethics for experts might suggest to nonexperts that there is temptation to violate professional standards for private ends. Thus, the very existence of an ethical code is a warning. To serve this end, the code of ethics needs to indicate where the dangers lie and what tempts the expert.

We begin the chapter by reviewing a pair of early discussions of the private and public incentives associated with experts. Frank Knight's discussion of economic experts is particularly valuable because he held a view of experts as truth seekers but he also realized that truth seeking was not incentive compatible. Instead of falling into Knight's pessimism, however, we will take this view as a first-best situation and ask what constraint blocks us from attaining it. Given that constraint, we can then think about a second-best solution.

Knight's important insight into "the reasons why economists write books and articles" led him to recognize, first, that economists should apply their models to themselves, thereby explicitly modeling researchers and experts as self-interested. Our approach has much in common with this. Second, he was acutely aware of the problem of seeking approbation from one's peers, the collective action problem in which the "competition for recognition and influence take the place of the effort to get things straight" (Knight 1933, p. xxvii). Knight's sometimes-intellectual opponent, A. C. Pigou, made the similar point that instead of seeking the truth, individual economists who are unconstrained by ethics simply posture and argue. In section 9.3 we locate the Knightian enterprise in a first-best world in which expertise is equivalent to truth seeking. Here we focus on John Rawls's appreciation for Knight's vision of truth seeking in Rawls's magisterial *Theory of Justice*. The first-best supposition of truth seeking fails when economists act as advocates for predetermined systems of belief. In section 9.4 we suggest why the Knight–Rawls notion of fully disinterested experts is so fragile, and we offer a suggestion to make the nontransparent pursuit of private ends itself transparent. We close with a proposed addition to the AEA guidelines to help the consumer deal with the motivated economist.

## 9.2 The Expert Economist's Dilemma, Historically Considered

Two important treatments of the collective action problem associated with economists as experts date from the early twentieth century. The first was offered by Knight in the 1933 "Preface to the Re-Issue" of *Risk, Uncertainty and Profit* in the London School of Economics reprints series of "Scarce Tracts." Pigou offered a second treatment a year later in his London School of Economics lecture in which he flamboyantly described the issue.[2]

Knight and Pigou are often correctly seen in oppositional terms. Knight's response to Pigou's problem of the divergence between private and social costs is rightly celebrated as the beginning of the LSE-Chicago analysis of the critical role of property rights in a competitive economy (Pigou 1918; Knight 1924; Coase 1993; Heckman 1997). As Ronald Coase tells us, he selected the title of his most famous article, "The Problem of Social Cost" in tribute to Knight's "Fallacies in the Interpretation of Social Cost" (Coase 1993, p. 250). But Knight and Pigou also share an important insight into the economics of economists as experts. In this context it becomes clear that just as they hold that the individuals studied by economists confront collective-action problems, so, too, do the economists themselves face these problems. This makes for a motivational homogeneity between the expert and the consumer, which, as noted in Chapter 1, we also take as foundational in analytical egalitarianism.

### 9.2.1 Frank Knight

Knight begins his preface by proposing to address what needs to be done to develop and improve received economic doctrine (Knight 1933, p. xi). Although there are very few specific targets of his preface – Pigou's treatment of uncertainty in an appendix of *Economics of Welfare* (xiv) and his confounding of the firm and plant (xxi) are exceptions – Knight's unhappiness with the larger enterprise of classical economics is quite clear and not especially surprising given his other writings of the period.

What *is* a surprise comes in his two-paragraph exercise in the economics of economics. In the first of these, he proposes to use the tools of economics to analyze the economist's own activity:

The first and main suggestion, looking towards a more relevant economics, is that the inquiry into motives might well, like charity, begin at home, with a glance at the

---

[2] Perhaps Knight and Pigou were inspired by considering what follows from failure of the motivational condition that J. Neville Keynes put forward when he described positive economics as the search for law. We print the motivational condition in bold to distinguish it from Keynes's italics. "We mean by a *law* a theorem, the statement of a uniformity, not a command enforced by sanctions. The law of supply and demand, the Ricardian law of rent, Gresham's law, and the like, may be given as examples of economic laws in the above sense. The validity of such laws is a purely theoretical question, **and our attitude towards them is not, or at any rate should not be, affected by our ethical or political views.**" Keynes (1891, p. 36) Keynes describes such motivated activity as advocacy.

reasons why economists write books and articles. These things are also commodities, produced competitively for a market, … the behaviour of economists provides evidence regarding the possibilities of settling questions – and of settling them rightly – by free discussion. (Knight 1933, xxvi)

Then Knight describes the collective action problem in which "Economics finds itself in a vicious circle":

To get recognition and have influence it descends to the public's level of thinking; then competition for recognition and influence take the place of the effort to get things straight; finally, success in this competition becomes the condition of membership in the profession itself. It is no doubt idle to say, now, that there "might have been" an economics profession made up of minds exclusively devoted to the problem-solving interest and working co-operatively at this task, instead of more and more hawking their wares competitively to the public by way of settling their "scientific" differences. (Knight 1933, xxvii–xxviii)

Knight's statement of the problem and his own solution to it were taken up by William Hutt in his 1936 *Economists and the Public*, but they seem to have been otherwise largely ignored.

### 9.2.2  A. C. Pigou

Lecturing at the London School of Economics in late 1934 on the role of economists in society, Pigou comes to the matter of controversy. Those who thought he might respond to Knight's criticism were in for a surprise, as Pigou accepted and actually sharpened Knight's point. Although "controversy up to a point serves, no doubt, to stimulate and clarify thought," Pigou argued that "controversy for its own sake is a prodigious waste of time" (Pigou 1935, p. 22). He then quoted a verse from Rudyard Kipling without explanation:

There are nine and sixty ways of constructing tribal lays,
And every single one of them is right!

Those in the audience who could place the verse in Kipling's poetic sketch of the hesitant steps away from a world of wars ("Neolithic Age"), might have foreseen some of what followed. Pigou pointed to a rule that J. M. Keynes urged on the occasion of the official obituary notice for Alfred Marshall:

It is not politic for us to lay down even the most general rules for one another: we may so soon be constrained to break those rules ourselves. Not so long ago one of my most distinguished colleagues urged his fellow-economists to "eschew the Treatise, pluck the day, fling pamphlets into the wind." A few years later he himself offered, and we gratefully received, a work with the title of Treatise and comprising two weighty tomes! (Pigou 1935, pp. 22–23)

After defending Marshall's generosity to the classics, Pigou clarified the point of the verse:

And there is yet another thing. Are we, in our secret hearts, wholly satisfied with the manner, or manners, in which some of our controversies are carried on? A year or two ago, after the publication of an important book, there appeared an elaborate and careful critique of a number of particular passages in it. The author's answer was, not to rebut the criticisms, but to attack with violence another book, which the critic had himself written several years before! Body-line bowling! The method of the duello! (1935, pp. 23–24)

The episode, now cited as witness to the decade-spanning dispute between Keynes and F. A. Hayek, is for Pigou an instance of the failure of economists to achieve their collective goal (attaining influence) as they understand it:[3]

That kind of thing is surely a mistake. It is a mistake, not merely in general and in the abstract, but also for a solid reason of State. Economists in this country lack the influence which – in their own opinion – they ought to have, largely because the public believes that on all topics they are hopelessly divided. Controversies conducted in the manner of Kilkenny cats do not help to dissipate this opinion. And yet in truth the opinion is largely mistaken! (1935, p. 24)

For Pigou, group influence depends on unanimity, but individual self-interest unconstrained by ethics leads to posturing and dissent. This was especially true in the arena of policy advice. Pigou described the demand for economic expertise:

… political partisans, I say, are accustomed to decide what they want to do first and to seek for arguments in favour of it afterwards. Economic reasoning is for them, not a means of arriving at the truth, but a kind of brickbat useful on occasions for inflicting injury on their opponents. (1935, pp. 8–9)

He continues with a story about an unnamed political figure who switched economic advice as policy changed and then another about his adventures in offering advice in the letters column of the *Times*. In the latter instance Pigou moved from being, in the judgment of the Prime Minister, "the great Cambridge economist" to a "mere academic theorist" in a twinkling of a policy shift! (1935, pp. 9–10). Next, he reviews the private incentives facing economists to gain influence through the sale of their theories for the sake of policy results:

Of course to students of detached mind this kind of thing is entertaining and quite harmless. But to a young man the ambition to play a part in great affairs is

---

[3]  F. A. Hayek (Hayek 1994, p. 47) quotes the passage as evidence of Keynes's reaction to his review of *Treatise of Money*. Bruce Caldwell offers an extensive discussion, Caldwell (1995, p. 26).

natural: and the temptation to make slight adjustments in his economic view, so that it shall conform to the policy of one political party or another, may be severe. As a conservative economist or a liberal economist or a labour economist he has much more chance of standing near the centre of action than he has as an economist without adjectives. But for the student to yield to that temptation is an intellectual crime. It is to sell his birthright in the household of truth for a mess of political pottage. (1935, pp. 10–11)

The only solution to this dilemma, which Pigou proposed, is what Kipling saw, a norm of tolerance and awareness, from which it followed that the public would be skeptical of advice.[4]

## 9.3  Experts as Truth Seekers: A First-Best Option

Knight's view is that experts ought to, but rarely do, participate in an objective exercise to find the best solution to social problems. Governance for Knight is not about trading interests. It is, instead, a discussion about how best to obtain agreed-upon ends. In *Theory of Justice* Rawls is completely clear that his understanding of expertise was fully aligned with Knight's view.[5] He depended on Knight at the critical moment in which the question arose about whether experts who discuss legislation aim at discovering the correct answer or simply at working out a compromise favored by a majority coalition. Rawls then provided a framework to think about the fair conduct of those who are concerned with discovering the correct answer but who are aware that they and others have other motivations.

For Knight, government by discussion involves majority rule and decision making by experts. We quote the long passage in which Rawls takes legislation in a just constitution as a procedure to arrive at the "best policy as defined by the principles of justice":

In the ideal procedure, the decision reached is not a compromise, a bargain struck between opposing parties trying to advance their ends. The legislative discussion

---

[4]  It perhaps intrigued the reader and certainly struck us as worthy of note, that both Knight's and Pigou's reflections offered in the space of a year on the collective action problem of economists have a London School of Economics [LSE] address. Whether this is purely coincidental or not, there is an LSE tradition of the 1930s that considers the role of the economist in the economy. William Beveridge's "Mock Trial of the Economists" and Hutt (1936) are additional examples (Levy and Peart 2014a).

[5]  Dennis Thompson (1987, pp. 102–05) discusses this "less-known part of a well-known theory of justice" (102) without taking up its Knightian foundation. His criticism of Rawls's thesis of principled legislation ("an inappropriate standard of representation") does not consider how the system might infect legislation because he takes the principles to be true.

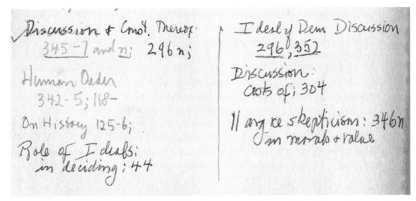

Figure 9.1. A portion of John Rawls's index to Frank Knight's *Ethics of Competition.* Reproduced by permission of Thomas Scanlon and Mrs. John Rawls for the Estate of John Rawls.

must be conceived not as a contest between interests, but as an attempt to find the best policy as defined by the principles of justice. I suppose, then, as part of the theory of justice, that an impartial legislator's only desire is to make the correct decision in this regard, given the general facts known to him. He is to vote solely according to his judgment. The outcome of the vote gives an estimate of what is most in line with the conception of justice.

If we ask how likely it is that the majority opinion will be correct, it is evident that the ideal procedure bears a certain analogy to the statistical problem of pooling the views of a group of experts to arrive at a best judgment. (Rawls 1971, pp. 357–58)

Rawls's footnote reveals the complexity of the issue. After the citation to Kenneth Arrow's *Social Choice* comes the reference to the critical argument in Knight:

For the notion of legislative discussion as an objective inquiry and not a contest between interests, see F. H. Knight, *The Ethics of Competition* (New York: Harper and Brothers, 1935), pp. 296, 345–347. In both cases see the footnotes. (Rawls 1971, p. 358)

The pages cited in *Justice* are marked for attention in Rawls's index in the rear inner lining of his copy of *Ethics of Competition.* These passages are from Knight's 1934 paper on nationalism, which has been (unfortunately) read in isolation from the introduction to the LSE reprint except perhaps by Hutt (1936). A small part of the index Rawls prepared for *Ethics* is reproduced here (Figure 9.1).

On the pages Rawls cites, he marked passages in red ink apparently as a mark of emphasis. He seems particularly taken by Knight's response to a skeptic who denies there is a "best" answer. Knight clearly worried that discussion aimed at discovering the correct answer might degenerate into the pursuit of one's interests. His proposed solution to the problem of partial interest corrupting the discussion of social goals was to appeal to fairness. The background assumption in footnote 1 (p. 345) is an appeal to impartiality. In the extensive footnote, to which Rawls paid close attention, Knight writes, "expression of personal preferences is not discussion and indeed leads definitely toward conflict." Thus, the role of agreement is worked into Knight's argument and seconded by Rawls.

Knight famously worried that growing income inequality would corrupt impartiality because those with more dollars would have a louder voice and members of each group would seek within-group approval. (We will return to this point in Chapter 12 when we consider the American jury system as a model of Knight's government by discussion.) His answer to this problem of potentially growing partiality is precisely the same in philosophical discussions as it is in the government of a competitive order. The player, as Knight puts it, must be more concerned to have a good game, to play by agreed-upon rules, than to win.

The question as we see it is whether this is sufficient to ensure the discussion is "fair." Our worry, expounded in more detail in section 9.4, is that without a more expansive code of ethics, enforced by spectators who are aware of the potential nontransparency of experts, experts will be insufficiently wedded to a norm of fair play to take part willingly in a competitive discussion, to play by the rules and to abide by the outcome. Knight sees this, too, and despairs.

## 9.4  Toward a (Partial) Solution to the Ethical Dilemmas of Expertise

As noted earlier, the problem of the misalignment of the public and private interests of experts has several dimensions. There is, first and perhaps most simply, the financial interests that accrue to the expert. An expert may be paid to provide expert advice by a client who wishes to obtain a particular kind of advice. We worry, however, about more than financial incentives. The misalignment of incentives may also involve approbation. If an expert is part of a group that favors one sort of system over another, the expert may be prone to what Smith referred to as the danger of favoring results that fit into a system over results that do not. Combining the idea of system with Knight and Rawls, the "objective inquiry" or the "best policy" may be contingent on a system. This would be akin to how James Buchanan reads Knight (Buchanan 1967), except that, instead of preferences for policies, we have preferences for a system.

System-specific answers, of course, will generally be local to issues and "best" answers that are far from the best may be the consequence of a false system. We have encountered examples of such expert failure earlier. In the case of forced sterilizations, the overall system was so-called racial betterment. Supposing an expert was committed to improving the race, the great dangers were race suicide and inherited criminality and a "best" policy might be the sterilization of the "unfit." If, instead, an expert was attached to a system of comparative economic growth in which Soviet overtaking was a near certainty, the "best" policy might be an early war against North Vietnam, a Soviet client state, as a way to prevent a later war against an "increasingly powerful" Soviet Union.[6]

It is common knowledge that Knight and Rawls worried about income going to those with extraordinary inherited abilities. For Knight, income inequality changes the rules of government by discussion; those with more income obtain a louder voice. Knight's concern with bias via inequality is largely a question of transparency. He worried that the arguments advanced by interested parties could not be checked by their opponents. And since the bias in the system is nontransparent, people would not come to the conclusion that the discussion was unfair. Consequently, the question of how the system is selected requires our attention.[7]

The Knightian vision of a fair game in which all the players are tempted by their several goals to cheat poses the question of what makes playing the game of greater importance than winning one round? What induces experts to propose their best attempt at the correct answer instead of their best attempt at an answer that maximizes their several individual interests? There is as we have argued no easy answer to this question. But given individual and social interests so rarely fully align, knowing the question is one step, perhaps, toward a second-best solution. As we have argued, experts function best when they are not fully trusted.

A Rawlsian potential solution now presents itself. Suppose the experts put themselves behind a veil of ignorance in which their future clients are unknown. Why would they do this? Perhaps if the consumers of expertise

---

[6] As illustration of the fragility with respect to false systems in the Knight–Rawls approach to politics, we can do no better than to notice that 1) Rawls himself toyed with eugenic concerns (Rawls [1971, p. 107) and 2) Brian Barry in his commentary on Rawls's work, asked whether we might give up liberty for the higher growth and the more abundant future in the Soviet Union (Barry 1973, pp. 73–74).

[7] This is not to say that inequality concerns go away in our approach. Rather, they come to us in system-specific fashion. In the eugenic era, poor girls were sterilized; in the Vietnam War, poor boys were drafted.

know the tricks of argumentation (of expertise), it would be harder for experts to impose a trick on them. But this would make the readers into experts of a sort. Making the nontransparency itself transparent is our second-best answer.

To reform economic advocacy we need to take the hardest step of all: to recognize, with Knight and Pigou, that experts share motivational structure with those we study. The consequence of this is that we need to put the economist in the model. We can see this by considering the "dirty-hands problem" of professional ethics, which asks whether the expert can "rightfully" overstate the evidence to press some noble "truth" (DeMartino 2011, pp. 132–33). Consider the cases discussed in the previous chapters. If an expert just *knew* that Jewish immigrants were inferior (or that the Soviet Union's economy just *had to be* growing faster than that of the United States) even though the data failed to corroborate these positions, so much worse for the data. The "dirty-hands problem" presumes that the client does not see this interior struggle between conflicting obligations, one to the "truth" and another to the client, because if the client were to see it, the nontransparency comes itself transparent. And knowing about the nontransparency the client might seek protection by finding methods to attenuate the influence of an expert's presuppositions.

Along with the American Economic Association and many other associations to which experts belong, we, therefore, suggest, as a preliminary matter, that it is critically important for experts to reveal information relevant to their financial interests. This at least begins to suggest to consumers what gap may exist between the experts' private and public interests. The AEA ethics guidelines ask for disclosures of financial temptations to bias. That experts face a temptation to choose their results in favor of a client who financially supports the research is now perhaps an uncontroversial claim.[8]

As noted at the outset, there may be other private reasons for a temptation to bias. An expert might, for instance, have nonmonetary ("sympathetic") connections with the advice seeker or with other experts who offer similar expertise. Or, a researcher might hold with a particular "system" as Smith put it, one that other experts favor. In today's parlance he or she might have ideological attachments or policy commitments, or commitments to governing principles for society. Commitments to "classical liberalism" or "social justice," for example, might influence an economist's

[8] The fact, however, that financial disclosure has only recently entered the economics discourse while there has long been a code of ethics in statistics and many other fields (Gorlin 1999), suggests that there has been more resistance to admitting that private interests might clash with the public interest in economics than in other disciplines.

model specification or choice of estimation technique, which, of course, in turn yield specific conclusions in favor of the presupposed (but hidden) commitment.

This is not to suggest that economists should refrain from having commitments – the impossible – but, instead, we maintain that the commitments themselves might constitute relevant information as the results (or advice) become public, are published in a journal, or are otherwise dispersed to a more general audience. Such sympathetic connections are more clearly revealed by detailing the history of one's work, including not least one's consulting history and the policy positions one has advocated in consulting and academic work. Indeed, the American Economic Association requires something close to this, requesting that authors reveal "paid or unpaid positions as office, director, or board member of relevant nonprofit organizations or profit making entities" (AEA 2012). Yet although this hints at the idea of group affiliations and attachment to systems of thought, the overall thrust of the AEA requirement is *financial* and as such is subject to the perverse incentives that Cain, Loewenstein, and Moore (2005) identified.[9] Although we recognize that the number and significance of such ideological affiliations are more difficult to assess and we have no intention of suggesting that one must reveal all affiliations one has ever had, we maintain that significant attachments also constitute important information for the consuming public. The point is to provide the public with as much information as is practically possible about the predictable temptations to bias that might exist among the experts whose results are otherwise quite difficult for the public to check.

## 9.5  Conclusion

Economists have occasionally recognized that they have enormous influence in the business of persuasion as well as the rewards associated with influence. Paul Samuelson's remark, quoted in Chapter 3, about the rewards associated with making his conclusions widely known speaks directly to the potential for influence and the nonmonetary reward that accrues from writing textbooks. For those whose expertise is prized, influence is gained by providing highly regarded advice. If the expertise is regarded as ill-informed or wrong, then the expert loses face or influence. Thus the expert will be

---

[9]  In the notes that follow the policy, the following sentence emphasizes just that: "The AEA policy is specifically focused on disclosure of 'conflicts of interest' that arise because of potential financial/material gains for the researcher."

asymmetrically motivated to accept confirming evidence and reject contra-dictory evidence. There is consequently a certain stickiness of models with respect to falsifying evidence. We have documented this stickiness in the context of the leading textbook comparisons, including that in Samuelson, of Soviet and American growth after 1960 (Chapter 6).[10] We have also doc-umented in Chapter 5 how one extremely talented expert statistician chose his methodology selectively in order better to obtain the results he sought.

Interestingly, our concern about the nonmonetary connections among those who give and receive expertise was shared by Coase. In 1968 Coase was accused of yielding to the sort of influence addressed in the AEA guide-lines, of advocating for the Zenith Corporation as a result of financial incen-tives, specifically, of being a hired advocate for Zenith. Coase responded with a letter now in the William Baroody Papers at the Library of Congress (Box 77) that flatly denied that there was any monetary connection between himself and Zenith. But he then went on to describe another reason for expert bias, the one we have identified, nonmonetary rewards that accrue from obtaining influence. Coase's letter turned the accusation around; he suggested that many false arguments that are advanced as a means to achieving the "public interest," as he put it, were actually in the private inter-est of the expert who put them forward. Of course, as a careful student of Smith, Coase knew all about motivation by a desire for approbation.

The foregoing has focused especially on problems that arise when there are nonmonetary incentives to bias one's advice, those that arise when the expert has a commitment to a particular group of experts or particular principles and policy stances. These are more intriguing and perhaps more difficult to deal with than simple financial incentives. First, it is likely the case that nonmonetary inducements to bias are more pervasive than are financial ones; second, it may be harder to detect bias associated with prior ideological commitments. Pigou and Coase agreed that the temptation to bias is especially prevalent in the giving of expert advice in public service. As these temptations concern the collective action of experts, there may be a role for reciprocity that is not captured in financial "conflict of interest" statements.

We emphasize in conclusion that our proposal is *not* that experts should remain neutral with respect to their own interests – something obviously

---

[10] In the context of a close examination of the methodology of economics, Mark Blaug (1980) concluded that economists' empirical research "is like playing tennis with the net down: instead of attempting to refute testable predictions, modern economists all too fre-quently are satisfied to demonstrate that the real world conforms to their predictions..." (p. 256).

impossible to attain – but, rather, that they render more fully transparent monetary and nonmonetary inducements to select evidence and estimation techniques. We live in a world of the second-best: since neutrality over results and full overlay of private and public interests will be impossible to attain, our proposed solution is more fully to disclose inducements to nonneutrality. Such a proposal allows the public to rely on experts with their eyes wide open, to know more about potential monetary and nonmonetary sources of bias associated with specific experts and expert recommendations. Although the temptations to bias may remain, knowing about them then allows consumers to act with awareness. In the next chapters, we shall offer a second proposal, an institutional reform that would more fully align the expert's interests with those of the public.

We return finally to the question of whether there is any way that a code of ethics might avoid the moral licensing problem associated with conflict of interest statements (Cain et al. 2005). The results in Cain et al. seem to be an instance of taking group goals to be exogenous. Indeed, the authors specify the underlying ethical issue as the possibility of the expert's self-enrichment at the client's expense. In that case, the danger of a conflict of interest statement is that if the experts need to detail potential corruption, and implicitly cast aspersions on their character, they might as well earn the aspersions. Although we do not deny that there are financial incentives to bias, we suggest that there is an additional underlying ethical issue – namely, the joint empowerment of clients and experts at the expense of others in society. Enrichment may, of course, follow but perhaps not.

The next two chapters take up the issue of such expert-client pairings. We suggest that ideological or sympathetic commonality distinguishes expert-client pairings, and such mutual interests are the cement of the pairing. Such mutuality might extend to other groups so that expert-client pairings are not the only group to consider. There is, most obviously, also the group of experts. Experts are connected by bonds of admiration and status and there is no reason to believe that they are unaware that the actions of some experts might have negative consequences for their community. In Chapter 10 we explore the problem of science and factional expertise. In Chapter 11, we offer a suggestion for agreed-upon procedures to follow regardless of the experts' affection for clients to come. These substantial institutional reforms take into account the endogeneity of group goals that we stressed in Part I earlier. Chapter 11 presents a model in which we can directly address the question of whether what we are calling a first-best solution (complete transparency) is in fact to be preferred to a second-best solution (a transparent nontransparency).

There is a larger issue. Knight, to whom we have deferred on many occasions, remarked (often) in a phrase attributed to the nineteenth-century American humorist, Josh Billings, that ignorance was not the problem as knowing so much that wasn't so. The larger lesson we draw is that the public must be aware of their ignorance. The most celebrated instance of asymmetric information, in which there is ignorance on one side of the market, is George Akerlof's model of the used-car market (Akerlof 1970). In such a case in which the nontransparency is known, defective cars are "lemons." But the public is aware of the nontransparency; since they know that they are unable easily to distinguish a lemon from a good used car, and sellers know that they are aware, warranties and other partial prudential solutions have evolved in the market. With a greater awareness of the economics of expertise, similar partial solutions will emerge over time.

## 10

# Mitigating the Consequences of Factional Expertise

There are no significant motives for attempting to obscure or conceal the truth in the natural sciences, while the social fields abound with such motives.

Gordon Tullock (2005, p. 158)

## 10.1 Introduction

At the beginning of the book, we set forth a central thesis, that all inquiry is motivated by desires common to all of us. When we touched on the problem of replicating published research, we presented one plausible explanation for this failure, that private incentives are not compatible with careful work. In this chapter we turn to another explanation. Chapter 9 closed with the observation that experts may align themselves with other experts in factions, and this forms our starting point in what follows. As we have throughout the book, we distinguish between the public goals of experts and their private goals. The private goals we take to be endogenous to a faction, and we continue to stress the dangers of neglecting these.

The chapter starts by considering a contribution of the economics of science by one of the founders of public choice, Gordon Tullock. Tullock's 1966 *Organization of Inquiry* is important to our purposes because he asks the question "Is economics a science?" and gives the answer "no" because the institutional structure of economics allows private goals to flourish in a way that a science does not. In economics, concealment is easier than in a science. Our argument will be that the great danger from faction occurs when this concealment is itself concealed. If the public is aware that expertise is divided, they can do something about it.

The larger context of Tullock's book is his long association with Karl Popper.[1] Popper famously laid out a vision of science in which the only goal is a desire for the truth (Popper 1974). This is expressed in his falsification principle. If a theory $T$ implies $x$ and we observed that $x$ is false, then $T$ is false. One motivated only by the goal of truth would reject $T$. We suppose everyone desires the truth; a public goal that we take as exogenous. Factions, however, have other goals, so a faction member might not reject $T$ preferring to direct attention somewhere else. In this context, the great challenge to Popper's view was, as he said, Thomas Kuhn's view that all science is factional, and the desire for truth is local to what Kuhn called a paradigm (Kuhn 1962; Popper 1970).

Suppose that Tullock is correct that the factional nature of economics depends on concealment. Is this concealment known? We have pointed to instances in our previous chapters in which attempts have been made to conceal this division. Because Nutter was perceived as "biased," an important economist dismissed in his textbook Warren Nutter's research that found the Soviet Union's economy was not a threat to overtake the American economy. The division among rating agencies discussed in Chapter 8 was concealed by the FDIC/NBER researchers as part of the contract with the agencies for agreeing to participate in the study.

Supposing we are aware of this concealment, what can we do about it? Frank Knight famously asserted that ignorance of an underlying distribution creates uncertainty. If factional expertise leads to concealed estimation procedures, then we can expect to be ignorant of the sampling distribution that results. Nonetheless, if we know that expert opinions differ significantly, one is led to ask what one can do about it. Our reading of Gilbert Harold's 1938 book on the use of ratings for investment purposes suggests that some expert-client pairs formed factions to take advantage of the larger public. We described in Chapter 8 two plausible solutions to this problem that prevailed early on, and we noted how such precautions eventually fell out of practice. In our final section of the chapter, we offer a simulation of Harold's solution and the NBER/ FDIC solutions as a way to illustrate the problem and some possible solutions to it.

---

[1]   In a letter to Popper of July 9, 1958 in which Tullock tells about his forthcoming fellowship at the University of Virginia, he expressed a hope to come to London to work on a book with the title *Organization of Inquiry*. This suggests a deeper and longer connection than what he later remembered (Tullock 2005, p. 1). Indeed, Jeremy Shearmur states that Tullock was present at Popper's lectures given at Emory University in 1956 for the Volker Fund. What Shearmur sees as "Republican" in his unpublished reconstruction of Popper's Emory lectures might feed into Tullock's view of the critical role of institutions.

## 10.2 Gordon Tullock and the "Racket"

In his 1966 *Organization of Inquiry* Gordon Tullock points to the incentives confronting economists relative to those of other disciplines. Since those incentives differ substantially in economics, where trades can happen (economic researchers are paid for their advice), and other disciplines, Tullock claims that economics is unscientific. Indeed, he calls economics a "racket."

So, Tullock invites us to consider economists' expressed views on tariffs. It has been long established, he argues, that free trade maximizes majority well-being. But, there will be a minority of the population who would be harmed by a removal of the tariff; they have an interest in hiring an economist to press their case:

The group which suffers concentrated injury, however, is likely to try to convince the majority that really they gain nothing and to hire economists for this purpose. Since there are always some such groups, there will always be economists who have been hired for this purpose. (Tullock 2005, p. 158)

Why does the majority of economists, whose reputation is surely harmed by such activity, put up with this racket?

Not all the advocates of tariffs, of course, are hired by "the interests." But the existence of people whose living does depend on finding arguments for tariffs and the further existence of another group who thinks that maybe, sometime in the future, they might need the assistance of either someone who believes in tariffs or an economist who is in this *racket* makes it possible for them to continue to publish, even in quite respectable journals. Thus a dispute which intellectually was settled over a century against still continues. (Tullock 2005, p. 158)

For Tullock, the real difference between the social sciences and the natural sciences, then, is a difference in motivation that results in greater non-transparency among economists: "… there are no significant motives for attempting to obscure or conceal the truth in the natural sciences, while the social fields abound with such motives." (2005, p. 158)[2]

Tullock's argument here is in the tradition of analytical egalitarianism that we have championed for the past decade. As we have explained earlier, analytical egalitarianism is our description of the Smithian insight that people are all essentially the same and it is luck, incentives, and history – notably the division of labor – that explains observed differences in outcomes: all type

---

[2] Since our interest is primarily in economic expertise, we leave aside the potentially fascinating question of whether trades occur in other disciplines so that Tullock's clean division between economics and science might need to be revisited.

differences are endogenous.[3] An operational version of analytical egalitarianism, a generalization of motivational homogeneity, specifies that the motivational assumptions employed inside economic models should be applied to the modelers themselves.[4] Motivational homogeneity was taken up by Tullock and James Buchanan in *Calculus of Consent*. There they held that (whether in the private or public sphere) people are motivationally the same, motivated by a messy combination of self- and other-regarding concerns. Most significantly for that project, they presumed that public officials are not a collection of beneficent overseers with all of our best interests at heart.

Tullock then extended that public choice insight of motivational homogeneity in the *Organization of Inquiry* to include *economists*. That addition, startling as it now seems, went almost unnoticed at the time; it has been resisted since. Perhaps the explanation for the neglect is that analytical egalitarian arguments often pass unnoticed in a world in which analytical hierarchy is common. Perhaps Tullock's insight was neglected because the argument applied to us. It is one thing to argue that public officials may potentially lack virtue and quite another to suggest that economists might be ethically challenged. Whatever the reason, as far as we can tell, Tullock's incentive-based characterization of economics as something other than a science has had no impact in the literature in the economics of science (Hands 1994; Wible 1998; Mäki 1999; Caldwell 2008; Diamond 2008). We would like to correct that neglect now.

It is interesting that on the matter of the motivation of economists, Tullock is a good deal more Hobbesian than is Buchanan in that Tullock is

[3] See Smith 1904, I.ii.4: "The difference of natural talents in different men is, in reality, much less than we are aware of; and the very different genius which appears to distinguish men of different professions, when grown up to maturity, is not upon many occasions so much the cause, as the effect of the division of labour. The difference between the most dissimilar characters, between a philosopher and a common street porter, for example, seems to arise not so much from nature, as from habit, custom, and education. When they came into the world, and for the first six or eight years of their existence, they were perhaps, very much alike, and neither their parents nor playfellows could perceive any remarkable difference. About that age, or soon after, they come to be employed in very different occupations. The difference of talents comes then to be taken notice of, and widens by degrees, till at last the vanity of the philosopher is willing to acknowledge scarce any resemblance. But without the disposition to truck, barter, and exchange, every man must have procured to himself every necessary and conveniency of life which he wanted. All must have had the same duties to perform, and the same work to do, and there could have been no such difference of employment as could alone give occasion to any great difference of talents."

[4] Peart and Levy (2005) demonstrate that analytical egalitarianism was overthrown late in the nineteenth century as notions of hierarchy and racial difference infected political economy. Analytical egalitarianism was revived in the 1950s at Chicago, the London School of Economics, and among the Austrians.

willing to bring economists inside the world of private motivation. Tullock worked in an old tradition in which there is no difference between passing bad money and passing bad arguments. Buchanan would agree to the equivalence, but he seems to have been more resistant than Tullock to the presumption that economists might pass off bad arguments. He might, however, have been coming around to Tullock's (and Peart and Levy's) view on this, in part as a result of his sharp unhappiness with the role of economists in the recent financial crisis (Buchanan 2010, 2011, 2012).

Hobbes's argument that one's ideas are an expression of one's interests worried many later thinkers. Smith in the eighteenth century and Richard Whately in the nineteenth century thought a great deal about how one might protect the public from being exploited with bad arguments (Levy and Peart 2007, 2010). If we are unaware of this tradition, we tend to overlook parts of Tullock's argument.

Tullock next asks why taxpayers might reasonably trust scientists, as opposed to economists, with resources on rather vague plans. His answer is that other scientists provide a great deal of social control over these scientists, thereby checking each result. The note he adds clarifies that he presumes good auditing procedures are in place: "Subject, of course, to the usual auditing procedures. Presumably there are as many potential embezzlers among ten thousand scientists as among ten thousand bankers" (Tullock 2005, p. 6). This explains trust with money. How about trust with ideas? Tullock sees an equivalent of auditing at work in that dimension as well:

> To repeat, scientists are not much better than other men, and there certainly are at least a few among them who would fake experiments if there was something to be gained there from. The … researcher has something to gain if he can get away with such a fraud. His income depends largely on the reputation he can develop, and this, in turn, depends on his "discoveries." It is obviously easier to produce an important and exciting article if one simply invents the facts reported than if one is confined to reality. This being so, the prevention of fraud depends on a detection apparatus. Part of the detection apparatus involves repetition. (2005, p. 124)

Tullock considers economics, as we have seen, to be a discipline in which the possibility of concealment is greater than in what he calls science. Suppose that Tullock is correct and differential auditing possibilities exist. What does this do to Michael Polanyi's argument (Polanyi 1962) that scientific opinion is uniform, an argument that assumes away "scientific faction" and other manifestations of endogenous goals? How are beliefs corrected in science? If there is a divergence in beliefs about how a problem is to be solved, then someone who sees the published incorrect answer can publish a correction. Transparency motivated by various sorts of rewards connects beliefs. Transparency allows the problem solutions to be compared. Polanyi appealed to an overlapping neighborhood of competence by which all problems in science are connected.[5]

All Polanyi needs is transparency.[6] When Tullock rehearses Polanyi's argument he *silently* provides the missing step of transparency and thus fails to impress his cleverness on the reader. To make the overlapping competence argument work, there must be data audits, results must be checked. Tullock says this over and over again. As Tullock sees it, economics allows concealment. Therefore, economics allows factions, it is not science, and it fails to possess Polanyi's efficiency properties.

One way to conceptualize this is to divide the world into gradations of expertise. A "secondary expert"– whose expertise does not quite match that of the primary or "research expert"– has interests that extend to the problems the primary expert is studying. Secondary-experts, for instance, might be those who read the experts' testimony or scientific papers with an educated eye, but who do not publish original research on the topic themselves. These are Polanyi's scientists who are not in the overlapping area of competence. We demonstrated in Chapter 5 that eugenics influenced economics in part because the economists in this domain – secondary experts such as Pigou – were convinced by the biologists. We noticed in Chapter 1 the seeming oddity of a television personality being the intellectual force in the recent antivaccination movement. Of course, she did not have the ability to publish on vaccination and autism in the *Lancet*, but she did discuss the findings. This is the account of science offered by Polanyi without Tullock's nonconcealment condition being satisfied.

## 10.3  Karl Popper on Scientific Faction

Polanyi's powerful argument for the uniformity of scientific opinion depends, as we have seen, on the supposition that every scientific argument can be checked by someone in a neighboring discipline and, therefore, a chain of checking is established which induces unanimity. This process would purge a science of private goals. It remains unclear whether this is a global or a local claim, whether unanimity spreads across the discipline or remains localized to a subgroup. Tullock's data auditing and replication requirement would make this overlapping checking a viable *global*

---

[5]  This is Mountifort Longfield's 1834 argument that established the equality of net advantages to employment in a competitive labor market without the requirement supposed by Smith for mobility. Longfield (1931).

[6]  The details are provided in Levy and Peart (2012).

argument. But suppose the data are not available for audit. Suppose there are four scientists, A, B, C, and D. A and B check each other, B and C check each other; but C checks A. The required data are shared among them. D is out of the loop and cannot check anyone, not because D is incompetent but D does not obtain the data. A, B, C form a noncompeting group of the sort that Polanyi's argument tried to deny.

Tullock writes that his *Organization of Inquiry* was inspired by the work of Karl Popper. Popper's work is often criticized for ignoring the role of factions, something that Kuhn famously described as "paradigms" (Kuhn 1962). When, in 1967, Popper wrote to Tullock expressing great delight at the receipt of a copy of *Organization of Inquiry* he told Tullock that he knew all about the sort of factionalized expertise that Tullock described.[7]

> Fallowfield, Manor Road,
> Penn, Buckinghamshire,
> England
> March 6th 1967

My dear Gordon,

What a marvelous surprise! Your book is really a charming, sane, and very excellent piece of work. I am happy that I am involved in it.

As to p vii, The Duke University is clearly solely responsible for calling my book on p. 48 <u>The Logic of Scientific Discovery</u> (right) but on p. 65 ... of <u>Scientific Inquiry</u> (wrong). What a Press! Incidentally, you praise Harold J. Katz, but in my <u>L. Sc. D</u> there is, so far as I know, a still more "strict" proof (in fact, several proofs). Incidentally, do you not know my <u>Conjectures and Refutations</u>? (Basic Books*). Tell me if you have not got them, and I shall ask Basic Books to send you a copy. It is, I think, the most readable of my books.

But as to your chapters VI, and VIII. Do you know that I know a very good theoretical physicist who has published many papers in highly reputed journals but cannot get the official quantum theorists to listen to him? He has developed a new non-linear relativistic field theory of particle interaction, and he has written a book on it, but cannot get the book published.

Do you ever come to England? I have been quite often in the U.S. but mainly in California; also in the Middle West and North-East.

Let me thank you again for the very enjoyable book.

> Yours, as ever,
> Karl (Popper)

---

\*   BB have also published <u>The Poverty of Historicism</u> which, if I remember well, you read in proofs; or did you only read the French Edn.

[7]   Tullock's book arrived after the Kuhn–Popper exchange in 1965 (Kuhn (1970); Popper (1970)). It thus remains an open question, whether Popper might have used the resources Tullock offered to make the case that the falsification principle, as well as other truth-seeking activities, depend on an institutional framework to make transparency incentive compatible.

## 10.4  Bringing Out the Best of Expertise

Tullock's overarching principle is that, to induce socially good results from purposive behavior, we need institutions to direct the purposes of individuals to the public good. In Chapter 8 we called attention to how the differential upward bias of the rating agencies seemed to be common knowledge when ratings entered regulation. We discussed two "plausible" – that is our conjecture since the underlying data have been lost! – statistical procedures to remove the bias from the ratings. The first, Harold's pessimistic estimator, was something that any aware investor might employ. The second, the NBER downward-rounded median, had the force of law. We argued that the FDIC/NBER agreement to conceal differences among the rating agencies led to the belief that any rating was as good as any other. And that led to rating shopping.

The question is how to bring out the best in expertise. If Tullock is correct about how the private incentives to bias occur within factionalized groups, we conclude that some experts may be more biased than others. One answer to the inclination to bias might be to use the least biased estimate. The discussion in Chapter 8, however, showed that Harold, suspecting bias, developed a different prudential estimate. As we showed there, he used the minimum of four estimates that he believed were biased upward. Harold did not discard any of the agencies perhaps because there was sufficient unpredictability in bias. Chapter 8 also showed that the economists and statisticians at the FDIC/NBER, who also suspected an upward bias in the ratings but were precluded from discussing the specifics of the data, adopted a variation on Harold's procedure, using the second lowest of the estimates. In that example, we, therefore, have two sets of estimates that mitigate against bias.

Thus, we have two examples of how we might try to get the best out of the experts, knowing that the expert raters have private incentives to bias. There are multiple ways to address Tullock's insight about the problem of factionalized expertise and bias. The question we address next is, Which performs better? Supposing we know that experts have incentives to bias and we have several means by which to mitigate against those incentives, which is the better way to do so? Put differently, supposing all estimates are biased, which one should we use?

Without either the NBER or the Harold data, how might we compare the properties of their estimates? To do so we construct below a model of estimation shopping in which four experts draw samples from a symmetrical heavy-tailed distribution and they compute sensible estimates of location. We could, of course, allow them each to propose their own favorite estimator, for example, one from the Princeton Robustness Study (Andrews et al. 1972), but for simplicity, suppose that each computes the sample median and then waits for reactions. All other things being equal, the estimates of the four will be the same. Suppose that, if the client asks nicely, the agency expert will also compute the sample mean and report as its estimate the higher of the two estimates, the sample median or mean. This of course does not guarantee that the agency judgment will be changed.

Suppose the agencies differ about how sympathetic they are with the client, that is, how frequently each will pick the maximum of the two estimates. Rater 1 will pick the maximum 50 percent of the time, Rater 2 will do so 30 percent of the time, whereas Raters 3 and 4 will do so only 15 percent of the time. Since Raters 3 and 4 follow the same rule, we can check the computations. Using Harold's data it was easy to distinguish the distribution of Fitch's and Moody's from Standard's. It was not so easy to distinguish Standard's from Poor's. This percentage is then the frequency with which the larger of the sample median or mean is reported.[8]

Consider how one might make reasonable adjustments if one were aware of the incentives to bias the ratings upward. We create a million realizations of four ratings and the Harold minimum with sample size 100 and then examine the sampling distribution. What is interesting is the skew of the four agencies that Harold reports and the de-skewing that the minimum produces. Using his procedure with our generating process we find the bias in the individual ratings is removed by the use of the minimum. Since the experiment supposes that the true underlying parameter is 0, the bias is simply the sample mean.

| Rating | Bias | Standard Deviation |
|--------|-------|--------------------|
| R1 | 0.058 | 0.19 |
| R2 | 0.035 | 0.18 |
| R3 | 0.018 | 0.16 |
| R4 | 0.018 | 0.16 |

[8] We used Shazam 11.1 (Whistler, White, Bates and Golding 2015) for the computations. The underlying distribution is a mixture of two normals, the celebrated Tukey distribution, a standard normal with probability 90% and a normal with mean 0 and standard deviation 10 with probability 10%. Each sample is size 100. We performed a million replications, which gives sufficient precision that the values of R3 and R4 are the same to three decimal places. The graphs seem to us sufficient, but the output as well as the code to generate the graphs are available upon request.

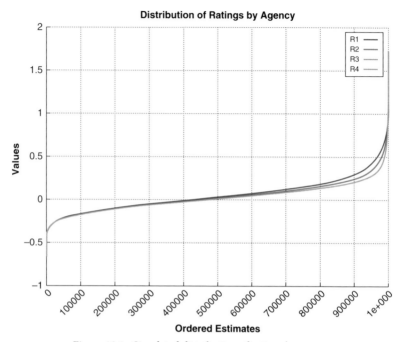

Figure 10.1. Simulated distribution of ratings by agency.

Figure 10.1 plots all four ratings. R3 and R4, as we designed the experiment, have the same distribution.

The question is whether we can do better than simply using R4, the least biased agency. The simulation next tells us that we can reduce both bias and standard error relative to using R1 by either of the procedures developed to deal with the biased ratings. RMin is our simulation of Harold's estimator; NBER is our simulation of the FDIC/NBER estimator, the second smallest value of the four estimates. Our simulation did not take into account the subtle integer characterization of the ratings.

| Rating Composite | Bias | Standard Error |
|---|---|---|
| R4 | 0.018 | 0.16 |
| RMin | 0.001 | 0.14 |
| NBER | 0.006 | 0.15 |

In Figure 10.2, we plot the most biased rating (R1) and both Harold's RMin and the "NBER" estimator. Clearly both Harold's and the NBER estimate perform better than the most biased rating (R1) at the tail of the distribution. The difference suggests how interesting it would be to have the real data to work with.

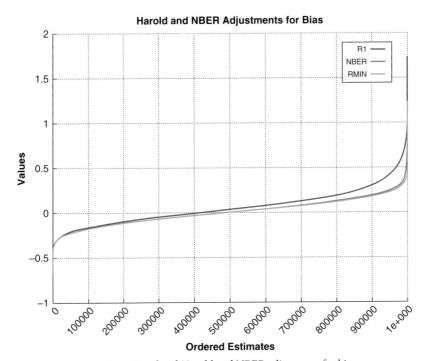

Figure 10.2. Simulated Harold and NBER adjustment for bias.

Finally, we consider the consequences of the "rating shopping" had the underlying agency ratings not changed. The "rating shopping" estimate (Figure 10.3) would be the maximum of the four. That would be an entirely implausible specification to apply to the procedures that contributed to the 2007 crisis. We have no doubt that the least biased agencies would lose business, but for our purposes, the simulation suggests the consequences of an inability to distinguish the agencies.

## 10.5  Conclusion

Tullock's challenge to the scientific status of economics depends on his claim that economics allows concealment. Although Tullock's own contribution seems to have been forgotten, the problem he pointed to has not gone away. We can point to recent developments that offer hope for improvement. In particular there is now a "replication network"[9] devoted solely to replication issues in economics. Of course, to be fair to our fellow economists,

---

[9]  http://replicationnetwork.com/

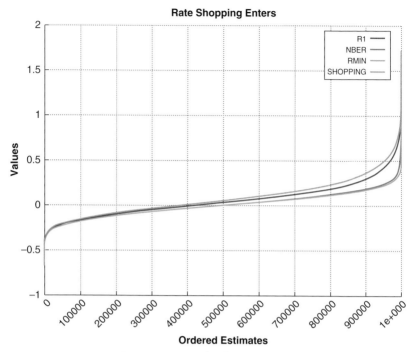

Figure 10.3. Simulated rate shopping.

there is the wide-ranging "Retraction watch" which covers the whole of scientific literature.[10]

Our major point in this chapter is that simple knowledge of the problem of data concealment helps. Neither Harold nor the NBER economic statisticians revealed any insight into how the rating agencies actually produced their estimates. Indeed, one suspects that the agreement between the agencies and the FDIC/NBER was precisely to preclude that sort of transparency! Yet noticing a difference among the agencies suggested a differential upward bias especially once we realize, as Harold informed his readers, that security dealers were able to complain to the rating agencies.

Knowledge of factional expertise opens the door for prudent procedures. This is a general property of nontransparent situations, which are themselves transparent. In Chapter 9 we made a distinction between the first-best case of complete transparency and the second-best case of a transparent

[10] http://retractionwatch.com/. As noted in footnote 2, it is also possible that other sciences are closer to economics than Tullock allows.

nontransparency. Here, we allowed that the incentive to bias varies with sympathetic connections among experts and clients, and we compared the properties of different rules to deal with bias. In Chapter 11 we shall ask in the context of a model of democratic decision making with expert advice whether moving from a transparent nontransparency to a full transparency makes any difference.

# 11

# Inducing Greater Transparency

In the case of economics, where the tradition of replicating previous academic studies is weaker than in the natural sciences, a study conducted for purposes of litigation is likely to receive more intense scrutiny than an academic study, even one published in a refereed journal.

Richard Posner (1999b, p. 94)

## 11.1 Introduction

The chapters in Part V bring together several themes we have developed with respect to the larger question of the role of experts and governance. We have argued that experts are motivated by private as well as public incentives, and we have explored the possibility that experts might form particularly strong sympathetic bonds within groups. In Chapter 10, the grouping we considered was within the community of experts. Here, we consider another group that forms as a result of sympathetic connections between the expert and the client(s). If experts and clients have common interests that do not fully overlap with those of the public, then the resulting expertise may be biased in favor of the client-expert small group at the expense of society writ large. In such situations, motivated nontransparencies may persist. What to do? Chapter 9 considered a substantial code of professional ethics to be created in full awareness of such expert–client pairings. To the extent that the code has motivational force, we encounter the endogeneity of group goals we have discussed previously. Chapter 10 explored an institutional framework in which such motivated nontransparency in estimation is itself transparent. Here, we consider an institutional framework, the American legal system, in which motivated nontransparency occurs and we propose a reform through which ethical behavior might be made incentive compatible.

Before we proceed with our analysis of bias, we need to be more precise about some terminology we took for granted earlier, the bias of an estimator. Intuitively, this is the average difference between the estimate and the true parameter of interest. Statisticians generally think of bias as a bad thing although, of course, it is important for our purposes to keep in mind that bias might be useful to someone who wants a particular outcome. Textbook discussions of these issues also focus on a measure of the precision of an estimate, the average squared deviation between the estimate and the true parameter of interest. Then, the higher the average squared deviation, the less we are being informed by the estimation procedure. That is not a good thing; indeed, it is something that statistical theory is at pains to minimize. What makes this appealing is the simple fact that the sign is removed by squaring the deviations so any interest in a high or a low estimate is washed out. By contrast, the bias has a sign.

In the case of expert witnesses when monetary damages are involved, a statistician has an interest in seeing things as the client would like them. But the danger of focusing exclusively on monetary incentives is that this neglects nonmonetary inducements to bias. It is true that monetary inducements are relatively easy to measure, but if ethicists neglect nonmonetary inducements, they will fail to find them. When we fill out conflict-of-interest statements, as we just did for a review in the *Journal of Economic Literature*, we are never asked who thanked us for writing an article. It may be that there is nothing to report – no one had an interest in the article in the first place! But since the question is never asked, potentially relevant information is not collected.[1] To help see nonmaterial motivation in what follows, we conduct the entire argument when "payment" occurs only in terms of approbation or approval.

One of the roles of statistical ethics, and perhaps the reason that it grew out of statistical consulting, is to clarify to practitioners that there may be aspects of the data that a client may want practitioners to ignore. We discuss the situation in detail in Section 11.2, but here we present a portion of the predicted internal dialogue of the young statistician who has come to an unhappy realization:

– This looks pretty much OK except for that oddity over there that the client doesn't really want to discuss. (Vardeman and Morris 2003, p. 23)

---

[1] As noted in Chapter 9, many conflict of interest policies emphasize disclosure of financial relationships; these may be significant improvements over nondisclosure, although the concerns laid out by Cain, Loewenstein, and Moore (2005) provide a cautionary note. Our goal in the following is to motivate a broader perspective in which we consider not only financial but also other motivations for cooperative behavior that may lead an investigator to choose a result that pleases the client.

We have used the phrase, *making the nontransparency itself transparent*, in other contexts. The dialogue just quoted is a marvelous instance of what we mean by the phrase! The question we ask in what follows is whether knowing there is something to worry about actually does some good. We suggest that if people know about a nontransparency, they can take steps to arm themselves against deferring too quickly to the expert.

In Chapter 8 we showed how both private and regulatory practice, in the period in which the nontransparency of the rating agencies was itself transparent, protected against such unguarded deference through a prudential use of competing sources of advice or estimates. Here, we consider the production of advice from the other side, from the perspective of the expert, and we demonstrate how in the absence of safeguards, ethical constraints or other transparency-inducing institutional arrangements, an expert may produce biased advice for the client. This result holds, we argue, even when the incentives to bias are *not* pecuniary, when the expert receives nothing more than approval from the client. Unlike the agency ratings that figured so prominently in Chapter 8, we suppose in what follows that we can obtain the underlying data and reproduce the estimate.

As we noted in Chapter 9, the American Economic Association [AEA] conflict of interest requirements ignore the nonpecuniary inducements for economists acting as experts to choose their results in the interest of their clients.[2] Widely discussed codes of ethics in statistical associations, such as those for the International Statistical Institute (1986) and the American Statistical Association (ASA 2000) describe such nonpecuniary issues associated with advising a client, but nothing like these has been adopted by economists or econometricians.

Why is this so? Perhaps because statistical ethics, in contrast to econometrics, arose in the process of a trading relationship, an explicit exchange referred to as "statistical consulting," in which the statistician trades expertise with a "client" for some other good thing, be it material income or coauthorship on a research project. Within the exchange setting, an explicit code of statistical ethics clarifies what is, and what is not, part of the bargain. Hence, the ASA's "Ethical Guidelines" contains sections on the statistician's "responsibilities" to "Funders, Clients, and Employers"; "Research Subjects"; and "Other Statisticians or Statistical Practitioners" (American Statistical Association 2000, pp. 6–9).

---

[2]   https://www.aeaweb.org/journals/policies/disclosure-policy.

In the next section, we review the historical record of statistical ethics, including its focus on the relationship between the expert and client and the serious attention given to nonpecuniary considerations. Next, we explore the implications of a model of sympathetic advice in which the expert advisor is explicitly connected to the client as well as the larger community of experts. This allows us to see how the client-expert relationship affects the expert's willingness to trade bias for efficiency. We then proceed to a simulation of the bias-efficiency trade-off faced by an expert.

## 11.2  Clients and Experts: The Statisticians' View

For statisticians, "client" is a general term. We quote from the formative discussion by Edward Deming:

The word client will denote the man or group of people who will use the results of the study. Or, the same word may denote an expert or group of experts in substantive fields … who are responsible to the man who will pay the bill for the study. (Deming 1965, pp. 1883–84)

Exchanges for money are no different than exchanges for coauthorship:

The same principles apply also to the statistician who works as a member of a research team. (Deming 1965, p. 1884)

In the discussion that led up to the creation of the 2000 ASA Code of Professional Ethics, John Gardiner described Edward Deming's practice from the viewpoint of a statistical consultant. In Gardiner's retelling, Deming was careful to stress what is *not* up for trade, and he was clear that expectations regarding the client-expert relationship and the expert's output should be clarified at the front end:

Statisticians proudly claim 'Ed' Deming as one of our heroes. He helped revolutionize industrial quality and productivity. He was also a stickler for the ethical practice of statistics. Among items featured in his personal code of conduct, which are not found in other statistical ethics sources:
Devote oneself to the statistics profession alone.
Set ethical rules with the client up front.
Limit own role as statistician only to those functions supported by statistical theory.
Draw conclusions only about the frame, not the population.
Retain exclusive publication control over statistical matter one reports.
Assure reports clearly state who did what in conducting the study and document all meaningful possible sources of error.

Prepare own expert testimony. (Lawyer can help clarify, but not originate, positions.)

Reserve right to break off an engagement without explanation. Do so if a client or colleague (on a joint study) does unacceptable work.

Retain all rights to statistical theory developed on an assignment to share them with the profession. (Gardiner 1996)

Deming himself clarified that the statistical consultant qua professional statistician was to have no interest in the substantive questions (the model) that interested his employer (Deming 1965). However, in an important article in *American Statistician*, Stephen Vardeman and Max Morris suggest that the "human element" in statistics arises from the fact that, all too often, the client has preferences over outcomes and the expert is emotionally attached to the client. This is the article we briefly quoted in section 11.1. It offers the following advice to the statistician whose client seeks a particular result:

If your assignment is to help with statistical consulting, you are already wrestling (at a "trainee" level) with some of the serious issues faced by one segment of our profession. Carefully consider and handle these now, as you begin to see how the "human element" of statistical consulting requires thoughtful and principled discipline. You're going to have to argue with yourself in conversations like:

What looks to me like the thing that should be done would take two hours to explain and several more hours of my time to implement, while this client would be happy with something less appropriate that I could explain in five minutes.

– This client really wants "A" to be true, but these data look inconclusive…

– This looks pretty much OK except for that oddity over there that the client doesn't really want to discuss. (Vardeman and Morris 2003, p. 23)

Supposing we know that things might not be what they seem to be, is there any way we can attenuate the temptation to bias that arises from such sympathetic connections between the statistician and the client?

## 11.3  A Model of Sympathetic Expertise

Consistent with the framework outlined in Chapter 1 we suppose in what follows that the expert has the same motivations as other people. Thus, we extend the insight of public choice economics – that policy makers are neither more nor less self-interested than the rest of us – to the modeling of expert advice giving, and we presume that experts are self-interested agents. Experts are separated from others by specialization and the division of labor (by expertise), as opposed to their innate character.

A common, and to our minds an unfair,[3] criticism of both classical and modern economics is that it depends on an unrealistic assumption that agents maximize material income. The context of this criticism is often the observation that people are altruistic, that they share with others for no apparent reason.[4] Economists have addressed such criticisms by developing a model in which a person obtains satisfaction not only from his or her own consumption but also from the consumption of others.[5] In our view, this newer approach has moved contemporary economics closer to its origins, and we see this as a good thing. People are connected to each other and, as Adam Smith wrote in 1759, the happiness of others matters to them. To model this more formally, economists have specified that one person's happiness depends on what he or she consumes *and* what others are able to consume.

This approach provides a powerful explanation for generous behavior. But we shall take a different approach here. Because, although Smith taught that the happiness (or, as an approximation, consumption) of others influences our happiness, he also wrote extensively about how our happiness is influenced by approbation or praise. Smith's insight is that people within various groups form sympathetic connections. Applied to experts and clients, this suggests that experts who are sympathetically connected to their clients may well be motivated to try to obtain praise or approval from the client. In what follows we develop a model that examines the implications of this approach.

Thus, following Smith, we augment the treatment of motivation that focuses exclusively on material motivation to include a second dimension, approval, or approbation. We, therefore, presume that experts are motivated by desires for material goods and for approval. What distinguishes the expert from other people is thus only the method (e.g., giving advice, testifying, advocating for policy) by which he or she satisfies these desires.

Although we recognize that there may be monetary gains to offering biased expertise, this is not our primary interest. Our contention is that

---

[3]   For examples of recent responses to this criticism, see notes 4 and 5. The criticism entirely neglects the significance of Adam Smith's idea of sympathy. That idea, once neglected by neoclassical economists, has been increasingly incorporated into experimental economics. See V. Smith (1998).

[4]   See Sen (1977).

[5]   There is an extensive literature on these developments; see *The Handbook of the Economics of Giving, Altruism, and Reciprocity* (Kolm and Ythier 2006).

even if these codes of ethics are in place and strictly enforced, the temptation to produce biased results may remain.[6] We focus, instead, on the continuing temptation in what follows. To isolate the effect of conflicting sources of approbation, we suppose that material income is invariant across all decisions.

To consider how approbation is produced, suppose that the expert belongs to several groups, each of which provides approbation. First, an expert is part of a community of experts – in this case a group of statisticians who are concerned with bias to the extent that it affects efficiency. Second, experts obtain approval from their clients and the client cares about bias in a particular direction. Thus, we have an expert and a client and they exchange. If material income is invariant to all decisions, they exchange approbation. The parameter values in the approbation production function may embody norms that are articulated in the two groups to which the agents belong.

The intuition behind our thinking should now be clear. The key to our formulation is that it does not focus on money payments but rather on sources of approval. When consultants or experts work with a client, they obtain satisfaction from the client's approval. So, experts are motivated by a desire to please their clients.

To develop this idea more formally, suppose the expert statistician is in group 1 and the client is in group 2. The expert's role is to come up with an estimate, and the client cares about what the expert is estimating and may wish to obtain a particular result. If so, then the client will approve of a biased estimate. In addition, the client desires an estimate that is obtained without too much uncertainty or one that is efficient.

But an expert receives approvals from his or her colleagues, too, from the group of which he or she is a member, of statisticians or economists. Here, approbation comes from each of two characteristics of the estimate, which we call bias (B) and statistical efficiency (E). Statistical efficiency as a measure does three things at once. It takes into account two reasons for an estimator's expected deviation from the underlying (true) value – variance plus the square of the bias. Neither the variance nor the square of the bias has

---

[6]   We do not claim that sympathetic motivation is independent of material motivation; indeed, in a more complicated motivational model, both material and sympathetic motivation can strengthen with habituation of the learning by doing sort. Our experimental research on leadership, discussed in Chapter 2, examined the consequence of randomized leadership. Intuitively, if affection grows with repeated dealings, an implication of Smith's view, then randomized expertise might be a way to reduce sympathetic bias. Of course, this will be costly for obvious reasons.

sign; thus, there is no easy way to distinguish what the client wishes in this respect. Efficiency compares this estimator with the variance for these two reasons. As is typically the case, only one estimate is reported, so the same B and E will be known to the client and the expert's colleagues. By assuming that material income is invariant to the choices we examine, changes in utility follow from and only from changes in approbation.

Our interest is in how much approbation the expert receives under different circumstances when there are two sources of approval, the client and fellow experts, and two characteristics that yield approval (or not), bias and efficiency. Fellow experts typically do not approve of a biased estimate unless the bias brings with it an increase in efficiency, but clients may approve of a biased estimate as long as the bias is in their direction, regardless of what it does to the efficiency. Bias can be a private good for the client. Both fellow experts and clients approve of an efficient estimate.

We can now think more concretely about the production of approval, A. Suppose approbation for the expert in group 1 is produced as described here, in a log additive form for the expert, a relation that our fellow economists will understand at a glance[7]

$$A_1 = (B^{\alpha_1} E^{\beta_1})^{1-\sigma} (B^{\alpha_2} E^{\beta_2})^{\sigma}$$

As noted, the disciplinary norm holds that $\alpha_1 = 0$ (experts do not approve of fellow experts producing bias) and only statistical efficiency matters for the production of disciplinary approbation. But approbation from the client follows a different rule, so $\alpha_2$ differs from 0. We assume that $\beta_1$ and $\beta_2$ are both positive.

In this context, the critical parameter is $\sigma$, the parameter that reflects approbation resulting from bias. Clients want bias and experts disapprove of bias. Thus, there are conflicting sources of approbation to consider. If this is the case, then the client may not have to offer any material income to induce the expert to provide a biased estimate. This result holds even if we allow the statistical investigator to play what is known as a "dictator game" with the client (Camerer and Thaler 1995; Hoffman, McCabe, and Smith 1996),[8] in

---

[7] To make the notation less dense, the text assumes that the bias is either positive or zero. It is a fair criticism that we are replacing material output with approbation but we do so to emphasize that it violates analytical egalitarianism to assume that experts are tempted only by money.

[8] Deming's articulation of the consultant's practice is consistent with a dictator game. One hires Deming for a statistical problem. Deming provides an answer. Full stop. But Deming's formulation, unlike ours, proceeds on the assumption that the client and expert are not sympathetically connected. Sympathy has been revived to motivate the

which he or she selects the estimate unilaterally for both other experts and the client and that is all there is.[9]

More than this, the preceding formulation that relies on sympathy speaks to the dynamics of cooperation and bias-seeking.[10] Over a period of association, $\sigma$ might increase as the client and expert come to know each other well and increasingly sympathize with each other's causes. As such, one would predict that the more an expert and a client have worked together, the more powerful the motivation toward bias. This suggests that disclosure policies should require reporting not only on relationships at a point in time but also over time, a point to which we return in the conclusion.

Some of these claims may initially appear counterintuitive. Often we think that cooperation is good, and we try to reduce incentives for competitive behavior. Rightly so: there are many contexts in which cooperation among agents is beneficial for society; nonetheless, there are important contexts in which such cooperation is not beneficial to the larger group.[11] The preceding model provides one demonstration of such a case, when loyalty between the client and experts works to the detriment of the group of experts as a whole and society at large.

An example of this sort of situation, drawn from the very highly competitive world of academic admissions, has been in the news recently. In 2013 *Forbes* removed four schools from its rankings because the magazine discovered that the schools sent them biased information on admissions. Even without knowing the details of the situation, the conclusion to be drawn from this is that some members of the university team were induced to provide other members of the team with biased results. Approval was initially

robust experimental finding that people cooperate even in a one-shot game of the sort we implicitly suppose in the text and when there is no material interest to do so (Sally 1995, 2001).

[9] This, of course, does not rule out the possibility of repeated interactions between an expert and clients; our point here is that, even in the instance of a one-shot game, the expert may feel sufficiently connected to the client to favor the client over the larger group.

[10] As Smith used the term, affection is simply the result of habitual sympathy (Levy and Peart 2013a).

[11] The prisoner's dilemma game is a key situation in which economists and others have pointed to the adverse effects of competing against the rival and the benefits instead of cooperating with the rival. That simple application has spawned considerable research into how to overcome the dilemma and obtain more cooperation. For overviews, see Axelrod (1984), Rapoport (1987), and Dixit and Nalebuff (2008). But in the prisoner's dilemma the rivals are just that, rivals, capable of imposing an externality on the other player; whereas, in the situation we have laid out in the text, both parties benefit directly from cooperating.

forthcoming. But the result, once known, clearly yielded disapproval from the larger community of admissions personnel and from the public.[12]

What is at issue here is the traditional problem of faction, discussed in Chapter 10, in which it is presumed (correctly in our opinion) that a person is a member of many groups.[13] The assumption that a person is a member of only one group – society – has forced the answer that cooperation is always a good thing, a result that is challenged when we introduce nested groups.[14] Our formulation, although not complex, allows for several such groups: experts, clients, and the public.

Sympathy, which induces cooperation between the expert and the client, is at the heart of the difficulty associated with bias. To see this, consider the unconcerned, reclusive expert, one for whom $\sigma = 0$. Without sympathy between the client and researcher, the research obtains no approval from the client. Approbation is produced only as a result of the combination of B and E he or she produces and the expert has no interest in producing bias unless bias were to enhance efficiency. Since the profession does not approve of bias, $\alpha_1 = 0$ and the expert will choose an estimate that maximizes statistical efficiency. Such a reclusive agent is consistent with Deming's formulation, and this conceptualization of an expert who is not sympathetically connected to the client is the textbook standard for considering expertise in economic and econometric education. It is so much the norm that, in fact, we generally fail to discuss ethics when we teach econometrics or discuss consulting with our students. Hence it took a long time to develop even minimal standards of ethics in the economics profession and many economists were drawn to such considerations only in the wake of publicity that showed economists in a poor light following the financial crisis of 2008. Nonetheless, the experimental evidence is overwhelming that agents are *not* reclusive, that Smith and those who followed his thinking were correct, and $\sigma>0$. Our view is that we should now apply this insight to experts.

---

[12] The story is available at www.forbes.com/sites/abrambrown/2013/07/24/why-forbes-removed-4-schools-from-its-americas-best-colleges-rankings/

[13] Although economists in the eighteenth and nineteenth century thought deeply about how individuals relate to the various groups of which they are members, attention to this problem waned early in the twentieth century. It was revived as public choice economists began to examine interest groups and interest group politics and experimental economists began experimentally to explore group and individual behavior. See Grossman and Helpman (2002), and Bornstein and Yaniv (1998).

[14] One reason for the continued interest in Smith is precisely the attention he paid to the problem of faction (Levy and Peart 2009a).

## 11.4  Governance by Jury

The larger theme of the book is the role of experts in democratic governance. To make this more concrete, in sections 11.5 and 11.6 we examine a particular democratic institution, the American judicial system in which contending experts present their clients' case to a jury of randomly selected ordinary people who decide on a monetary award of damages. This occurrence, which seems routine, provides several insights into the role of experts in providing advice. First, we can take it for granted that the jury does not fully understand the competing models offered by experts. They do, however, understand that the experts are working for clients and that there is a good reason to expect experts on both sides to present biased estimates. Thus, the nontransparency of the experts' cases is itself transparent. Moreover, there is competition and there are rules that require narrowly defined replication.

We shall begin our examination of the problem of governance by reiterating some of the key points developed by Frank Knight and John Rawls in the middle of the twentieth century. As we noted in Chapter 3, Knight argued that democracy is "government by discussion," a phrase that as he acknowledged, aptly catches the difficulty of real democratic action.[15] How does a large group (society) actually engage in a discussion? A randomly selected jury might be the solution, but first it is important to make clear that the Knight–Rawls formulation supposes that discussion aims at discovering the correct answer rather than determining a compromise position to best satisfy different preferences. In such a situation, unanimity is unattainable so Knight and Rawls settle for people having fair discussion, and equal voices in the discussion. One major impediment to this goal that worried Knight and Rawls, as we saw in Chapter 9, is differential power in such discussions. Specifically, they feared that a growing inequality of income allowed some voices to be louder than others so that the discussion

---

[15] Knight (1951, p. 28): "Democratic action is *hard*. It means government by discussion, and the organization of discussion itself, as I said before, involves the main problems. Not much intercommunication is even theoretically possible. As the world is built, the cards are heavily stacked in favor of centralization. Even in one direction, communication is bad enough; among economists, for instance, the typical reply to a criticism is, 'but I didn't say that.' I myself have been made a bad example for views I supposed I was arguing against all through the years. As to inter-communication – even with two persons there is an insoluble problem of dividing the time for both between speaking and listening; and it is said to give rise sometimes to friction, even causing dissolution of the holy marriage bond. With larger numbers, the limitation increases rapidly … "

would be changed from an attempted discovery of the correct answer to satisfying the interests of the dominant group.

More than this, the so-called terms of discussion would change without the public even realizing that the differential in power was responsible for it. Such an insight, we suggest, has much in common with the very real concerns today about "crony capitalism." Any characterization of governance today in western democracies must recognize that the principle of equal weighting of votes has been corrupted by the distortion that results when money purchases influence. The reforms we put forward here and in Chapter 12 would, we suggest, do much to mitigate against these concerns. It would be quite difficult to purchase influence in the arrangement we propose in Section 11.6.

As we have noted, the American legal system seems an ideal case to consider such motivated estimation in a competitive context because, although the motivation for nontransparencies is all too obvious, the nontransparency of expert witnesses is itself transparent. Those who hire an expert know that the expert will serve their interests to the extent that they are able to do so within the bounds of the law, without committing fraud. Here, we ask whether an institutional reform akin to final-offer arbitration might make transparency incentive compatible. By this we mean that, in such a setting, the experts will find that transparency is their best course of action. More formally, the condition for incentive compatibility we employ is one that, loosely speaking, provides for large gains while making potential losses very small – that is, one of minimax loss.[16]

The intuition underscoring the rule we propose in section 11.6 is that we constrain experts to use existing data, and then we choose the estimate they put forward that results in the smallest bootstrap variance. This has the appealing characteristic that it constrains experts to use the actual, as opposed to a possible, distribution. It is in line with our strong support for aggregated experience as opposed to theory.[17] With this announced rule we

---

[16] The relationship between expected utility and minimax decision theory is subtle. L. J. Savage's contribution to the Princeton Robustness study, the estimator LJS, is a minimax estimator varying a theme due to Peter J. Huber (Andrews et al. 1972, p. 2C3). On Huber's original paper, see Savage (1972, p. 291): "An important nonpersonalistic advance in the central problem of statistical robustness." Independent development of minimax methods in robust statistics and robust macroeconomic theory is discussed by Stephen Stigler (Stigler 2010).

[17] We have elsewhere developed the idea that the proverbial wisdom of ordinary people can be viewed as a robust estimator. This can be viewed as an extension of Francis Galton's insight that we can view a majority-rule decision process as if it were the sample median (Peart and Levy 2005).

find transparency on the part of experts is prudent: it is in the self-interest of the experts to be transparent.

## 11.5  Is Transparency Incentive Compatible?

In the context we consider, contending clients hire expert econometricians to press their case before a jury. We suppose both that clients are motivated by a desire to report an estimation that maximizes their well being and they can find sympathetic experts whose preferences come to mirror their own. Here, a statistician $s$ chooses the estimator $b$ of a parameter and, as explained earlier, the statistician is motivated to choose an estimate that his or her client desires. We suppose that $s$'s understanding of the first moment of $b$ is $E(b)^s$. The estimate is *transparent* if, for an arbitrary reader $t$, $E(b)^s = E(b)^t \, \forall t$ and nontransparent when the equality fails. The definition can be generalized to an arbitrary moment. If moments do not exist, transparency is attained if both the writer and reader understand the failure of absolute convergence. As long as we have full transparency, an estimate can be biased without raising ethical questions.[18] So, for instance, a client may wish to obtain an optimistic report. Then, if an expert were to choose an optimistic estimator and the client knows that the estimate is optimistic, there would be no ethical problem of the sort that Cain et al. (2005) consider. The client is not being exploited. Although admittedly the client is being helped to produce the best result for the client, this is known by all. In Chapter 8 we encountered an example of this on the other side, when (initially, at least) all knew and accepted that the estimate of sound investments was a prudent, or pessimistic, estimate because individual ratings were biased upward.

Structural equation estimation is a natural test ground for thinking about nontransparency because the identifying restrictions flow from a possibly unobservable theoretical insight. It is not a coincidence that structural equation estimation is also fertile ground to study nontransparent estimation because for a long time conventions did not require the researcher to document the consequences of different selections of instrumental variables.[19]

---

[18]  In the discussions leading up to the American Statistical Association (2000), great care was taken to distinguish an estimate in which the bias is transparent, as defended by Bayesians, from an estimate in which the bias is not transparent.

[19]  One of the most promising developments in this regard is the model uncertainty literature associated with Steven Durlauf, for example Brock, Durlauf, and West (2007). In addition to helping motivate a turn toward specification robustness in theoretical macroeconomics, this also has the nice property of offering a citation to replicable work so that scholars now

To control the dimension of the problem, we assume that the underlying error distribution is known.

To make this more concrete, consider a demand and supply system (D&S) of the following structure:[20]

$$Quantity = \beta_1 + \beta_2\, Price + \beta_3\, Income + \eta \qquad (D)$$

$$Price = \alpha_1 + \alpha_2\, Quantity + \alpha_3 Cost + \alpha_4 Weather + a_5\, Politics + \varepsilon \qquad (S)$$

We suppose that the client has preferences over the estimated value of $\beta_2$. The researcher is required by convention to report only $D$, mentioning $S$ casually. In this example, we face a deep problem of how to distinguish a movement along a curve from a movement of the curve. Since it is so difficult to identify the difference, economists refer to this as the identification problem. When one teaches simultaneous equation estimation, it is common to draw a picture that shows the mess that results when a variable shifts both curves at the same time. We need variables that shift only one curve. Thus, the answer that has been offered, is to find a variable that shifts one curve but not the other. In textbook econometrics, in which the econometrician is assumed to be motivated only by the truth (efficient estimates), we proceed directly from the model specified to its estimation. Assuming there is no incentive to bias the results, the textbooks suggest that the coefficient of Cost, Weather, and Politics should be supposed to be 0 in the $D$ equation, and the coefficient of Income should be supposed to be 0 in the $S$ equation. Those are the requisite identifying restrictions. The resulting estimation technique, two-stage least squares, has nice properties when the errors come from a normal distribution.

But what about experts for whom bias is a private good? Seeking bias, one can choose whether to include one, two, or three exogenous variables from $S$. The reported estimate is the result of computing all possible combinations that identify a system and then choosing one. As we specified in section 11.3, we suppose that the client and the sympathetic expert want both bias and statistical efficiency. We measure the efficiency of estimator $i$ by the minimum mean square error (MSE*) of the estimates considered relative to the MSE of estimator $i$; thus, MSE*/MSE$_i$.

---

have an incentive to provide the data (Dewald, Thursby, and Anderson 1986). Previously, it was common knowledge that a positive replication was not publishable, which made data sharing not incentive compatible (Feigenbaum and Levy 1993). Durlauf tells us that, even so, it is distressingly difficult to pry data out of authors. We return to that concern in Chapter 12.

[20] The error terms are standard normal. The values of the $\alpha$ terms are 1; $\beta_1 = 10$; $\beta_2 = -1$; $\beta_3 = 3$.

We have created a case in which narrow and broad replication diverge. By changing identifying restrictions – the variables whose coefficients are supposed to be zero in either equation – we can bias the result in our preferred direction. If we are asked to provide the data, as we would be in a discovery context, we would likely *not* provide the variables that we had strategically omitted in the estimation.

A simulation is provided below to offer some idea of the ease with which biased estimates can be generated by such a selection procedure.[21] There are several technical details. First, what is the distribution of the exogenous variables? If they are omitted, they not only change the error distribution but also the degree of overidentification, which dramatically changes the property of two-stage least squares [2SLS] estimates (Phillips 1983). In the case considered, all exogenous variables are assumed to be a standard normal. Thus, omitting an exogenous variable in search of a biased outcome will not change the normality of the resulting errors. Had we allowed the exogenous variables to be nonnormal then we would violate the spirit of our assumption of a known (normal) distribution.

We consider two types of search. First, there is an unconstrained search for the maximum (minimum) value of the estimates of $\beta_2$. In the Tables 11.1 and 11.2, these are called "Max" and "Min." Second, there is a search that is constrained by the desire to have at least two exogenous variables in the supply curve. These are called "C Max" and "C Min." This will suggest how much the researcher might be willing to give up in terms of efficiency to get bias. 100,000 experiments for N=25, 100, 400, 1600 were performed in Shazam.

All the simultaneous estimates are replicable "two-stage least squares" estimates or as inefficient two-stage least squares although only 2SLS and OLS are transparent. The divergence between the reported estimate and the transparent 2SLS estimate can be thought of as transparency bias. Such bias persists through the case of N=1600.[22]

Although the bias declines in absolute value as N increases, the reduction in bias from increasing N by a factor of four can be held in check by moving from the C-max (C-min) to Max (Min). This suggests that the problem of convergence will depend on how the possible models increase as N

---

[21] The idea was suggested by Paul David at an Economics of Science meeting at Notre Dame in 1997.
[22] Experiments on a smaller scale had bias persisting through N=6,400. Using median expectation instead of mean expectation also generates bias.

Table 11.1. *Bias-seeking in simultaneous equations*

|  | N=25 | | N=100 | | N=400 | | N=1600 | |
|---|---|---|---|---|---|---|---|---|
|  | Bias | Efficiency | Bias | Efficiency | Bias | Efficiency | Bias | Efficiency |
| OLS | 0.40 | 0.35 | 0.40 | 0.08 | 0.40 | 0.02 | 0.40 | 0.02 |
| 2SLS | 0.03 | 1.00 | 0.01 | 1.00 | 0.00 | 1.00 | 0.00 | 1.00 |
| C Min | −0.21 | 0.27 | −0.09 | 0.48 | −0.04 | 0.54 | −0.02 | 0.54 |
| C Max | 0.17 | 0.58 | 0.08 | 0.66 | 0.04 | 0.63 | 0.02 | 0.63 |
| Min | −1.74 | 0.00 | −0.22 | 0.14 | −0.09 | 0.21 | −0.04 | 0.21 |
| Max | 1.87 | 0.00 | 0.16 | 0.32 | 0.08 | 0.30 | 0.04 | 0.30 |

Normal Exogenous Variables 100,000 Replications.

increases. The simulation considered only exogenous variables that were truly included in the structure.[23]

Taking into account the transparency of the nontransparent, but predictably biased, procedures employed by both sets of experts, the literature on the economics of expert witnesses has supposed that the jury decision will be made on the basis of an average of such biased estimates. This is the intuitively appealing idea of "splitting the difference" with an expectation that the resulting estimate will be less or even unbiased. The conclusion of Froeb and Kobayashi (1996) for the case of biased experts before a jury is that the average of their estimates will be unbiased. In this, they are followed by Judge Richard Posner who contends that this property of a competitive procedure makes the idea of a court-appointed expert witness unwarranted:

The use of a court-appointed expert is problematic when (for example, in the damages phase of the case) the expert witness's bottom line is a number. For then, in the case of opposing witnesses, the trier of fact can "split the difference," after weighting each witness's estimate by its plausibility. Posner (1999a, p. 1539)

Table 11.1 shows that, roughly speaking, the policy determined by the average of Min and Max or by the average of C-Min and C-Max will be unbiased. If the nontransparency is itself transparent, then there is something we can do about it. This confirms in a technical setting the argument

[23] We leave the problem of identifying the system by employing random numbers for future research. The problem of pseudo-identification raises theoretical questions that emerged at the dawn of simultaneous equation estimation and seems to have reappeared in a new guise. We benefited from conversations with Adolph Buse about weak-identification and with Arthur Goldberger about pseudo-identification.

Table 11.2. *The expert's dilemma*

| | 2SLS | | C-Min | | Min | |
|---|---|---|---|---|---|---|
| | Bias | Efficiency | Bias | Efficiency | Bias | Efficiency |
| 2SLS | 0.00 | 1.00 | −0.02 | 0.81 | −0.05 | 0.50 |
| C-Max | 0.02 | 0.88 | 0.00 | 0.97 | −0.03 | 0.73 |
| Max | 0.04 | 0.64 | 0.02 | 0.92 | −0.01 | 0.86 |

Normal Exogenous Variables, N=400; 250,000 Replications.

we have pressed in our case studies earlier: if we know about a nontranspar-ency, a rule may evolve to help us deal with it.

Can we do better than splitting the difference? Table 11.2 demonstrates that such a policy will have a higher variance than a policy determined by both using 2SLS. Thus, we create the familiar prisoner's dilemma in a statistical context. Although it is in the interest of each statistician consid-ered separately to engage in selective underreporting of results, it is in the interest of the statisticians considered as a group not to underreport. This is shown by the result that the diagonal elements, in which conduct is recipro-cal, are roughly unbiased, but the cells where statisticians do not reciprocate have lower statistical efficiency.

The optimistic conclusion of Froeb and Kobayashi (1996) and followed by Posner (1999a), depends on their exclusive focus on the problem of bias. But if variance is also an issue, because one worries about the efficiency of the process, then their optimism about the unrestricted competitive pro-cess of expert witnesses seems unwarranted and the situation is more com-plicated than they suggest. A rule that constrains experts to report only 2SLS results would have a smaller variance than the competitive process modeled earlier.

The problem occurs because the expert witness knows that the jury splits the difference between competing estimates. This gives the experts an incentive to go as far in their clients' directions as replication, in the narrow sense, allows. The question then becomes whether we can alter the institu-tion so that the incentives change.

## 11.6 Making Transparency Incentive Compatible

Let us reflect on the challenge posed by Judge Posner. Just what might a court-appointed expert witness, (see Tullock 1980), do to improve a com-petitive outcome? Here we consider a statistical variation on the widely discussed principle of final-offer arbitration (Crawford 1979; Ashenfelter and Bloom 1984; Ashenfelter et al. 1992). The best known example of final-offer arbitration is that employed in major league baseball. When salary disputes arise about a baseball player's salary, the arbitrator is allowed to pick only one of the two contending offers, that is, he or she is not allowed to split the difference. Let us think about reform in which the court expert is allowed to recommend only one model, not to propose a compromise between models.[24]

The court-appointed expert would have similar motivations as the experts hired by the contending parties. As a court-appointed consultant, however, he or she would be rewarded only for a reduction in variance, not for the increase in bias. Can this reduction in variance be accomplished without supposing the court expert to be more knowledgeable than the clients' experts? The question is whether we can construct a rule that changes the incentives of the clients' experts and makes transparency incentive compatible.

The rule we propose to induce transparency is this: the court-appointed expert takes each of the contending models, bootstraps them, and then chooses the model with the smaller bootstrap variance. Unlike the general case of final-offer arbitration, in which the judgment depends on the possibly unknown preferences of the arbitrator, *we suppose that the rule is common knowledge*. The question is then whether this rule makes transparent estimation a prudent decision, a minimax strategy. First, we examine the asymptotic problem and, second, the finite sample problem. Not surprisingly, the former is easier than the latter.

*Asymptotics*. Bootstrap standard errors of 2SLS are consistent in the D&S context we have supposed (Freedman 1984). Therefore, if one expert proposes an inefficient 2SLS estimate, the other expert who proposes the efficient 2SLS estimate will, by our rule, prevail because the bootstrap standard errors, as consistent estimates of the standard error, will reveal which of the competing estimates is more efficient. Transparency thus bounds the loss at 2SLS. Transparency is safe, the prudent strategy. If one expert proposed a biased and, therefore, inefficient estimate, he or she would risk his or her opponent, producing a biased but somewhat less inefficient estimate. Any report other than transparency risks a larger loss. Nontransparency is not safe. The reporting of the transparent 2SLS estimate, therefore, minimizes one's maximum loss and makes transparent estimation incentive

---

[24] This idea was suggested by John Miller at the George Mason Statistics Department Seminar in 2002.

compatible. The results of Freedman (1984) made into a rule and applied to our D & S estimation thus prove:

Theorem. The rule makes transparent estimation minimax in the D&S estimation situation considered.

*Finite samples.* Freedman (1984) gives reason for optimism for the application of bootstrap in the finite sample case. We return to the D&S context earlier. In our setup, as one moves from 2SLS to C-Min/C-Max and then to Min/Max the number of identifying restrictions falls; hence, the number of existing moments falls. As the bootstrap estimate of variance is not a robust technique, and thus sensitive to tail mass, as the moments vanish, the tail mass increases. Thus the estimated value of the 2SLS estimates will be predictably lower than the bootstrap variance of C-Min/C-Max, which, in turn, will be predictably lower than the bootstrap variance of Min/Max. When the number of existing moments is the same, the results are not so obvious. If C-Min competes with C-Max, then C-Min has probability P of prevailing. If Min competes with Max, then Min has probability Q of prevailing. There is no reason to believe that either P = 1 – P or Q = 1 – Q.

Would making the decision on the basis of the bootstrap variance introduce transparency in the game of expert witness? Unlike the general problem of final-offer arbitration where the knowledge of the arbitrator's preferences is problematic, here the decision rule for the court-appointed expert can be taken as common knowledge.[25] Could the court now see which of the two estimates is associated with the smaller variance? The game of expert witness is now that pictured in Figure 11.1.

The first column presents the three possible choices made by the advocates of the "high" side. The second column presents the three possible choices made by the advocates of the "low" side. The third column is the outcome that results for each pair of plays. If either player prefers the certainty of 2SLS to the gamble associated with reporting C-Min/C-Max or Min/Max, then for that player, reporting 2SLS is a minimax loss strategy. This result is consistent with what is known about final-offer arbitration in general: there is safety in being reasonable.[26]

---

[25] Ashenfelter and Bloom (1984, p. 112) point out how the conclusions in Crawford (1979) depend critically upon this assumption.

[26] Ashenfelter et al. (1992, p. 1427): "risk averse bargainers can mitigate the risks inherent in FOA [final-offer arbitration] by submitting more reasonable offers while CA [conventional arbitration] offers less scope for mitigation of risk. One way to interpret the conventional wisdom that FOA is riskier than CA is that, by preventing the arbitrator from compromising, the middle of the distribution of arbitrator's preferred outcomes is

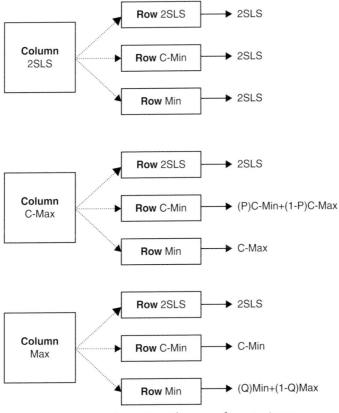

Figure 11.1. The game of expert witness.

The game in Figure 11.1 was simulated using N=400 and 10K replications. The cells in the game on each of the 10K replications were filled in with the contending estimate that had the smallest bootstrap standard error. In this case, as could be predicted from Figure 11.1, the side preferring small numbers can only improve on 2SLS when it plays C-Min and the other plays Max. For this side, 2SLS is minimax. And this suffices to induce transparency. The results are presented in Table 11.3.

## 11.7 Conclusion

We have argued throughout this book that a transparent nontransparency is a minimal requirement in expert consulting. We are not so worried about

eliminated as potential arbitration awards. This by itself would increase risk. However, FOA also eliminates the tails of the distribution, and this decreases risk."

Table 11.3. *Induced transparency by minimizing bootstrap variance*

|        | 2SLS | | C-Min | | Min | |
|--------|------|-----------|-------|-----------|------|-----------|
|        | Bias | Efficiency | Bias | Efficiency | Bias | Efficiency |
| 2SLS   | 0.00 | 1.00 | 0.00  | 1.00 | 0.00 | 1.00 |
| C-Max  | 0.00 | 1.00 | 0.03  | 0.64 | 0.04 | 0.64 |
| Max    | 0.00 | 1.00 | −0.04 | 0.51 | 0.06 | 0.31 |

Normal Exogenous Variables, N=400; 10,000 Replications.

experts taking advantage of clients as we are about the expert–client pair taking advantage of those unaware of the dangers this poses, and we have suggested that the insight about motivated inquiry is a warning to adopt prudential methods. Transparency represents a significant step toward the establishment of an effective code of ethics for economists who sell their expertise to clients. Thus, it is no surprise that the ASA and the AEA statements on expert conduct encourage statisticians in the first instance and economists in the second to follow transparent procedures.

In Chapter 9 we suggested without further attempt at proof that, although full transparency is first-best, a transparent nontransparency is second-best. The model construction reported in Tables 11.2 and 11.3 makes this case. The institutional features that constrain expert witnesses in the legal system of the United States have much to recommend themselves for consideration in democratic procedures. First, there is discovery, which rules out fraud, so we may presume that the estimates offered to the jury are replicable in a narrow sense. Second, the bias of the experts is obvious as is the nontransparency of the procedures used by the experts. Third, there is competition. The literature makes the case that a jury that simply splits the difference of the competing estimates will remove the bias. We reproduced this result in Table 11.2.

The question is whether we can improve this institutional set up. The splitting-the-difference rule leads to more extreme estimates by both sides, an evidentiary arms race. In section 11.6 we described a simple rule change similar to final-offer arbitration, and we demonstrated that this new rule, known to all, would induce transparency among experts. The rule involved a court-appointed expert who is allowed to recommend only one model, rather than splitting the difference. In the case of the expert witness, such an institutional set up is not out of the question. The cost of implementing such a rule would be minimal and the benefits, we presume to hope, would be substantial since it removes some of the nontransparency out of the judicial system. Our reform proposal improves the norm of splitting the difference: we demonstrated that by allowing the court-appointed expert to pick only the model with the smaller variance, and we induced transparency on the part of the contending experts.

The more serious question of the ethics of expertise is to remind experts that, even though they are members of a research community, a policy-making group, or expert witnesses, they are also part of a larger community. One way to think about severe sanctions or trial by resampling, which we proposed earlier, is that they remind the expert of this each and every time he or she takes on a new project.

How might we take advantage of this insight outside of the legal context? Experts testify or attempt to persuade the public in many diverse settings about the advantages of their recommended course of action. They testify before Congress. They produce reports for the public. They write articles for other scientists and for the public. At least in some of these situations, disclosure rules could be more stringent and binding. Testimony before a Congressional committee could certainly be made conditional on disclosure. Needless to say, testimony under oath would impress experts about the importance of transparency. In addition, the public could be made more fully aware of the contending experts' affiliations. Full disclosure of data and estimation techniques not used in the study would go a long way toward enabling prudential reliance on the experts' testimony. Perhaps, in addition, a mechanism might be developed, as described in section 11.6, to choose the recommendation of one of the contending experts. Parties might, for instance, be invited to precommit to allowing a third party to choose an estimate. We return to this thought in our Conclusion in which we put forward an additional proposal.

# PART VI

# CONCLUSION

12

# Vox Populi?

Experts often get their reputations in narrow specialties and are no better in solving problems outside their area of expertise than a random citizen off the street. But we expect them to have an absolute advantage over less accomplished people on all topics.

Vernon Smith (2008, p. 186)

## 12.1 Returning to Discussion

We began this book with a study of an old and now mostly lost tradition in economics, that of discussion. Indeed, we argued in Chapter 2 that the discussion tradition provides the means by which group goals may be discovered, assessed, and revised at each step along the way. By way of discussion – an essential piece of the sort of democratic process we strongly favor – group goals become endogenous to the discussion, to the wishes and desires of the group. We sketched in Chapter 2 how experimental evidence confirms the significance of discussion.

More than this, those who take part in the discussion are members of the group as opposed to someone above the fray, supposedly uninfluenced by the incentives that affect the public. As long as the expert is a discussant as everyone else is – being neither more powerful nor having no more votes than others[1] – discussion places the expert within the group. The expert may have special information or talent, but he or she is subject to the same motivational forces as are all people. Our view, detailed in Chapter 1 and

---

[1] Thus, we specify that the expert is a Robbinsonian voter, as Paul Samuelson put it in the epigram quoted in Chapter 4. This characterization implies that experts are not able to purchase influence, thus addressing Frank Knight's and John Rawls's concerns about the distribution of wealth and power.

emphasized repeatedly throughout the book, is that it is time for economists to apply their models to themselves, to place the economist as expert within the same framework as the public. Such a view is consistent with the tradition outlined in Chapters 2 and 3, but it contrasts with what followed. With the rise of new welfare economics, discussed in Chapter 4, the role for discussion largely fell away, and the economist as expert was positioned outside of the economy and the attendant motivational structure. Experts thereafter largely assessed and then testified about whether a policy might possibly increase total welfare.

Our concern with that process, outlined in Chapter 4, is that if norms are exogenous, not to be discussed or changed, then experts might testify "scientifically" about how to obtain larger output or to lower costs. The goals themselves fall largely outside the expert's analysis; efficiency rules as the metric for analysis, and the expert is presumed to be motivated only by truth seeking. If, by contrast, experts recognize that the goals themselves are subject to analysis and discussion, then the expert becomes one of many competing and motivated voices talking through a discussion of both the superstructure itself as well as actions within the superstructure. Efficiency no longer can be held up as *the* determinative criterion in this discussion; instead, competing and perhaps conflicting goals will be put forward. In a long, deliberative process, consensus emerges, but it may not. Beliefs change slowly. In such a case, continued discussion may be the best possible outcome, at least for now and until consensus emerges.

In Chapters 5 and 6 we examined some of the more egregious results of presuming that group goals need not be discussed. The eugenics movement may perhaps be the most terrifying example of expert judgment simply overrunning the desires of the public. It also provided a striking instance of how experts may respond to the incentives to obtain specific results, as when Karl Pearson abandoned his statistical principles in order to "prove" the result he sought. A major theme of this book is that experts, like the rest of us, are sometimes sympathetic with an approach or an outcome (a "system") and it is imperative for the public to be aware of this fact. Chapter 6 further emphasized that expert judgments are sticky with respect to disconfirming evidence; as when the Soviet economy repeatedly failed to catch up to the United States despite supposedly growing faster. Chapter 7 offered another study of the self-interested expert and there we focused on the nontransparency sometimes associated with expertise. Chapter 8 reviewed evidence that informal rules and techniques may emerge to deal with the temptation to bias; but they can also be forgotten. Experts are more likely to make ethical missteps, we argued there, when all is based on blind trust between the expert and the client and transparency is lacking.

Our larger point is that the public should be aware of such motivations and temptations to bias, so that we can take steps to prevent being overly deferent to the expert. The passage from Vernon Smith that serves as epigram to this chapter suggests the danger of constrained deference to experts (Smith 2008, p. 186). Outside a range of issues, experts simply are not more competent than anyone else. Smith's judgment is based on a half century of research in the experimental economics he pioneered. The temptation to deference, it seems to us, comes from the belief that any scientist will give the same expert advice. This is what one might believe from a reading of Michael Polanyi's 1962 "The Republic of Science," discussed in Chapter 10, in which he argued for the uniformity of scientific understanding. Of course, with specialization, any scientist would only be competent in a little area but, Polanyi pointed out, there is sufficient overlap so that a chain of competence can be created. Perhaps so, but in economics, perhaps not. We saw in Chapter 4 that both Frank Knight and A. C. Pigou held that such a uniformity did not characterize economics. In 1966 Gordon Tullock, without knowledge of either Knight's or Pigou's argument, argued that economics is not a science in Polanyi's sense because economists conceal results, techniques, or roads not taken. There, too, we provided a means by which to assess differentially biased estimates.

Why would the expert conceal things? One answer that we have stressed throughout the book is sympathy for a system, for a client, or for one's group. Of course, there may instead be material motivation but we stress sympathy because that is what we consider to be the glue of faction. Faction has long been viewed as the great problem of republican governance. A central text of the American founding is James Madison's tenth essay in the *Federalist Papers*. The question he addressed is how to break up faction without destroying liberty.

Today, the danger to democracy may well be expert faction, especially factions among those who are powerful. If experts arrived at their opinions independently, then we would not expect systematic error. The logic of the scientific community that Polanyi developed shows precisely why we would not expect independence. We observe deference. And, in a world without complete transparency, we can predict faction. With faction, of course, we get systematic error, such as the predictions we have seen in Chapters 5 and 6 about the "danger" of racial degeneracy, or of the Soviet overtaking of the American economy.

What can be done? The first step is to think about experts as sympathetically connected with clients or with a system. This step is obvious in the context of the American legal system discussed in Part V: experts are connected with clients. Chapter 9 sketched a proposal for an expert code of ethics that might alert the public about the allegiances of the expert. From that understanding comes another modest recommendation put forward in Chapter 11 for the public (both American and Canadian!): the legislative process ought to have something akin to the discovery procedure in litigation. This would allow unfriendly eyes to check the results. Our simulation of the game of expert witness did not suppose that a discovery procedure would do more than force narrowly defined replication. That and an awareness of bias clarified through a code of ethics, as suggested in Chapter 9, might be good enough.

We emphasize once more that our proposal is *not* that experts should remain neutral with respect to their own interests – something obviously impossible to attain – rather that they render more fully transparent monetary and nonmonetary inducements to select evidence and estimation techniques. We live in a world of the second best: since neutrality over results and full overlay of private and public interests will be impossible to attain, our proposed solution is more fully to disclose inducements to nonneutrality. Such a proposal allows the public to rely on experts with their eyes wide open, to know more about potential monetary and nonmonetary sources of bias associated with specific experts and expert recommendations. Although the temptations to bias may remain, knowing about them then allows consumers to act with awareness.

Mutuality of interests distinguishes expert-client pairings and cements the pairing. Such mutuality might extend to other groups so that expert-client pairings are not the only group to consider. In addition, there is most obviously the group of experts. Bonds of admiration and status connect experts, and there is no reason to believe that they are unaware that the actions of some experts might have negative consequences for their community. In Chapter 10 we explored the problem of science and factional expertise. In Chapter 11, we offered a suggestion for agreed upon procedures to follow, regardless of the experts' affection for clients to come. These substantial institutional reforms take into account the endogeneity of group goals that we stressed in Part I.

Throughout this book we have argued that a transparent nontransparency is a minimal requirement for ethical procedures in expert consulting. As noted in Chapter 9, this warns the public to adopt prudential methods. Transparency represents a significant step toward the establishment of an effective code of ethics for economists who sell their expertise to clients. Although we worry about experts taking advantage of clients, we are also concerned with the expert–client pair that takes advantage of those who are unaware of the dangers. Thus, it is no surprise that the ASA and the AEA statements on expert conduct encourage statisticians in the first instance and economists in the second to follow transparent procedures. In Chapter 9, we made the case that, although full transparency is first best, a transparent nontransparency is second best.

Chapter 11 examined how the institutional facts constraining expert witnesses in the US legal system have much to recommend themselves in other contexts involving experts. First, there is discovery, which rules out fraud, so we may presume that the estimates offered to the jury are replicable in a narrow sense. Second, the bias of the experts is obvious, as is the nontransparency of the procedures that affects the bias. Third, there is competition. We then described a simple rule change and we demonstrated that this new rule would induce transparency among experts. The rule involved a court-appointed expert who is allowed to recommend only one model, rather than splitting the difference. In the case of the expert witness, such an institutional setup is not out of the question. The cost of implementing such a rule would be minimal and the benefits, we presume to hope, would be substantial since it removes some of the nontransparency out of the judicial system. The fact that the nontransparency is itself transparent has allowed an informal norm of splitting the difference to attenuate bias. Our reform proposal, however, improves splitting the difference; we demonstrated that by allowing the court-appointed expert to pick only the model with the smaller variance, we induced transparency on the part of the contending experts.

The larger role of the ethics of expertise is to remind experts that, even though they are members of a research community, policy-making group, or expert witnesses, they are also part of a larger community. One way to think about severe sanctions or trial by resampling, which we proposed earlier, is that they remind the expert of this each and every time he or she takes on a new project.

How might we take advantage of this insight outside of the legal context? We suggested in Chapter 11 that there are many other situations in which experts testify or in other ways attempt to persuade the public about the advantages of their recommended course of action. They testify before Congressional hearings. They produce reports for the public. They write articles for other scientists and for the public to consume. At least in some of these situations, disclosure rules could be more stringent and binding.

Testimony before a Congressional committee could certainly be made conditional upon disclosure. Needless to say, testimony under oath would impress experts as to the benefits of transparency.

Outside of such an austere context, the audience could be made more fully aware of the contending experts' affiliations. Full disclosure of data and estimation techniques not used in the study would go a long way toward enabling prudential reliance on the experts' testimony. Perhaps, in addition, a mechanism could be developed, as in Chapter 11, to choose the recommendation of one of the contending experts. Parties might, for instance, be invited to precommit to allowing a third party to choose an estimate.

## 12.2 A Radical Proposal

We opened the book with a passage from Knight's presidential address to the American Economic Association in which he called attention to the two great difficulties with implementing government by discussion. First, there are too many people to have a real discussion and, secondly, even if that problem can be solved there is no structure to the discussion to insure fair play.

Perhaps we can do more to address Knight's concerns with the analysis of the legal system in Chapter 11. What makes the jury system the paradigm of democracy for us is twofold. First, it is important to note that the group selected is small and is selected randomly, without regard to influence or income. This speaks directly to the large number problem in discussion that rightly worried Knight, and to the questions related to distortions that arise in crony capitalism and regulatory capture. Second, there is a procedure by which experts are involved and the evidential basis of their testimony is subject to discovery. Might it be possible to extend the jury system to that of regulation? Instead of appointed regulatory bodies with their experts making decisions, where the only people with a voice in the matter have a particular interest in the issues, we propose that decisions be made by people, randomly selected, who have the issues explained to them by contending experts.

This would address the problem of one manifestation of the collective action problem associated with determining group goals – namely, regulatory capture. Consider the thought experiment: if Uber were to be banned because of the damage to taxi companies' medallion asset values, we would each be worse off by $100 or less. To testify with some credibility against such a proposal would take at least a week's work. Private cost-benefit calculations thus instruct us to do nothing. On the other hand we can confidently predict that the taxi companies would present experts offering plausible calculations showing the world will end if Uber is allowed to compete freely. Uber would also find experts to present calculations showing just the opposite. In the present regulatory system old firms may well have an advantage over new firms. Incumbents and regulators know each other. Under our proposal that advantage would be reduced, since the randomly selected members of the public would be less prone to be connected with established firms.

More than that, regulatory oversight by jury would extend government by discussion to a much greater portion of American life. There would of course remain an enormous number of details to work through but the greatest merit would be to put the question on the table: Do we as a people believe in democracy or do we believe in rule by experts? Late in his life, when Francis Galton discovered that democracy as he visualized it had remarkable statistical properties, he endorsed an egalitarian presupposition to entitle his article, "*Vox populi.*" His readers could be expected to add the familiar tag, "*Vox Dei.*" Our proposal, consistent with the others sketched earlier, is simply to allow the voice of the people to be heard more clearly as they discuss and assess expert views and evidence with their eyes wide open to the motivations and group allegiances of the experts who contend for attention and, ultimately, approval.

# Bibliography

## Unpublished Manuscripts

### The Authors' Collections

John Rawls's Marginal Notes on Frank Knight. 1951. *Ethics of Competition.* 2nd impression. New York: Augustus Kelley.

John Rawls's Marginal Notes on Lionel Robbins. 1949. *An Essay on the Nature and Significance of Economic Science.* 2nd edn, revised and extended. London: Macmillan.

### Cambridge University

Charles Darwin Correspondence Project.

Transcription of Calendar number: 10988, draft of a letter from Charles Darwin to Charles Bradlaugh, June 6, 1877, supplied to D. M. Levy and S. J. Peart, October 6, 2004.

### Dwight Eisenhower Presidential Library

Arthur Burns Papers. www.eisenhower.archives.gov/Research/Finding_Aids/PDFs/Burns_Arthur_Papers.pdf

### George Mason University Libraries. Special Collections and Archives

Clark Warburton Papers, 1920–1979, available from http://sca.gmu.edu/finding_aids/warburton.html

### Library of Congress, Manuscript Division

William J. Baroody Papers, available from http://memory.loc.gov/service/mss/eadxmlmss/eadpdfmss/2008/ms008097.pdf

### London School of Economics Archives

[R. A. "Pat" Adams Collection.] LSE History Project Photographs/16.

### National Archives

www.nationalarchives.gov.uk/

### Stanford University. Hoover Institution.

Gordon Tullock Papers. Hoover Institution, Stanford University, available from www
.oac.cdlib.org/findaid/ark:/13030/kt787034zq/entire_text/
V. Orval Watts Papers. Hoover Institution, Stanford University, available from http://
pdf.oac.cdlib.org/pdf/hoover/83064.pdf

### University of Liverpool Library.

John Fraser Collection, available from www.liv.ac.uk/library/sca/colldescs/fraser.html

### University of Virginia.

Small Special Collections, University of Virginia, President's Papers.

## Court Decision

Abu Dhabi Commercial Bank, King County, Washington, Together and On Behalf of All
Others Similarly Situated, v. Morgan Stanley & Co. Incorporated, Morgan Stanley & Co.
International Limited, The Bank of New York Mellon (F/K/A The Bank of New York),
Qsr Management Limited, Moody's Investors Service, Inc., Moody's Investors Service
Ltd., Standard And Poor's Ratings Services and the McGraw Hill Companies, Inc. 08
Civ. 7508 (SAS). Southern District of New York (September 2, 2009).

## Published Work

Ackley, Gardner. 1961. *Macroeconomic Theory*. New York: Macmillan.
  1978. *Macroeconomics: Theory and Policy*. New York: Macmillan.
Akerlof, George P. 1970. "The Market for 'Lemons': Quality Uncertainty and the Market
Mechanism." *Quarterly Journal of Economics* 84: 488–500.
Alchian, Armen A. and William R. Allen. 1964. *University Economics*. Belmont, CA:
Wadsworth Publishing.
Allais, Maurice. 1966. "A Restatement of the Quantity Theory of Money." *American
Economic Review* 56: 1123–1157.
Allen, William R. 1977. "Economics, Economists, and Economic Policy: Modern
American Experiences." *History of Political Economy* 9: 48–88.
American Banker. August 12, 1936. "Rating Services Only Advisory." *American Banker*
101: 2.
American Economic Association. 2012. "American Economic Association Adopts
Extensions to Principles for Author Disclosure of Conflict of Interest." Available from
www.aeaweb.org/PDF_files/PR/AEA_Adopts_Extensions_to_Principles_for_
Author_Disclosure_01-05-12.pdf
American Statistical Association. 2000. *Ethical Guidelines for Statistical Practice*.
Alexandria, VA.
Andrews, David F. et al. 1972. *Robust Estimates of Location*. Princeton: Princeton
University Press.

Angner, Erik. 2006. "Economists as Experts: Overconfidence in Theory and Practice." *Journal of Economic Methodology* 13: 1–24.

Arnstein, Walter L. 1965. *The Bradlaugh Case: A Study in Late Victorian Opinion and Politics*. Oxford, UK: Clarendon Press.

Arrow, Kenneth J. 1963. *Social Choice and Individual Values*. 2nd edn. New York: John Wiley.

——— 1971. *Some Models of Racial Discrimination in the Labor Market*. Santa Monica, CA: Rand Corporation.

Ashenfelter, Orley and David E. Bloom. 1984. "Models of Arbitrator Behavior: Theory and Evidence." *American Economic Review* 74: 111–124.

Ashenfelter, Orley, et al. 1992. "An Experimental Comparison of Dispute Rates in Alternative Arbitration Systems." *Econometrica* 60: 1407–1433.

Ashraf, Nava, Colin F. Camerer, and George Loewenstein 2005. "Adam Smith, Behavioral Economist." *Journal of Economic Perspectives* 19: 131–145.

Axelrod, Robert. 1984. *The Evolution of Co-operation*. New York: Basic Books.

Bach, George Leland. 1954–1980. *Economics: An Introduction to Analysis and Policy*. Englewood Cliffs: Prentice-Hall.

Backhouse, Roger E. 1988. *Economists and the Economy: The Evolution of Economic Ideas*. Oxford, UK: Blackwell.

Balliet, Daniel. 2010. "Communication and Cooperation in Social Dilemmas: a Meta-Analytic Review." *Journal of Conflict Resolution* 54: 39–57.

Banton, Michael. 1977. *The Idea of Race*. London: Tavistock Publications.

Barber, William. 1995. "Chile con Chicago: A Review Essay." *Journal of Economic Literature* 33: 1941–1949.

Barry, Brian. 1973. *The Liberal Theory of Justice: A Critical Examination of the Principle Doctrines in Theory of Justice by John Rawls*. Oxford, UK: Clarendon Press.

Bernstein, Michael A. 2004. "Statecraft and Its Retainers: American Economics and Public Purpose after Depression and War." In *The Social Sciences Go To Washington: The Politics of Knowledge in the Postmodern Era*, edited by Hamilton Cravens. Picsataway, NJ: Rutgers University Press, 41–60.

Binmore, Kenneth G. 1994. *Game Theory and the Social Contact: Playing Fair*. Cambridge, MA: MIT Press.

Blanchard, Olivier Jean. 2008. "Neoclassical Synthesis." In *The New Palgrave's Dictionary of Economics*, edited by Lawrence Blume and Steven Durlauf. 2nd edn. New York: Palgrave. Available online from www.dictionaryofeconomics.com/article?id= pde2008_N000041

Blaug, Mark. 1980. *The Methodology of Economics*. Cambridge, UK: Cambridge University Press.

Bonner, Hypatia Bradlaugh. 1895. *Charles Bradlaugh; A Record of His Life and Work*. 2nd edn. T. F. Unwin, London.

Bornstein, Gary and Ilan Yaniv. 1998. "Individual and Group Behavior in the Ultimatum Game: Are Groups More 'Rational' Players?" *Experimental Economics* 1: 101–108.

Bowles, Samuel. 2008. "Policies Designed for Self-Interested Citizens May Undermine the 'Moral Sentiments': Evidence from Economic Experiments." *Science* 320 (5883): 1605–1609.

Brady, Gordon. 2008. "The NBER Soviet Study." Summer Institute for the History of Economics. Fairfax, VA: George Mason University.

Brandis, Royall. 1968. *The Principles of Economics*. Homewood, IL: Irwin.

Breiner, Laurence A. 1979a. "The Career of the Cockatrice." *Isis* 70: 30–47.

1979b. "Herbert's Cockatrice." *Modern Philology* 77: 10–17.

Brock, William A., Steven N. Durlauf, and Kenneth D. West. 2007. "Model Uncertainty and Policy Evaluation: Some Theory and Empirics." *Journal of Econometrics* 136: 629–664.

Buchanan, Allen. 2002. "Social Moral Epistemology." *Social Philosophy and Policy* 19: 126–151.

2007. "Institutions, Beliefs and Ethics: Eugenics as a Case Study." *Journal of Political Philosophy* 15: 22–45.

Buchanan, James M. 1954. "Individual Choice in Voting and the Market." *Journal of Political Economy* 62: 334–343.

1959. "Positive Economics, Welfare Economics, and Political Economy." *Journal of Law and Economics* 2: 124–138.

1967. "Politics and Science: Reflections on Knight's Critique of Polanyi." *Ethics* 77: 303–310.

2003. "Public Choice: Politics without Romance." *Policy* 19: 13–18.

2004. "The Status of the *Status Quo*." *Constitutional Political Economy* 15: 133–144.

2010. "Chicago School Thinking: Old and New." Summer Institute for the History of Economics. University of Richmond.

2011. "Ideology or Error: Economists and the Great Recession." Summer Institute for the History of Economics. University of Richmond.

2012. "Institutional Sources of Fiscal Tragedy." Summer Institute for the History of Economics. University of Richmond.

Buchanan, James M., and Warren J. Samuels. 2008. "Politics as Exchange or Politics as Power: Two Views of the Government." In *The Street Porter and the Philosopher*, edited by Sandra J. Peart and David M. Levy. Ann Arbor: University of Michigan Press, 15–40.

Buckley, William F., Jr. 1951. *God and Man at Yale: The Superstitions of "Academic Freedom."* Chicago: Regnery.

Burns, Jennifer. 2009. *Goddess of the Market: Ayn Rand and the American Right*. New York: Oxford University Press.

Burtchett, Floyd F. 1939. "Review of Gilbert Harold Bond Ratings as an Investment Guide." *Annals of the American Academy of Political and Social Science* 202: 222–224.

Cain, Daylian M., George Loewenstein, and Don A. Moore. 2005. "The Dirt on Coming Clean: Perverse Effects of Disclosing Conflicts of Interest." *Journal of Legal Studies* 34: 1–25.

Caldwell, Bruce. 1995. "Introduction" In *Contra Keynes and Cambridge: Essays, Correspondence*, edited by F. A. Hayek. Chicago: University of Chicago Press, 1–48.

2008. "Gordon Tullock's *The Organization of Inquiry*: A Critical Appraisal." *Public Choice* 135: 23–34.

Camerer, Colin F., and Richard H. Thaler. 1995. "Anomalies: Ultimatums, Dictators and Manners." *Journal of Economic Perspectives* 9: 209–219.

Campbell, John Angus. 1989. "The Invisible Rhetorician: Charles Darwin's 'Third Party' Strategy." *Rhetorica: A Journal of the History of Rhetoric* 7: 55–85.

Carlyle, Thomas. 1841. *On Heroes, Hero-Worship, the Heroic in History.* J. Fraser: London.
  1849. "Occasional Discourse on the Negro Question." *Fraser's Magazine for Town and Country* 40: 670–679.
  1867. *"Shooting Niagara – and After."* London: Chapman and Hall.
Chandrasekhar, Sripati. 1981. *"A Dirty, Filthy Book."* Berkeley: University of California.
Coase, Ronald H. 1960. "The Problem of Social Cost." *Journal of Law and Economics* 3: 1–44.
  1991. "The Institutional Structure of Production." Lecture to the memory of Alfred Nobel, December 9, 1991. Available at www.nobelprize.org/nobel_prizes/economic-sciences/laureates/1991/coase-lecture.html
  1993. "Law and Economics at Chicago." *Journal of Law and Economics* 36: 239–254.
Colander, David. 2009. "What was 'It' that Robbins Was Defining?" *Journal of the History of Economic Thought* 31: 437–448.
Colander, David C., and Harry Landreth, eds. 1996. *The Coming of Keynesianism to America: Conversations with the Founders of Keynesian Economics.* Cheltenham, UK: Edward Elgar.
  1998. "God, Man, and Lorie Tarshis at Yale." In *Keynesianism and the Keynesian Revolution in America,* edited by Omar Hamuda. Cheltenham, UK: Edward Elgar, 59–72.
Cole, Arthur H. 1949. *The Great Mirror of Folly (het groote tafereel der dwaasheid): An Economic-Bibliographical Study.* Boston: Baker Library of Harvard Business School.
Crawford, Vincent P. 1979. "On Compulsory-Arbitration Schemes." *Journal of Political Economy* 87: 131–159.
Curtis, Lewis P., Jr. 1968. *Anglo-Saxons and Celts.* Bridgeport, CT: Conference on British Studies at the University of Bridgeport.
Daniell, David. 2003. *The Bible in English: Its History and Influence.* New Haven: Yale University Press.
Darwin, Charles. 1964. *On the Origin of Species by Natural Selection, or the Preservation of Favoured Races in the Struggle for Life,* edited by Ernst Mayr. Cambridge, MA: Harvard University Press. Originally published in 1859 in London by John Murray.
  1871. *The Descent of Man, or Selection in Relation to Sex.* London: John Murray.
Darwin, George. 1873. "On Beneficial Restrictions to Liberty of Marriage." *The Contemporary Review* 22: 412–426.
Davenport, Guy. 1980. *Archilochos, Sappho, Alkman: Three Lyric Poets of the Late Greek Bronze Age.* Berkeley: University of California Press.
De Bruyn, Frans. 2000a. "Reading *Het groote tafereel der dwaasheid*: An Emblem Book of the Folly of Speculation in the Bubble Year 1720." *Eighteenth-Century Life* 24: 1–42.
  2000b. "*Het groote tafereel der dwaasheid* and the Speculative Bubble of 1720: A Bibliographical Enigma and an Economic Force." *Eighteenth-Century Life* 24: 62–87.
  2013. *Het Groote Tafereel Der Dwaasheid* and Its Readers, Then and Now." In *The Great Mirror of Folly: Finance and Culture, and the Crash of 1720,* edited by William N. Goetzmann, Catherine Labio, K. Geert Rouwenhorst and Timothy G. Young. New Haven, CT: Yale University Press, 21–34.
DeMartino, George. 2011. *The Economist's Oath: On the Need for and Content of Professional Economic Ethics.* Oxford, UK: Oxford University Press.

2015. "Harming Irreparably: On Neoliberalism, Kaldor-Hicks, and the Paretian Guarantee." *Review of Social Economy* 73: 315-340.

Deming, W. Edwards. 1965. "Principles of Professional Statistical Practice." *The Annals of Mathematical Statistics* 36: 1883–1900.

Desmond, Adrian. 1994. *Huxley: The Devil's Disciple*. New York: M. Joseph.

Dewald, William G., Jerry Thursby, and Richard G. Anderson. 1986. "Replication in Empirical Economics: The *Journal of Money, Credit, and Banking* Project." *American Economic Review* 76: 587–603.

Diamond, Arthur M. 2008. "The Economics of Science." In *The New Palgrave Dictionary of Economics Online*, edited by Stephen. N. Durlauf and Lawrence E. Blume. New York: Palgrave Macmillan. Available online at www.dictionaryofeconomics .com/article?id=pde2008_E000222 doi:10.1057/9780230226203.1491

Dixit, Avinash and Barry Nalebuff. 2008. "Prisoners' Dilemma." In *The Concise Encyclopedia of Economics*, edited by David R. Henderson. Liberty Fund, Inc. Library of Economics and Liberty [Online] available at www.econlib.org/library/ Enc/PrisonersDilemma.html

Dobbs, Betty Jo Teeter. 1975. *The Foundations of Newton's Alchemy or "The Hunting of the Greene Lyon."* Cambridge, UK: Cambridge University Press.

1990a. *Alchemical Death & Resurrection: The Significance of Alchemy in the Age of Newton*. Washington, DC: Smithsonian Institution.

1990b. "From the Secrecy of Alchemy to the Openness of Chemistry." In *Solomon's House Revisited: The Organization and Institutionalization of Science*, edited by Tore Frängsmyr. Nobel Symposium 75. Canton, MA: Science History Publications, 75–94.

Düppe, Till. 2011. *The Making of the Economy: A Phenomenology of Economic Science*. Lanham, MD: Lexington Books.

Duvendack, Maren, Richard W. Palmer-Jones, and W. Robert Reed, 2015. "Replications in Economics: A Progress Report." *Economics Journal Watch* 12: 164–191.

Easterly, William. 2013. *The Tyranny of Experts: Economists, Dictators and the Forgotten Rights of the Poor*. New York: Basic Books.

Elder, Gregory P. 1996. *Chronic Vigour: Darwin, Anglicans, Catholics and the Development of a Doctrine of Providential Evolution*. Lanham, MD: University Press of America.

Eliade, Mircea. 1972. *The Forge and the Crucible*. Translated by Stephen Corrin. 2nd edn. Chicago: University of Chicago Press.

Elzinga, Kenneth G. 1992. "The Eleven Principles of Economics." *Southern Economic Journal* 58: 861–879.

Erasmus, Desiderius. 1904. *The Epistles of Erasmus: From His Earliest Letters to His Fifty-First Year Arranged in Order of Time*. Translated by Francis Morgan Nicholas. London: Longmans, Green.

1979. *In Praise of Folly*. Translated by Clarence H. Miller. New Haven, CT: Yale University Press. Originally published in 1509 in Latin.

1999. *Colloquies*. Translated and annotated by Craig R. Thompson. Volumes 39 and 40 of *Collected Works of Erasmus*. Toronto: University of Toronto Press. Originally published in Latin in 1518.

Farrant, Andrew, and Edward McPhail. 2013. "Torturing the Data to Make It Confess? Friedman, and the Chilean 'Generals.'" Working Paper.

Feigenbaum, Susan, and David M. Levy. 1993. "The Market for (Ir)reproducible Econometrics." *Social Epistemology* 7: 215–232.

Fels, Rendigs. 1961–1966. *The Challenge to the American Economy: An Introduction to Economics.* Boston: Allyn and Bacon.

Fiorito, Luca, and Sebastiano Nerozzi. 2009. "Jacob Viner's Reminiscences from the New Deal (February 11, 1953)." *Research in the History of Economic Thought and Methodology* 27–A: 75–136.

Fisher, Irving. 1930. *The Theory of Interest.* New York: Macmillan.

Flandreau, Marc, Norbert Gaillard, and Frank Packer. 2009. "Rating Performance, Regulation and the Great Depression: Evidence from Government Securities." Available at http://papers.ssrn.com/sol3/papers.cfm?abstract_id=1433924

Ford Foundation. 1949. *Report of the Study for the Ford Foundation on Policy and Program.* Detroit, MI: Ford Foundation.

Forrer, Kuniko. 2013. "*Het Groote Tafereel Der Dwaasheid:* A Bibliographical Interpretation." In *The Great Mirror of Folly: Finance and Culture, and the Crash of 1720,* edited by William N. Goetzmann, Catherine Labio, K. Geert Rouwenhorst and Timothy G. Young. New Haven, CT: Yale University Press, 35–52.

Fraine, Harold G., and Melvin W. Brethouwer. 1944. *The Corporate Bond Project: Organization and Methods. Part I of Organization and Administration of the Corporate Bond Project.* New York: National Bureau of Economic Research.

Francis, Mark. 2007. *Herbert Spencer and the Invention of Modern Life.* Ithaca NY: Cornell University Press.

Freedman, David A. 1984. "On Bootstrapping Two-Stage Least-Squares Estimates in Stationary Linear Models." *Annals of Statistics* 12: 827–842.

Frehen, Rik, William N. Goetzmann, and K. Geert Rouwenhorst. 2013. "Finance in the Great Mirror of Folly." In *The Great Mirror of Folly: Finance and Culture, and the Crash of 1720,* edited by William N. Goetzmann, Catherine Labio, K. Geert Rouwenhorst and Timothy G. Young. New Haven, CT: Yale University Press, 63–88.

Fried, Rebecca. 2015. "No Irish Need Deny: Evidence for the Historicity of NINA Restrictions in Advertisements and Signs." *Journal of Social History* 49: 1–25.

Friedman, Milton. 1942. "The Inflationary Gap: II. Discussion of the Inflationary Gap." *American Economic Review* 32: 314–320.

 1957. *A Theory of the Consumption Function.* Princeton, NJ: Princeton University Press.

 1962a. *Capitalism and Freedom.* Chicago: University of Chicago Press.

 1962b. "Should There Be an Independent Monetary Authority?" In *In Search of a Monetary Constitution,* edited by Leland Yeager. Cambridge, MA: Harvard University Press, 219–243.

 1991. "Say 'No' to Intolerance." *Liberty* 4: 17–2018.

Friedman, Milton, and Rose Director Friedman. 1998. *Two Lucky People: Memoirs.* Chicago: University of Chicago Press.

Friedman, Milton, and George J. Stigler. 1946. *Roofs or Ceilings?: The Current Housing Problem.* Irvington-on-Hudson, NY: Foundation for Economic Education.

 1952. "Roofs or Ceilings?" In *Readings in Economics,* edited by Paul A. Samuelson, Robert L. Bishop, and John R. Coleman. New York: McGraw-Hill, 161–169.

Froeb, Luke M., and Bruce H. Kobayashi. 1996. "Naive, Biased, yet Bayesian: Can Juries Interpret Selectively Produced Evidence?" *Journal of Law, Economics and Organization* 12: 257–276.

[F. S.] 1926. "Annals of Eugenics." *Journal of the Royal Statistical Society* 89: 147–151.

Galton, Francis. 1883. *Inquiries into Human Faculty and Its Development*. London: Macmillan.

———. 1907a. "One Vote, One Value." *Nature* 75: 414.

———. 1907b. "Vox Populi." *Nature* 75: 450–451.

Gardiner, John. 1996. "What and Where Are Statistical Ethics." Presented at the Joint Statistical Meetings. Chicago. Available at www.tcnj.edu/~asaethic/asaweb2.html

Gleeson, Janet. 1999. *Millionaire: The Philanderer, Gambler, and Duelist Who Invented Modern Finance*. New York: Simon & Schuster.

Godwin, W. 1801. *Thoughts Occasioned by the Perusal of Dr. Parr's Spital Sermon*. London: Taylor and Wilks.

Goetz, Charles. 1991. *Uncommon Common-Sense vs. Conventional Wisdom: The Virginia School of Economics*. Fairfax, VA: Center for Study of Public Choice.

Goetzmann, William N. et al., eds. 2013. *The Great Mirror of Folly: Finance and Culture, and the Crash of 1720*. New Haven, CT: Yale University Press.

Good, Irving J. 1983. "Rational Decisions." In *Good Thinking: The Foundations of Probability and Its Applications*. Minneapolis: University of Minnesota Press, 3–14. Originally published in 1952 in the *Journal of the Royal Statistical Society.*

Gorlin, Rena A., ed. 1999. *Codes of Professional Responsibility*. Washington, DC: Bureau of National Affairs.

Gorman, William G. 1955. "The Intransitivity of Certain Criteria Used in Welfare Economics." *Oxford Economic Papers* 7: 25–34.

Gould, Stephen J. 1981. *The Mismeasure of Man*. New York: Norton.

———. 2002. *The Structure of Evolutionary Theory*. Cambridge, MA: Harvard University Press.

Greenspan, Alan. 2005. Testimony of Chairman Alan Greenspan: The Economic Outlook before the Joint Economic Committee, U.S. Congress. Available at www.federalreserve.gov/BOARDDOCS/TESTIMONY/2005/200506092/default.htm

Greenwald, Anthony G. and Lisa A. Cooper. 2006. "Implicit bias: Scientific foundations." *California Law Review* 94: 945–967.

Greg, William R. 1868. "On the Failure of 'Natural Selection' in the Case of Man." *Fraser's Magazine for Town and Country* 78: 353–362.

———. 1875. *Enigmas of Life*. Boston: James R. Osgood.

Grossman, Gene M. and Elhanan Helpman. 2002. *Special Interest Politics*. Cambridge, MA: MIT Press.

Gruber, Jacob W. 1960. *A Conscience in Conflict: The Life of St. George Jackson Mivart*. New York: Columbia University Press.

Halpern, Joseph Y., and Leandro C. Rêgo. 2009. "Reasoning about Knowledge of Unawareness." *Games and Economic Behavior* 67: 503–525.

Hammond, Daniel J., and Claire H. Hammond, eds. 2006. *Making Chicago Price Theory: Friedman-Stigler Correspondence 1945–1957*. New York: Routledge.

Hands, D. Wade. 1994. "The Sociology of Scientific Knowledge: Some Thoughts on the Possibilities." In *New Perspectives in Economic Methodology*, edited by Roger Backhouse. London: Routledge, 75–106.

Harberger, Arnold C. 1954. "Monopoly and Resource Allocation." *American Economic Review* 44: 77–87.

Harcourt, Geoffrey C. 1995. "Lorie Tarshis: 1911–1993: In Appreciation." *Economic Journal* 105: 1244–1255.

Harold, Gilbert. 1938. *Bond Ratings as an Investment Guide*. New York: Ronald Press.

Harrod, Roy F. 1938. "Scope and Method in Economics." *Economic Journal* 48: 383–412.

Hayek, F. A. 1994. *Hayek on Hayek: An Autobiographical Dialogue*, edited by Stephen Kresge and Leif Wenar. London: Routledge.

Heckman, James J. 1997. "The Intellectual Roots of the Law and Economics Movement." *Law and History Review* 15: 327–332.

———. 2005. "Interview with James Heckman." *Federal Reserve Bank of Minneapolis*. Available at //www.minneapolisfed.org/publications/the-region/interview-with-james-heckman

Heilbroner, Robert L. 1968–1970. *The Economic Problem*. Englewood Cliffs: Prentice Hall.

Herrnstein, Richard J., and Charles Murray. 1994. *The Bell Curve: Intelligence and Class Structure in American Life*. New York: Free Press.

*Het Groote Tafereel Der Dwaasheid &c.* 1720 [?] [State 1] Amsterdam. LC HG 6006 G82.

———. 1720 [?] [State 2] Amsterdam. LC HG 6006 G822.

———. 1720 [?] [State 2] Amsterdam. Available online at the Harvard Business School www .library.hbs.edu/hc/ssb/recreationandarts/tafereel.html

———. 1720 [?] [State 3] Amsterdam. LC HG 6006 G8.

Hickman, W. Braddock. 1952. *Trends and Cycles in Corporate Bond Financing*. Princeton, NJ: Princeton University Press.

———. 1953. *The Volume of Corporate Bond Financing since 1900*. Princeton, NJ: Princeton University Press.

———. 1958. *Corporate Bond Quality and Investor Experience*. Princeton, NJ: Princeton University Press.

Hickman, W. Braddock, and Elizabeth T. Simpson. 1960. *Statistical Measures of Corporate Bond Financing since 1900*. Princeton, NJ: Princeton University Press.

Hicks, John R. 1939. "The Foundations of Welfare Economics." *Economic Journal* 49: 696–712.

———. 1941. "The Rehabilitation of Consumers' Surplus." *Review of Economic Studies* 8: 108–116.

Hitchens, George P. 1944. *The Record of Issue and Extinguishment Characteristics of Corporate Bonds, 1900–38*. Part III of *The Corporate Bond Project: Organization and Methods*. New York: National Bureau of Economic Research.

Hochstrasser, Julie Berger. 2013. "Print Power: Mad Crowds and the Art of Memory in *Het Groote Tafereel Der Dwaasheid*." In *The Great Mirror of Folly: Finance and Culture, and the Crash of 1720*, edited by William N. Goetzmann, Catherine Labio, K. Geert Rouwenhorst, and Timothy G. Young. New Haven, CT: Yale University Press, 191–206.

Hoffman, Elizabeth, Kevin A. McCabe, and Vernon L. Smith. 1996. "Social Distance and Other-Regarding Behavior in Dictator Games." *American Economic Review* 86(3): 653–660.

Houser, Daniel, et al. 2014. "Raising the Price of Talk: An Experimental Analysis of Transparent Leadership." *Journal of Economic Behavior and Organization* 105: 208–218.

Howson, Susan. 2011. *Lionel Robbins*. Cambridge, UK: Cambridge University Press.

Hunt, James. 1864. *The Negro's Place in Nature: A Paper Read before the London Anthropological Society*. New York: Van Eurie, Horton.

Hutt, William H. 1936. *Economists and the Public*. London: Jonathan Cape.

International Statistical Institute. 1986. "Declaration on Professional Ethics." *International Statistical Review* 54: 227–242.

Ioannidis, John P. A. 2005. "Why Most Published Research Findings Are False." PLOS Medicine. Available at http://journals.plos.org/plosmedicine/article?id=10.1371/journal.pmed.0020124

Jensen, Richard 2002. "'No Irish Need Apply': A Myth of Victimization." *Journal of Social History* 36: 405–429.

Jonson, Ben. 1974. *The Alchemist*, edited by Alvin B. Kernan. New Haven: Yale University Press. Originally printed in London in 1611.

Jung, Carl G. 1967. *Alchemical Studies*. Princeton, NJ: Princeton University Studies.

Kaldor, Nicholas. 1939. "Welfare Propositions of Economics and Interpersonal Comparisons of Utility." *Economic Journal* 49: 549–552.

Keith, Arthur. 1917. "Presidential Address. How Can the Institute Best Serve the Needs of Anthropology." *Journal of the Royal Anthropological Institute of Great Britain and Ireland* 47: 12–30.

Keynes, John Maynard. 1972. "Newton the Man." In *Essays in Biography*. Volume 10 of the *Collected Writings of John Maynard Keynes*, edited by Elizabeth Johnson and Donald Moggridge. London: Macmillan, 363-374. Originally prepared for the Newton Tercentenary Celebrations at Trinity College, Cambridge in 1946.

Keynes, J. Neville. 1891. *The Scope and Method of Political Economy*. London and New York: Macmillan.

Kindleberger, Charles P. 2000. *Manias, Panics and Crashes: A History of Financial Crises*. 4th edn. New York: John Wiley.

Kinzer, Bruce L., Ann P. Robson, and John M. Robson. 1992. *A Moralist In and Out of Parliament: John Stuart Mill at Westminster, 1865-1868*. Toronto: University of Toronto Press.

Kipling, Rudyard. 1895. "Neolithic Age." Available at www.kipling.org.uk/poems_neolithic.htm

Klaus, Václav. 2013. "Hayek and My Life. In *F. A. Hayek and the Modern Economy: Economic Organization and Activity*, edited by Sandra J. Peart and David M. Levy. New York: Palgrave Macmillan.

Klein, Naomi. 2007. *The Shock Doctrine: The Rise of Disaster Capitalism*. New York: Picador.

Knight, Frank H.1924. "Some Fallacies in the Interpretation of Social Cost." *Quarterly Journal of Economics* 38: 582–606.

   1933. *Risk, Uncertainty and Profit*. London: London School of Economics. Originally published in 1921 in Boston by Houghton Mifflin Company.

   1939. "Theology and Education." *American Journal of Sociology* 44: 649–683.

   1947. "Social Science and the Political Trend." In *Freedom and Reform: Essays in Economics and Social Philosophy*. New York: Harper, 19–34. Originally published in in 1934 in the *University of Toronto Quarterly*.

   1947. *Freedom and Reform*, New York: Harper and Brothers.

   1951. *Ethics of Competition*, 2nd impression. New York: Augustus Kelley.

   1951. "The Rôle of Principles in Economics and Politics." *American Economic Review* 41: 1–29.

Kolchinsky, David. 2010. "Statement and Testimony before the Financial Crisis Inquiry Commission." Available at www.fcic.gov/hearings/pdfs/2010-0602-Kolchinsky.pdf

Kolm, Serge-Christophe, and Jean Mercier Ythier, eds. 2006. *Handbook of the Economics of Giving, Altruism and Reciprocity.* Amsterdam: Elsevier.

Kuhn, Thomas S. 1962. *The Structure of Scientific Revolutions.* Chicago: University of Chicago Press.

———. 1970. "Logic of Discovery or Psychology of Research?" In *Criticism and the Growth of Knowledge,* edited by Imre Lakatos and Alan Musgrave. Cambridge, UK: Cambridge University Press, 1–23.

Kuznets, Simon. 1942. *Uses of National Income in Peace and War.* New York: National Bureau of Economic Research.

Laidler, David. 1993. "Hawtrey, Harvard, and the Origins of the Chicago Tradition." *Journal of Political Economy* 101: 1068–1103.

Lane, Rose Wilder. 1947. "Review of Lorie Tarshis's *Elements of Economics.*" *Economic Council Review of Books* 4: 1–8.

Lemmon, Edward J. 1977. *An Introduction to Modal Logic: The Lemmon Notes,* edited by Krister Segerberg. Oxford, UK: Blackwell.

Leonard, Thomas C. 2003. "More Merciful and Not Less Effective Eugenics and American Economics in the Progressive Era." *History of Political Economy* 35: 687–712.

———. 2005. "Eugenics and Economics in the Progressive Era." *Journal of Economic Perspectives* 19: 207–224.

———. 2016. *Illiberal Reforms: Race, Eugenics and American Economics of the Progressive Era.* Princeton, NJ: Princeton University Press.

Lerner, Abba P. 1944. *The Economics of Control: Principles of Welfare Economics.* New York: Macmillan.

Levy, David M. 1978. "Some Normative Aspects of the Malthusian Controversy." *History of Political Economy* 10: 271–285.

———. 1999. "Christianity and Malthusianism: The Invisibility of a Successful Radical." *Historical Reflections/Réflexions Historiques* 25: 61–93.

———. 2001. *How the Dismal Science Got Its Name: Classical Economics and the Ur-Text of Racial Politics.* Ann Arbor: Michigan.

Levy, David M., and Sandra J. Peart. 2002. "Galton's Two Papers on Voting as Robust Estimation." *Public Choice* 113: 357–365.

———. 2005. "The Theory of Economic Policy in British Classical Political Economy: A Sympathetic Reading." *History of Political Economy* 37 Supplement: *The Role of Government in the History of Economic Thought* 120–42.

———. 2007. "Counterfeiting Truth: Statistical Reporting on the Basis of Trust." In *Game Theory and Linguistic Meaning,* edited by Ahti-Veikko Pietarinen. Oxford, UK: Elsevier, 39–48.

———. 2008a. "An Expert Induced Bubble." *Reason.* Available at http://reason.com/archives/2008/09/30/an-expert-induced-bubble

———. 2008b. "George J. Stigler: January 17, 1911–December 1, 1991." *The New Palgrave's Dictionary of Economics,* edited by Lawrence Blume and Steven Durlauf. 2nd edn. New York: Palgrave. Available at http://www.dictionaryofeconomics.com/article?id=pde2008_S000262

———. 2008c "Socialist Calculation Debate." *The New Palgrave's Dictionary of Economics,* edited by Lawrence Blume and Steven Durlauf. 2nd edn. New York: Palgrave. Available at www.dictionaryofeconomics.com/article?id=pde2008_S000535

2009a. "Adam Smith and the Place of Faction." In *The Elgar Companion to Adam Smith*. Edited by Jeffrey Young. Cheltenham, Glos, UK, Edward Elgar, ch 18, 335–345.

2009b. "Sympathy, Evolution and *The Economist*." *Journal of Economic Behavior & Organization* 71: 29–36.

2010. "Richard Whately and the Gospel of Transparency." *American Journal of Economics and Sociology* 69: 166–182.

2011. "Soviet Growth and American Textbooks: An Endogenous Past." *Journal of Economic Behavior and Organization* 78: 110–125.

2012. "Tullock on Motivated Inquiry: Expert-Induced Uncertainty Disguised as Risk." *Public Choice* 153: 163–180.

2013a. "Adam Smith on the State: Language and Reform." In *Oxford Handbook on Adam Smith*, edited by Christopher Berry, Maria Paganelli, and Craig Smith. Oxford, UK: Oxford University Press, 372–392.

2013b. "Learning from Scandal about What We Know and What We Think We Know." *Homo Oeconomicus* 20: 283–314.

2014a. " 'Almost Wholly Negative: The Ford Foundation's Appraisal of the Virginia School." Available at http://papers.ssrn.com/sol3/papers.cfm?abstract_id=2485695

2014b. "Ronald Coase and the Fabian Society: Competitive Discussion in Liberal Ideology." http://papers.ssrn.com/sol3/papers.cfm?abstract_id=2472130

2014c. "William Beveridge's 'Mock Trial of the Economists': Experts and Liberalism." http://papers.ssrn.com/sol3/papers.cfm?abstract_id=2377314

2015a. "Learning from Failure: A Review of Peter Schuck's *Why Government Fails so Often: And How It Can Do Better*." *Journal of Economic Literature* 53: 667–674.

2015b. "Sympathy Caught between Darwin and Eugenics." In *Sympathy: A History*, edited by Eric Schliesser. Oxford, UK: Oxford University Press, 323–358.

Levy, David M., Sandra J. Peart, and Margaret Albert. 2012. "Economic Liberals as Quasi-Public Intellectuals: The Democratic Dimension." *Research in the History of Economic Thought and Methodology* 30: 1–116.

Levy, David M, et al. 2011. "Leadership, Cheap Talk and *Really* Cheap Talk." *Journal of Economic Behavior and Organization* 77: 40–52.

Lipsey, Richard G. 1963–1966. *An Introduction to Positive Economics*. London: Weidenfeld and Nicolson.

2008. "Assessments of the Soviet Union: Who Got It Right and Who Got It Wrong." Presented at the Summer Institute for the History of Economics. Fairfax VA.

Lipsey, Richard G., and Kelvin Lancaster. 1956–1957. "The General Theory of Second Best." *Review of Economic Studies* 24: 11–32.

Lipsey, Richard, Gorden R. Sparks, and Peter O. Steiner. 1978. *Economics*. Toronto: Harper & Row.

Lipsey, Richard G., and Peter O. Steiner. 1966–1981. *Economics*. New York: Harper & Row.

Little, Ian M. 1952. "Social Choice and Individual Values." *Journal of Political Economy* 60: 422–432.

1957. *A Critique of Welfare Economics*. 2nd edn. Oxford, UK: Oxford University Press.

Longfield, Mountifort. 1931. *Lectures on Political Economy, Delivered in Trinity and Michaelmas Terms in 1833*. London: London School of Economics and Political Science. Originally published in 1834 in Dublin by Richard Milliken and Son.

Lorimer, Douglas. 1978. *Colour, Class and the Victorians*. Leicester: Leicester University Press.

Machlup, Fritz. 1965. "Why Economists Disagree." *Proceeding of the Philosophical Society* 109: 1–7.

1978. "If Matter Could Talk." In *Methodology of Economics and Other Social Sciences*. New York: Academic Press, 309–32.

Mäki, Uskali. 1999. "Science as a Free Market: A Reflexivity Test in an Economics of Economics." *Prospectives on Science* 7:486–509.

Mackay, Charles. 1932. *Memoirs of Extraordinary Popular Delusions*. New York: L. C. Page. Originally published in 1841 in London. The 1852 edition with the "numerous engravings" was published in London by Office of the National Illustrated Library.

Matthews, R. C. O. 1991. "The Economics of Professional Ethics: Should the Professions Be More Like Business?" *Economic Journal* 101: 737–750.

Mayer, Thomas. 1972. *Permanent Income, Wealth, and Consumption*. Berkeley: University of California.

1980. "Economics as a Hard Science: Realistic Goal or Wishful Thinking?" *Economic Inquiry* 18: 165–78.

1993. *Truth versus Precision in Economics*. Aldershot, Hants, England; Brookfield, Vt., USA: E. Elgar.

Mayr, Ernst. 1991. *One Long Argument: Charles Darwin and the Genesis of Modern Evolutionary Thought*. Cambridge, MA: Harvard University Press.

McCloskey, Deirdre. 2010. *Bourgeois Dignity: Why Economics Can't Explain the Modern World*. Chicago: University of Chicago Press.

McConnell, Campbell R. 1960–1990. *Elementary Economics: Principles, Problems and Policies*. New York: McGraw-Hill.

Mehrling, Perry. 2011. *Comments on Levy & Peart, "Prudence with Biased Raters."* History of Economics Society. Notre Dame.

Mill, John S. 1850. "Negro Question." *Fraser's Magazine for Town and Country* 41: 25–31.

1973. *A System of Logic Ratiocinative and Inductive Being a Connected View of the Principles of Evidence and the Methods of Scientific Investigation, Volumes 7-8 Collected Works of John Stuart Mill*, edited by J. M. Robson. Toronto: University of Toronto Press. Originally published in 1843 by J. W. Parker, London.

1965. *The Principles of Political Economy with Some of Their Applications to Social Philosophy. Volumes 2–3 of The Collected Works of John Stuart Mill*, edited by J. M. Robson. Toronto: University of Toronto Press. Originally published in 1848 by J. W. Parker, London.

1977. *On Liberty, Essays on Politics and Society, Volume 18 Collected Works of John Stuart Mill*. Edited by J. M. Robson. Toronto: University of Toronto Press, 213–310. Originally published in 1859 by John W. Parker, London.

1981. *Autobiography. Autobiography and Literary Essays, Volume 1 of the Collected Works of John Stuart Mill*, edited by John M. Robson and Jack Stillinger. Toronto: University of Toronto Press. Originally published in 1873 in London by Longmans, Green, Reader, and Dyer.

1984. "Inaugural Address Delivered to the University of St Andrews," *Essays on Equality, Law, and Education*. Volume 21 *Collected Works of John Stuart Mill*,

Edited by J. M. Robson. Toronto: University of Toronto Press, 215–58. Originally published in 1867 by Longman, Green. Reader, and Dyer, London.

1986. "Romilly's Public Responsibility and the Ballot." *Newspaper Writings, Volume 25 of The Collected Works of John Stuart Mill*, edited by Anne Robson. Toronto: University of Toronto, 474–475. Originally published in 1865 in *Reader*.

Montes, Leonidas. 2015. "Friedman's Two Visits to Chile in Context." Summer Institute for the Study of the History of Economics. University of Richmond.

Morgan, Mary S., and Margaret Morrison, eds. 1999. *Models as Mediators: Perspectives on Natural and Social Sciences*. New York: Cambridge University Press.

Morgenson, Gretchen, and Joshua Rosner. 2011. *Reckless Endangerment: How Outsized Ambition, Greed and Corruption Led to Economic Armageddon*. New York: Times Book.

Munk, Nina. 2013. *The Idealist: Jeffrey Sachs and the Quest to End Poverty*. New York: Doubleday.

Murphy, Antoin. 1997. *John Law: Economic Theorist and Policy Maker*. Oxford, UK: Oxford University Press.

2012. "The First Stock Market Collapse: Perspectives from John Law and Richard Cantillon." *History of Economics Society*. St. Catharines, Ontario: Brock University.

National Bureau of Economic Research. 1941. *The Corporate Bond Project, a History and Description, a Work Projects Administration Study Sponsored by the Federal Deposit Insurance Corporation, Supervised by the National Bureau of Economic Research*. New York: NBER.

Newman, William R. 2004. *Promethean Ambitions: Alchemy and the Quest to Perfect Nature*. Chicago: University of Chicago Press.

Newman, William R., and Lawrence M. Principe. 1999. "Alchemy vs. Chemistry: The Etymological Origins of a Historiographic Mistake." *Early Science and Medicine* 3: 32–65.

Nummedal, Tara. 2007. "On the Utility of Alchemical Fraud." In *Chymists and Chymistry: Studies in the History of Alchemy and Early Modern Chemistry*, edited by Lawrence M. Principe. Canton, MA: Science History Publications, 173–180.

2009. *Alchemy and Authority in the Holy Roman Empire*. Chicago: University of Chicago Press.

Nussbaum, Martha. 1997. *Cultivating Humanity*. Cambridge, MA: Harvard University Press.

2010. *Not for Profit: Why Democracy Needs the Humanities*. Princeton, NJ: Princeton University Press.

Nutter, G. Warren. 1957. "Some Observations on Soviet Industrial Growth." *American Economic Review* 47: 618–630.

1962. *The Growth of Industrial Production in the Soviet Union*. Princeton, NJ: National Bureau of Economic Research.

1969. *The Strange World of Ivan Ivanov*. New York and Cleveland: World Publishing.

1983a. "Economic Warfare." In *Political Economy and Freedom: A Collection of Essays*, edited by Jane Couch Nutter. Indianapolis: Liberty Press 222–236. Originally given to the National War College (Washington DC) in 1958.

1983b. "The Soviet Stir: Economic Crisis and Response." In *Political Economy and Freedom*, edited by Jane Couch Nutter. Indianapolis: Liberty Press, 181–188. Originally presented in 1964 to the House Committee on Foreign Affairs.

O'Connor, J. F. T. 1936. "Law Department." *Federal Reserve Bulletin* 22: 191–198.

Ospovat, Don. 1981. *The Development of Darwin's Theory: Natural History, Natural Theology, and Natural Selection, 1838-1859.* Cambridge, UK: Cambridge University Press.

Ostrom, E., Walker, J., and Gardner, R. 1992. "Covenants With and Without a Sword: Self-governance is Possible." *American Political Science Review* 86: 404–417.

Palyi, Melchior. 1938. "Bank Portfolios and the Control of the Capital Market." *Journal of Business* 11: 70–111.

Partnoy, Frank. 2002. "The Paradox of the Credit Ratings." In *Ratings, Rating Agencies and the Global Financial System*, edited by Richard M. Levich, Giovanni Majnoni, and Carmen M. Reinhart. Boston: Kluwer, 65–84.

Pearson, Karl. 1936. "Method of Moments and Method of Maximum Likelihood." *Biometrika* 28: 34–59.

Pearson, Karl, and Margaret Moul. 1925. "The Problem of Alien Immigration into Great Britain, Illustrated by an Examination of Russian and Polish Jewish Children." *Annals of Eugenics* 1: 5–55, 56–127.

Peart, Sandra J. 1995. *The Economics of W. S. Jevons.* London: Routledge.

——— 2000. "Irrationality and Intertemporal Choice in Early Neo-Classical Thought." *Canadian Journal of Economics* 3: 175–188.

——— 2009. "We're All 'Persons' Now: Classical Economists and their Opponents on Marriage, the Franchise and Socialism." *Journal of History of Economic Thought* 31: 3–20.

——— 2015. *Hayek on Mill: The Mill-Taylor Friendship and Related Writings. Volume 16 of The Collected Works of F. A. Hayek.* Chicago: University of Chicago Press.

Peart, Sandra J., and David M. Levy. 2005. *The 'Vanity of the Philosopher': From Equality to Hierarchy in Post-Classical Economics.* Ann Arbor: University of Michigan Press.

——— 2008a. "Darwin's Unpublished Letter at the Bradlaugh–Besant Trial: A Question of Divided Expert Judgment." *European Journal of Political Economy* 24: 243–253.

——— 2008b. "Discussion, Construction and Evolution: Mill, Buchanan and Hayek on the Constitutional Order." *Constitutional Political Economy* 19: 3–18.

——— 2013. "Hayek and the Individualists." In *F. A. Hayek and the Modern Economy: Economic Organization and Activity*, edited by Sandra J. Peart and David M. Levy. New York: Palgrave Macmillan.

Phillips, J. Ronnie. 1995. *The Chicago Plan and New Deal Banking Reform.* Armonk, NY: Sharpe.

Phillips, Peter C. B. 1983. "Exact Small Sample Theory in the Simultaneous Equations Models." In *Handbook of Econometrics*, edited by Zvi Griliches and Michael D. Intriligator. Amsterdam: Elsevier, 449–516.

Pigou, Arthur C. 1907. "Social Improvement and Modern Biology." *Economic Journal* 17: 358–369.

——— 1918. *The Economics of Welfare.* London: Macmillan.

——— 1935. *Economics in Practice.* London: Macmillan.

Place, Francis. 1930. *Illustrations and Proofs of the Principle of Population*, edited by Norman E. Himes. London: Allen & Unwin. Originally published in 1822 in London by Longman, Hurst, Rees, Orme, and Brown.

Plato. 1930. *Republic.* Translated by Paul Shorey. Cambridge, MA: Loeb Classical Library.

Polanyi, Michael. 1962. "The Republic of Science: Its Political and Economic Theory." *Minerva* 38: 1–21.

Popper, Karl R. 1970. "Normal Science and Its Dangers." In *Criticism and the Growth of Knowledge*, edited by Imre Lakatos and Alan Musgrave. Cambridge UK: Cambridge University Press, 51–58.

——— 1974. *Logic of Scientific Discovery*. Translated by Julius Freed and Lan Freed. 7th revised impression. London: Hutchinson. English translation of the 1935 German language original was published in London in 1959 by Hutchinson.

——— 1983. *Realism and the Aim of Science*, edited by W. W. Bartley III. London: Routledge.

Posner, Richard A. 1999a. "An Economic Approach to Legal Evidence." *Stanford Law Review* 51: 1477–1546.

——— 1999b. "The Law and Economics of the Economic Expert Witness." *Journal of Economic Perspectives* 13: 91–99.

Principe, Lawrence M., and William R. Newman. 2001. "Some Problems with the Historiography of Alchemy." In *Secrets of Nature: Astrology and Alchemy in Early Modern Europe*, edited by William R. Newman and Anthony Grafton. Cambridge, MA: MIT Press, 385–431.

Principe, Lawrence M., and Lloyd De Witt. 2002. *Transmutations – Alchemy in Art: Selected Works from the Eddleman and Fisher collections at the Chemical Heritage Foundation*. Philadelphia: Chemical Heritage Foundation.

Putnam, Hilary. 2004. *The Collapse of the Fact / Value Dichotomy and Other Essays*. Cambridge: Harvard University Press.

*The Queen v. Charles Bradlaugh and Annie Besant. June 18, 1877.* 1878. London: Freethought Publishing, [2 Q.B.D, 569; reversed 3 Q.B.D., 607].

Quine, W. V. 1969. *Set Theory and Its Logic, 2nd edn*. Cambridge, MA: Harvard University Press.

Rainger, Ronald. 1978. "Race, Politics, and Science: The Anthropological Society of London in the 1860s." *Victorian Studies* 22: 51–70.

Rand, Ayn. 1995. *Letters of Ayn Rand*, edited by Michael S. Berliner. New York: Penguin.

Rapoport, Anatol. 1987. "Prisoner's Dilemma." In *The New Palgrave: A Dictionary of Economics*, edited by John Eatwell, Murray Milgate, and Peter Newman. Available at www.dictionaryofeconomics.com/article?id=pde1987_X001756#citations

Rawls, John. 1955. "Two Concepts of Rules." *Philosophical Review* 64: 3–32.

——— 1958. "Justice as Fairness." *Philosophical Review* 67: 164–194.

——— 1971. *A Theory of Justice*. Cambridge, MA: Harvard University Press.

——— 1999. "Justice as Reciprocity." In *Collected Papers*, edited by Samuel Freeman. Cambridge, MA: Harvard University Press, 190–224. Originally published in 1971 in *John Stuart Mill: Utilitarianism, with Critical Essays*, edited by Samuel Gorowitz.

——— 2000. *Lectures on the History of Moral Philosophy*, edited by Samuel Freeman. Cambridge, MA: Harvard University Press.

——— 2007. *Lectures on the History of Political Philosophy*, edited by Samuel Freeman. Cambridge, MA: Harvard University Press.

Reder, Melvin W. 1982. "Chicago Economics: Permanence and Change." *Journal of Economic Literature* 20: 1–38.

Reinhart, Carmen M., and Kenneth Rogoff. 2009. *This Time It's Different*. Princeton, NJ: Princeton University Press.

Richards, Robert J. 1992. *The Meaning of Evolution: The Morphological Construction and Ideological Reconstruction of Darwin's Theory*. Chicago: University of Chicago Press.

Robbins, Lionel. 1938. "Interpersonal Comparisons of Utility: A Comment." *Economic Journal* 48: 635–641.

    1949. *An Essay on the Nature and Significance of Economic Science.* 2nd edn., revised and extended. London: Macmillan.

    1952. *The Theory of Economic Policy in English Classical Political Economy.* London: Macmillan.

    1971. *The Autobiography of an Economist.* London: Macmillan.

    1981. "Economics and Political Economy." *American Economic Review* 71: 1–10.

Romer, Paul M. 2015. "Mathiness in the Theory of Economic Growth." *American Economic Review* 105: 89–93.

Rosenberg, Nathan and L. E. Birdzell Jr. 1986. *How the West Grew Rich: The Economic Transformation of the Industrial World.* New York: Basic Books.

Rostow, W. W. 1960. *The Stages of Economic Growth: A Non-Communist Manifesto.* Cambridge, MA: Cambridge University Press.

Rubinstein, Ariel. 2000. *The Economics of Language: Five Essays.* Cambridge, UK: Cambridge University Press.

Ruse, Michael. 1999. "Afterwards: Two Decades Later." In *The Darwin Revolution: Science Red in Tooth and Claw.* 2nd edn. Chicago: University of Chicago Press.

Sachs, Jeffrey D. 1991. "Crossing the Valley of Tears in East European Reform." *Challenge* 34: 26–31.

    2005. *The End of Poverty: Economic Possibilities for Our Time.* New York: Penguin.

Sally, David. 1995. "Conversations and Cooperation in Social Dilemma: A Meta-Analysis of Experiments from 1958 to 1992." *Rationality and Society* 7: 58–92.

    2001. "On Sympathy and Games." *Journal of Economic Behavior and Organization* 44: 1–30.

Samuels, Warren J. 2005. "Melchior Palyi: An Introduction and Bibliography." *Research in the History and Methodology of Economics* 23: 305–306.

Samuelson, Paul A. 1943. "Further Commentary on Welfare Economics." *American Economic Review* 33: 604–607.

    1948–80. *Economics: An Introductory Analysis.* New York: McGraw-Hill.

    1965. *The Foundations of Economic Analysis.* Student edition. New York: Antheneum.

    1997. "Credo of a Lucky Textbook Author." *Journal of Economic Perspectives* 11: 153–569.

Samuelson, Paul. A., and Anthony Scott. 1966–1971. *Economics: An Introductory Analysis.* Toronto: McGraw Hill.

Savage, Leonard J. 1972. *The Foundations of Statistics.* 2nd edn. New York: Dover.

Schama, Simon. 1987. *The Embarrassment of Riches: An Interpretation of Dutch Culture in the Golden Age.* New York: Alfred A. Knopf.

    2000. "Money Unconfined: 'I Invest, He Speculates, They Gamble.'" In *Great Bubbles,* edited by Ross B. Emmett. London: Pickering and Chatto, vol. 1, 130–61. Originally published in The *Embarrassment of Riches* in 1988 in Berkeley by the University of California Press.

Schuck, Peter. 2014. *Why Government Fails So Often: And How It Can Do Better.* Princeton, NJ: Princeton University Press.

Schumpeter, Joseph A. 1954. *A History of Economic Analysis.* New York: Oxford.

Sellink, Manfred. 2007. *Bruegel: The Complete Paintings, Drawings and Prints.* Belgium: Ludion.

Sen, Amartya K. 1977. "Rational Fools: A Critique of the Behavioral Foundations of Economic Theory." *Philosophy & Public Affairs* 6: 317–344.

1979. "The Welfare Basis of Real Income Comparisons." *Journal of Economic Literature* 17: 1–45.

1995. "Rationality and Social Choice." *American Economic Review*, 85: 1–24.

2012. "What happened to Europe?" *New Republic*, August 2. Available at www.new republic.com/article/magazine/105657/sen-europe-democracy-keynes-social-justice

2013. "On James Buchanan," http://lijian267.blog.sohu.com/252974528.html

Silk, Leonard S. 1972. "Truth vs. Partisan Political Purpose." *American Economic Review* 62: 376–378.

Simons, Henry C. 1934. *A Positive Program for Laissez Faire*. Chicago: University of Chicago Press.

Skousen, Mark. 1997. "The Perseverance of Paul Samuelson's Economics." *Journal of Economic Perspectives* 11: 137–152.

Smith, Adam 1790. *The Theory of Moral Sentiments*. 6th edition. Available at www .econlib.org/library/Smith/smMS.html. Originally published in 1759 by A. Millar, London.

1904. *An Inquiry into the Nature and Causes of the Wealth of Nations*, edited by Edwin Cannan. Available at www.econlib.org/library/Smith/smWN .html. Originally published in 1776 by W. Strahan and T. Cadell, London.

1982a. *Essays in Philosophical Subjects*. Edited by W. P. D. Wightman and J. C. Bryce. Indianapolis: Liberty Fund. Originally published in 1795 in London by T. Cadell Jun and W. Davies.

1982b. *Lectures on Jurisprudence*, edited by Ronald L. Meek, David D. Raphael and Peter. G. Stein. Indianapolis: Liberty Fund. Originally published in 1978 by Oxford University Press, Oxford.

Smith, Vernon L. 1998. "The Two Faces of Adam Smith." *Southern Economic Journal* 65: 1–19.

2008. *Rationality in Economics: Constructivist and Ecological Forms*. New York: Cambridge University Press.

Spieth, Darius. 2013. "The French Context of *Het Groote Tafereel Der Dwaasheid*: John Law, Rococo Culture, and the Riches of the New World." In *The Great Mirror of Folly: Finance and Culture, and the Crash of 1720*, edited by William N. Goetzmann, Catherine Labio, K. Geert Rouwenhorst and Timothy G. Young. New Haven, CT: Yale University Press, 219–234.

Stepan, Nancy. 1982. *The Idea of Race in Science*. Hamden, CT: Archon Books.

1991. *The Hour of Eugenics: Race, Gender and Nation in Latin America*. Ithaca, NY: Cornell University Press.

[Stephens, Frederic George]. 1873. *Catalogue of Prints and Drawings in the British Museum, Division I, Political and Personal Satires*. London: British Museum.

Stigler, George J. 1943. "New Welfare Economics." *American Economic Review* 33: 355–359.

1945. "The Cost of Subsistence." *Journal of Farm Economics* 25: 303–314.

1946. *Theory of Price*. New York: Macmillan.

1948. Review of *Foundations of Economic Analysis*. *Journal of the American Statistical Association* 43: 603–605.

1961. "The Economics of Information." *Journal of Political Economy* 69: 213–225.

1966. *Theory of Price*. 3rd edn. New York: Macmillan.

1975. "Editorial Comment." *Journal of Political Economy* 83: 1295-1296.

1988. *Memoirs of an Unregulated Economist*. Chicago: University of Chicago Press.

Stigler, George J., and Gary S. Becker. 1977. "De Gustibus Non Est Disputandum." *American Economic Review* 67: 76–90.

Stigler, Stephen M. 1986. *The History of Statistics: The Measurement of Uncertainty before 1900*. Cambridge, MA: Harvard University Press.

1999. *Statistics on the Table: The History of Statistical Concepts and Methods*. Cambridge, MA: Harvard University Press.

2010. "The Changing History of Robustness." *American Statistician* 64: 277–281.

Su, Huei-Chun, and David Colander. 2013. "A Failure to Communicate: The Fact-Value Divide and the Putnam-Dasgupta Debate." *Erasmus Journal for Philosophy and Economics* 6: 1–23.

Suzumura, Kotaro, and Paul Samuelson. 2005. "An Interview with Paul Samuelson: Welfare Economics, 'Old' and 'New', and Social Choice Theory." *Social Choice and Welfare* 25: 327–356.

Sylla, Richard. 2002. "An Historical Primer on the Business of Credit Rating." *Ratings, Rating Agencies and the Global Financial System*, edited by Richard M. Levich, Giovanni Majnoni and Carmen M. Reinhart. Boston: Kluwer, 19–40.

Tarshis, Lorie. 1947. *The Elements of Economics: An Introduction to the Theory of Price and Employment*. Boston: Houghton Mifflin.

1967. *Modern Economics*. Boston: Houghton Mifflin.

Terborgh, George W. 1945. *The Bogey of Economic Maturity*. Chicago: Machinery and Allied Products Institute.

Tetlock, Philip E. 2005. *Expert Political Judgment: How Good Is It? How Can We Know?* Princeton, NJ: Princeton University Press.

Thacker, Paul D., and Charles Seife. 2015. "The Fight over Transparency: Round Two." Available at https://archive.is/4kflm

Thompson, Dennis E. 1987. *Political Ethics and Public Office*. Cambridge, MA: Harvard University Press.

Thorndike, Lynn. 1958. *A History of Magic and Experimental Science: The Seventeenth Century*. New York: Columbia University Press.

Thornton, Henry. 1939. *An Enquiry into the Nature and Effects of the Paper Credit of Great Britain (1802): Together with His Evidence Given Before the Committees of Secrecy of the Two Houses of Parliament in the Bank of England, March and April, 1797, Some Manuscript Notes, and His Speeches on the Bullion Report, May 1811*, edited by F. A. Hayek. London: George Allen and Unwin. Originally printed in 1802 in London by J. Hatchard.

Trani, Eugne P. and Robert D. Holsworth. 2010. *The Indispensable University: Higher Education, Economic Development and the Knowledge Economy*. Lanham, MD: Rowman & Littlefield.

Tukey, John W. 1986. "The Future of Data Analysis." *Philosophy and Principles of Data Analysis: 1949–1964. Volume 3 of The Collected Works of John W. Tukey*, edited by Lyle V. Jones. Monterey: Wadsworth & Brooks, 391–484. Originally published in 1962 in the *Annals of Mathematical Statistics*.

Tullock, Gordon. 1980. *Trials on Trial: The Pure Theory of Legal Procedure*. New York: Columbia University Press.

2005. *The Organization of Inquiry. Volume 3 of Selected Works of Gordon Tullock*, edited by Charles K. Rowley. Indianapolis: Liberty Fund. Originally published in 1966 in Durham, N.C. by Duke University Press.

Tyndale, William, Trans. 1992. *Tyndale's Old Testament*, edited by David Daniell. New Haven, CT: Yale University Press. The translation from the Hebrew was originally published between 1530 and 1537 in Antwerp by Merten de Keyser.

Valdes, Juan Gabriel. 2008. *Pinochet's Economists: The Chicago School of Economics in Chile*, paperback edition. Cambridge, UK: Cambridge University Press.

Vardeman, Stephen B. and Max D. Morris. 2003. "Statistics and Ethics: Some Advice for Young Statisticians." *American Statistician* 57: 21–26.

Viner, Jacob. 1927. "Adam Smith and Laissez-Faire." *Journal of Political Economy*, 35: 198–232.

1937. *Studies in the Theory of International Trade*. New York: Harper and Brothers.

1962. "The Necessary and the Desirable Range of Discretion to Be Allowed to a Monetary Authority." In *In Search of a Monetary Constitution*, edited by Leland Yeager. Cambridge, MA: Harvard University Press, 244–274.

Viscusi, W. Kip and Ted Gayer. 2015. "Behavioral Public Choice: The Behavioral Paradox of Government Policy." *Harvard Journal of Law and Public Policy* 38: 973–1007.

Vorzimmer, Peter J. 1970. *Charles Darwin: The Years of Controversy*. Philadelphia: Temple University Press.

Voth, Hans-Joachim. 2013. "Blowing Bubbles: Rational Exuberance in the South Sea and Mississippi Bubbles." In *The Great Mirror of Folly: Finance and Culture, and the Crash of 1720*, edited by William N. Goetzmann, Catherine Labio, K. Geert Rouwenhorst and Timothy G. Young. New Haven, CT: Yale University Press, 89–97.

Wald, Abraham. 1950. *Statistical Decision Functions*. New York: John Wiley.

Wallace, Alfred Russel. 1864. "The Origin of Human Races and the Antiquity of Man Deduced from the Theory of 'Natural Selection.'" *Journal of the Anthropological Society of London* 2: clviii–clxxxvii.

1871. "The Development of Human Races under the Law of Natural Selection." *Contributions to the Theory of Natural Selection*. 2nd edn. London: Macmillan and Co., 303–331.

1900. "Human Selection." *Studies Scientific & Social*. London: Macmillan, 509–526. Originally published in 1890 in *Fortnightly Review*.

1913. *Social Environment and Moral Progress*. London: Cassell.

Wallas, Graham. 1898. *The Life of Francis Place, 1771–1854*. London: Longmans, Green.

Warlick, M. E. 2006. "Fluctuating Identities: Gender Reversals in Alchemical Imagery." In *Art & Alchemy*, edited by Jacob Warnberg. Copenhagen: Museeum Tusculanum Press, University of Copenhagen, 103–123.

Webb, Sidney. 1910. "Eugenics and the Poor Law: The Minority Report." *The Eugenics Review* 2: 233–241.

Weisbrot, Mark, and Dean Baker. 2004. "Applying Economics to Economists: Good Governance at the International Financial Institutions." CEPR Briefing Paper. Available at https://docs.google.com/viewer?url=http%3A%2F%2Fwww.cepr.net%2Fdocuments%2Fpublications%2Fifi_2004_07.pdf

Whately, R. 1832. *Introductory Lectures on Political Economy.* 2nd edn. London: B. Fellowes.

White, Eugene. 2013. "The Long Shadow of John Law on French Public Finance: The Mississippi Bubble." In *The Great Mirror of Folly: Finance and Culture, and the Crash of 1720,* edited by William N. Goetzmann, Catherine Labio, K. Geert Rouwenhorst and Timothy G. Young. New Haven, CT: Yale University Press, 99–105.

White, Lawrence J. 2002. "The Credit Rating Industry: An Industrial Organization Analysis." *Ratings, Rating Agencies and the Global Financial System,* edited by Richard M. Levich, Giovanni Majnoni, and Carmen M. Reinhart. Boston: Kluwer, 19–40.

2010. "The Credit Rating Agencies." *Journal of Economic Perspectives* 24: 211–226.

Whistler, Diane, K. J. White, David Bates and Madeline Golding. 2015. *Shazam 11.* Cambridge UK: Shazam Analytics.

Wible, James. 1998. *The Economics of Science: Methodology and Epistemology as if Economics Really Mattered.* London: Routledge.

Wilson, John. 1881. *Studies of Modern Mind and Character at Several European Epochs.* London: Longman, Green and Co.

Wolf, Charles. 1979. "A Theory of Nonmarket Failure: Framework for Implementation Analysis." *Journal of Law and Economics* 22: 107–139.

Woodward, Richard T., and Richard C. Bishop. 1997. "How to Decide When Experts Disagree: Uncertainty-Based Choice Rules in Environmental Policy." *Land Economics* 73: 492–507.

Yeager, Leland B. 1976. "Economics and Principles." *Southern Economic Journal* 42: 559–571.

Young, Robert J. C. 1995. *Colonial Desire: Hybridity in Theory, Culture, and Race.* London: Routledge.

Ziliak, Stephen T., and Deirdre N. McCloskey. 2008. *The Cult of Statistical Significance: How the Standard Error Costs Us Jobs, Justice, and Lives.* Ann Arbor: University of Michigan Press.

# Index

Academic admissions, bias in, 218–19
Akerloff, George, 13, 196
*The Alchemists* (Jonson), 140–41,
    141n6, 154–55
Alchemy
    basilisk imagery and, 147–49
    Erasmus on, 144–45, 149–55, 149n22
    *Great Mirror of Folly* and, 144–49
    Keynes on, 144
    Mississippi Bubble and, 139–41, 144
    rooster imagery and, 147–49
    Smith on, 140
Alchian, Armen, 125–28, 128n16
Allais, Maurice, 145n12
Allen, William, 125–28, 128n16
Altruism, 215
*American Banker,* 172–73
American Economic Association (AEA)
    economic experts and, 179–80, 183, 184,
        192, 193, 239 (*See also* Revised code of
        ethics)
    overview, 240
    statisticians and, 212, 230
American Statistical Association (ASA), 212,
    213, 230, 239
*American Statistician,* 214
Analytical egalitarianism, 7, 24, 199–200
Angner, Erik, 7n10
*Annals of Eugenics* (Pearson), 105
Approbation
    bias and, 216–18
    Smith on, 215
    statistical efficiency and, 216–18
Archilochos, 10
Arnold, Matthew, 14n21

Arrow, Kenneth J.
    on discussion, 37–38
    on exogeneity of goals, 37
    generally, 9n11, 18, 189
    on new welfare economics, 50, 70, 83, 85
    Samuelson and, 84
    on savings, 60–61, 67
ASA. *See* American Statistical
    Association (ASA)
Ashenfelter, Orley, 228n26
Asymmetric information, 14n23
Asymptotics, 227–28
Autism, vaccination and, 5, 11n17, 13, 202

Bach, George, 115, 122–23, 129–30
Baker, Dean, 24n36
Banking Act of 1935, 161–62
Banque Royale, 141–43
Barber, William, 15n24
Becker, Gary, 145n12
Bentham, Jeremy, 76, 92–93
Berlin, Isaiah, 10
Besant, Annie, 35n15, 93, 97–103, 103n16,
    105, 108
Bias
    in academic admissions, 218–19
    approbation and, 216–18
    concealment of (*See* Concealment of bias)
    discussion and, 137–38
    economic experts and, 194
    implicit bias, 34n9
    Knight on, 237
    least biased estimates, 204–8
    Mississippi Bubble and (*See* Mississippi
      Bubble)